TAPESTRY
Mirror of History

DEDICATED to
the memory of my father
WILLIAM GEORGE THOMSON (1865–1942)
who from childhood fought to surmount
great physical disabilities
and in middle life was the first
Director of Weaving at the Dovecot
Tapestry Studios, Edinburgh, and wrote
the first standard international
reference works in English
A History of Tapestry
and
Tapestry Weaving in England

TAPESTRY
Mirror of History

Francis Paul Thomson OBE

CROWN PUBLISHERS, INC.,
New York

© Francis Thomson 1980.

Printed in Great Britain

First published in the U.S.A. by
Crown Publishers, Inc., New York.

Published simultaneously in Canada
by General Publishing Company Ltd.

Library of Congress Cataloging in Publication Data

Thomson, Francis Paul.
  The history of tapestry and tapestry making.

  1. Tapestry—History.   2. Textile industry—History.
I. Title.
NK3000.T38   746.3'9   78-1469
ISBN 0-517-53415-0

Contents

List of Illustrations

Colour

Black and White

Preface

Thirty years after the Royal Windsor Tapestry Manufactory opened its doors to start weaving in 1876, the first comprehensive *History of Tapestry* in the English language was published in London. One hundred years after the Windsor Manufactory—despite its short life—initiated a century of tapestry renaissance, the third edition of *A History of Tapestry* was out-of-print.

A suggestion was made that I should replace my father's *magnum opus* in a shorter form: one that would serve the interests of the general reader and the needs of the specialist.

Benefiting from archaeological and general historical research of recent years, this volume attempts to sketch the history of tapestry-like fabrics from prehistoric times to the present day. The popular definition of 'tapestry' has broadened since the 1950s, so an attempt is made also to depict the best of modern tapestry of many countries in terms of the older formal definitions. It is hoped that the reader will decide what is 'good' tapestry and then help to influence public opinion. Is it still essential to precede flawless weaving with inspired and well-planned design on paper? Or are today's weavers so multi-disciplined that anything they evolve on their loom is likely only to exalt the 'elegant art'? Are materials and structures not made on a loom entitled to be called tapestry?

Within the formal limits given above, I have tried to illustrate tapestry of all periods, using pictures never brought together before under one cover—and to introduce a little humour. I am grateful for the opportunity to rectify misconceptions regarding the origins and early history of the Dovecot Tapestry Studios in Corstorphine, near Edinburgh, Scotland; I have drawn on family and other material not published before.

I have been pressed to depart from my customary standards of word choice and methods of expressing—for example—measurements, with the object of facilitating comprehension equally among English language readers not steeped in the British version of it. The *Glossary* of archaic or unusual terms (Appendix 2) is designed especially to aid readers of English as a foreign language.

The preparation of this volume would have been impossible without help and encouragement from people in many countries. I cannot thank them enough. I am deeply indebted to my wife, Ester Sylvia Thomson, for making translations from Swedish, Norwegian, Danish, German and French, for undertaking historical research and for checking the manuscript.

Watford, England 1979   Francis Paul Thomson

Note
Tapestry measurements are in the form of height × width.

1 The Nature of Tapestry

Tapestry has been called 'the elegant art'. It has also been called 'the mirror of civilization'. More accurately tapestry should be called 'the mirror of history'. Its origins extend back some 400 000 years, to the time when man's ancestors were learning how to make tools.

Elegance with popularity attracts imitation, and the name of the article is liable to be borrowed to describe something not quite the same and very often inferior. The word 'tapestry' has suffered this fate, and so it is necessary initially to ask: what is tapestry?

The name *tapestry* is derived from the Greek ταπης and the Latin *tapetium*. But during the last 600 years it has also been known in the English-speaking world by any of the following names: *arras, arrass, arrazi, arres, aubusson, Flemish drapery, gobelin, hanging, tæped, tæpped, tapeccery, teped, tapesry, tapesserie, tapetion, tapetium, tapis, tapisery, tapisserie, tapissery, tapistry, tapistrye, tapstry.*

True tapestry is defined by the structure of the material. In the strict sense, *tapestry* should be used only to describe a hand-woven material of ribbed surface resembling rep, but into which the design is woven during manufacture, so that it forms an integral part of the textile. This may be woven on either of two types of loom:

1. on a high-warp, or 'haute-lisse', or upright loom with vertical warps
2. on a low-warp, or 'basse-lisse', or low loom with horizontal warps and foot-pedals.

The resulting fabric from either loom is virtually the same.

A classical definition of tapestry was given by William Morris (1834–96), the pre-Raphaelite and Founder of the Merton Abbey Tapestry Workshops in south London:

It may be looked upon as a mosaic of pieces of colour made up of dyed threads, and is capable of producing wall ornament of any degree of elaboration within the proper limits of duly considered decorative work. As in all wall decoration, the first thing to be considered in the designing of it is the force, purity and elegance of the silhouette of the objects represented, and nothing vague or indeterminate is admissable. Depth of tone, richness of colour, and exquisite gradation of tints are easily to be obtained in tapestry; and it also demands that crispness and abundance of beautiful details which was the especial characteristic of fully developed Mediaeval Art.

The *Novo Dizionario Scolastico* published in 1892 defined tapestry as '... an ornamental cloth woven with wool and gold thread, telling a story'. In more recent times *The Shorter Oxford Dictionary on Historic Principles* gives the definition:

A textile fabric decorated with ornamental designs or pictorial subjects, painted, embroidered, or woven in colours, used for wall hangings, curtains, etc.; especially, such a decorated fabric in which a weft containing ornamental designs in coloured wool or silk, gold or silver thread, etc. is worked with bobbins or broaches, and pressed close with a comb, on a warp of hemp or flax stretched in a frame. Often loosely applied to imitative textile fabrics.

The more general 'imitative fabrics' are:

Appliqué: a fabric composed of pieces of material cut to various shapes and sewn either by hand or by machine, or embroidered, to adhere to the surface of other material often of a different colour or texture.

Batik: a cloth dyed by a method that originated in Java but that has been adopted in the West, and is also known as 'resist-dyeing'. Parts of the cloth that are to remain the original colour are coated with wax applied in a molten state, or with flour paste, before the cloth is dipped in the dye-vat.

Collage: this is an ornamental or pictorial fabric built up by stitching or sticking shapes of paper or other material, including objects such as a hat or eyeglasses to a cloth, net, cardboard or other material, which may itself be part of the final design.

Crochet: effect is similar to lace but a hook and single strand of yarn is used.

Embroidery: an embroidered fabric may be produced by hand or by machine and consists of stitchwork with a needle and thread, to create ornament or pattern on a canvas, muslin or other base, or backing material, so as to cover it in whole or in part. Various types of stitches may be used such as chain-stitch or cross-stitch and also various kinds and colours of thread.

Gauze or *Netting*: this is an open-weave fabric made so that it is semi-transparent and has an evenly-woven appearance, or is composed of knotted threads.

Knitting or *Lace*: both fabrics are made by making a variety of stitches repeatedly so that the thread of one is looped into the thread of the next. Knitting is accomplished by needles or bobbins, which may be either straight or circular and manipulated by hand, or it may be done by machine. Lace is also made by hand or machine.

Macramé: this is a fabric built up with plain, or knotted, or cord-like strands of wool, raffia and the like and stitched to provide ornament, outline, contrast, substance, or other characteristic to the fabric.

Rugs and *Carpets*: a common characteristic of nearly all is that they are woven on a strong base of jute, linen, hemp, nylon or cotton and have free ends of wool, silk, cotton or nylon on the 'right' or used side to make pile, the tufts being held in the base material by a knot, or by blending and spinning or, in recent times, by thermoplastic welding or adhesive.

Rya Rugs: these originated in Northern Scandinavia in Viking times and in the original form are composed of a fairly tightly woven fabric of cotton, wool or linen, into which is knotted long-stranded tufts, usually of wool, with free ends facing outwards to make a pile. Much used as wall decoration.

Tie and Die: a coloured fabric made by a 'resist' technique of three varieties: (1) fabric not to be coloured in the dye-vat is bound and sewn to protect it; (2) some parts may be screened off from the dye by tying a suitably-shaped object to them; or (3) parts to be protected from the dye are folded and rolled, or pleated, before being bound.

Sampler: a cloth usually of canvas over which a student stitches and, or, fixes examples of work, or does an exercise in embroidery.

'Tapestry' stitchwork: the making of designs by means of a needle and thread

on open-pattern canvas, or doing likewise but with a hooked tool which threads the yarn through the base material.

Upholstery or furnishing 'tapestry' : like machine-made 'tapestry', this is usually rather hard-wearing cotton or linen material, which may be either printed or made from coloured threads, and woven on a machine so that as much of the warp as of the weft is seen.

The above are the major 'imitative fabrics'. Perhaps one of the easiest ways to recognize true tapestry, apart from its characteristic ribbed surface, is the fact that many pieces have little or none of the warp showing.

Looms

The high-warp and the low-warp looms are the two types that have gained greatest favour over the centuries. The common characteristics of both are:

   1.   a strong framework of wood or, in modern times, of metal or plastic

   2.   two rollers, each fitted with a winding handle, and a ratchet-and-pawl mechanism that limits movement to one turning direction until the mechanism is disengaged

   3.   long, parallel threads comprising the warp, stretched from one roller to the other with means for fixing the threads to each roller until it is desired to release them

   4.   one roller to act as a 'store' for warp, and the other on to which the tapestry is wound as it is woven

   5.   means of making easy access by hand to alternate threads of the warp, in order to intertwine the threads of weft between them, and thus to build up construction of the tapestry.

The basic components of a high-warp loom are shown in 1. 2 shows a small model loom viewed from the reverse side, i.e., the face of the tapestry is shown. For clarity, the framework of the loom shown in 1 is omitted. It will be seen that the warp threads—or strings—are parallel and vertical

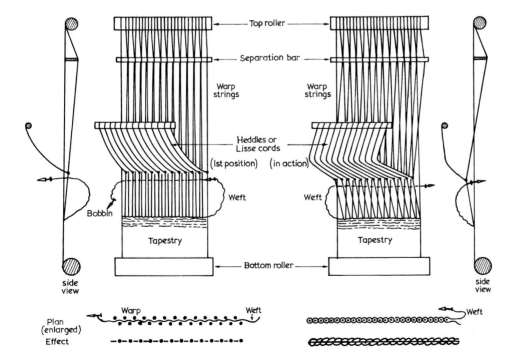

1 A simplified high-warp or upright tapestry loom, drawn by W. G. Thomson (*Author's copyright reserved*)

13

2 The front of a small tapestry loom, showing the face of the tapestry. The mirror, which would have its back to the reader, has been removed so that the design traced on to the warps may be seen more clearly above the woven edge of the tapestry. The loops of the heddles encircle alternate warps, just below the upper bar (*Victoria and Albert Museum; Crown Copyright*)

and pass from the upper roller (the warp 'store') to the lower roller (the 'tapestry' roller). Near to the top, the warp threads are divided by a separating rod or cross-bar into two ranks. Each thread, from left to right, is numbered, and the threads represented by even numbers are placed behind the bar while those with odd numbers are placed in front of the bar. A shuttle, spindle or bobbin, filled with weft thread, is passed behind each alternate warp thread from right to left. In its passage the bobbin (also known as the shuttle or spindle) lays down a thread of weft between the warp strings (or thread), depositing in front of each alternate warp a tiny dot of weft. With his left hand the weaver then pulls the heddles (or lisse cords) attached to the rank of warp threads behind the separator bar until they project well in front of the original row (*see* 1). On its return journey from left to right the bobbin passes in front of threads of warp it formerly passed behind, and they in turn are covered with weft as the first were. The double pass of weft may now be pushed together with a blunt-edged tool, called a 'scraper', or compacted by a box-wood or ivory comb until it forms an almost even line across the full width of warp threads. Repeat the operation several times and a cloth is formed which has the distinctive ribbed appearance of tapestry, with the warps entirely covered by the weft threads. This is an example of plain weave. By altering the colour of the weft (i.e., by taking bobbins wound with threads of other colours), and by plucking particular warps forward and interleaving the weft with respect to them only, the weaver reproduces the lines and masses of the design. The warp is the foundation of the tapestry and may be made of wool, linen (flax), hemp, cotton, silk, nylon or even wire. The weft may be made of fibres of a single coloured thread, or of a combination of coloured threads twisted together, made of wool (sheep, goat, alpaca, etc.), silk, cotton, linen, man-made fibres, gold, silver or other metallic threads. The author learned to weave on a loom similar to that shown in 2. Students at modern art or technical institutes learn to weave on a simple frame without rollers, but with a means of keeping the warp taut.

A low-warp loom has a heddle or lisse cord encircling each of both the even- and odd-numbered warps, each rank of which can be displaced with respect to the other by the weaver pressing on first one, and then the other, of two foot-pedals. The left pedal advances the odd-numbered warps with respect to the even-numbered ones, and vice versa. Consequently, both hands of the weaver are free to pluck particular warp strings or to interleave the weft bobbin, or to manipulate scraper and comb, although some looms are fitted with a reed, which is like a comb extending across the width of the loom. If equipped thus, the loom is probably making ordinary cloth rather than tapestry.

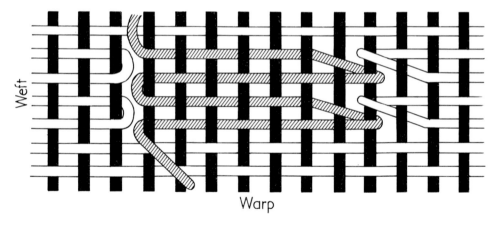

Weft

Warp

3 Tapestry-weaving is more complicated than it may appear. The pick (row) of weft extending across the width of the warps at top and bottom demonstrates plain weave. Where two different-coloured areas have a vertical or a diagonal boundary there are several ways of making a clean line of colour difference. The example at the left employs the slit technique, the disadvantage being that if slits are many or large the tapestry is weakened and the slit has to be sewn up by hand. It is easy to avoid a slit. The weft threads may be dovetailed around a warp thread, as shown by the example at the right; variations of this technique are 'comb' and 'sawtooth' dovetailing; the former entails alternating single weft threads, and the latter involves patches of wefts from one side and then from the other. This method gives a very strong but rather uneven texture. A better technique is to loop the different-coloured wefts through each other (chain-link fashion), between the two warps marking the colour boundary. There are several variations, such as laying a pick of plain weave, or of dovetailing, in very thin but strong thread, like linen or hemp, which will be lost in the thickness of the weft of wool, silk and so on. Twill weave results from passing the weft alternately in front and behind two or more warps, each pick being staggered by one or two warps to right or left, to produce a diagonal ribbed effect. The test of a weaver's skill is whether the finer design details keep their shape for 500 years or so (*Author's copyright*)

15

Plate 3 The characteristic ribbed texture of traditional tapestry is clearly seen in this view of a weaver passing a blue weft thread through the shed formed by alternate warps. Bobbins hanging by their weft threads, at the left, will be used for weaving when the design dictates use of the weft colour wound on each of them (*Victorian Tapestry Workshop, Australia*)

Plate 4 Weavers at work on a high-warp loom often raise their modular seats as the weaving line of the tapestry rises, and so eliminate frequent adjustments to the warp and tapestry rollers, thus helping to maintain warp tension more evenly, and concurrently enjoying the opportunity to see a greater expanse of finished tapestry before it is wound on to the bottom roller. Tapestries in this workshop are woven from the front. A cartoon detail stands at the left (*Victorian Tapestry Workshop, Australia*)

twentieth century and especially in workshops where weaving is done from the front of the tapestry, it is more customary to place it near the weaving face.

7. As the level of woven tapestry builds up on the loom, weavers use a succession of boxes to raise their seating position until a height is reached at which it is convenient to wind down another length of warp and to wind up the woven tapestry on its roller (*see* Plate 4).

8. The workshop mark, designer's and, or, weaver's mark is usually woven into a border or a selvedge—i.e., the tapestry is 'signed'.

9. When the tapestry is finished it is cut off the loom and, for the first time, seen in its complete state, although work may still have to be done on the piece such as stitching in weft ends. It is not unusual for the workshop to have a small celebration.

A weaver at work on a low-warp loom is shown in 5. There is an initial slight difference of warp and weft tension between tapestries woven on different types of loom. This is apparent when the tapestry is cut off and shows where a change of colour occurs, but after a time the tension should relax and the distinction disappear. Eighteenth century weavers put a single red thread, the thickness of a line, in the top or bottom selvedge of a tapestry woven on a low-warp loom. The selvedge colour is usually the same for all tapestries of a particular manufactory, which may also weave it in a slight but distinctive pattern although all in the same colour, further to identify the piece with the workshop. The primary purpose of the selvedge is to provide a strong, neutral border that will eliminate any need to bind the tapestry to prevent it from fraying, or from loosening its border texture density.

A tapestry with much fine detail may have, say, 10 warps per centimetre (10 w/cm), or 25 warps per inch (25 w/in), and a hundred or more colour shades. Depending on its design and application, a tapestry cheaper to produce might still be adequate with only 5 w/cm (14–15 w/in) and only twenty colours. Inexpensive ways of creating dramatic effect are heavily dependent on close co-operation between designer and weaver, who must be masters of their craft. These cheaper ways include using more than one thickness of yarn for weft, making a shaded effect by weaving in strokes of lighter coloured weft that penetrates into the darker coloured areas, and the reverse, with the resulting production of half-tones or 'hatchings'. Sometimes a very thin and entirely different weft thread is woven between areas of different colour to provide a physical boundary not apparent to the eye except as a stark colour or tonal change. Silk and man-made fibre wefts give a sheen that enhances highlights; metallic threads such as silver or gold give a sense of warmth and richness in combination with suitable colours. A slit purposely left between small details of different colour heightens emphasis, but too many slits weaken the structure of the textile. Interlocking threads as depicted in 3 are a skilled alternative to slits. If the interlocking is done carelessly, uneven tensions will produce bulging; and there is always the temptation for a lazy weaver to make, for example, a diagonal line in the form of a number of steps instead of interlocking one warp at a time to left or right, so as to produce an even diagonal.

During the latter part of the twentieth century, much has been made of so-called 'three-dimensional tapestry' as if it were a new phenomenon. It is not. All textiles are three-dimensional and, because of its characteristically ribbed surface, tapestry looks more three-dimensional than other textiles. But some

4 This is part of the cartoon for the *Peter and the Wolf* tapestry depicted in Plate 45 and shows how the design is outlined for copying or tracing on to the warps of the loom. The numbers and letters encode the weft thread colours and tints the weaver should use (*Gabriella Hajdal, Budapest; photograph Karoly Szelenyi*)

5 This weaver is working at a low-warp loom. The cartoon lines are clearly seen just below the warps, through which the bobbin of weft thread is passed to make the tapestry. The separation of alternate warps, to make the shed through which the bobbin is passed, is operated by foot pedals. The weaver selects the separated warps between which the weft is to be laid and passes the bobbin (*Nürnberger Gobelin Manufaktur, Federal Republic of Germany*)

very capable designers and weavers have created a new conception of three-dimension using plane design and colours alone. They have produced the three-dimensional visual effect in pictorial and landscape tapestries, and in some with plane patterns or figures which appear to recede into the tapestry fabric. This is art. The so-called 'three-dimensional tapestries' rely almost entirely on physical displacement of parts of the fabric, and there is the ever-present question: is it the same 'tapestry' when somebody who is neither the designer nor weaver has been required to disturb the original arrangement in the process of cleaning? One tends to feel much the same about this sort of stuff as William Morris felt about the Gobelins manufactures of the mid-nineteenth century, and which he expressed in his lecture, *The Lesser Arts of Life*.

There is insufficient space in this book to describe all the techniques of weaving in great detail. There are books devoted to the subject. The foregoing is but an introduction.

The Legendary Origins of Tapestry

Archaeological research on ancient sites in recent times has shown that a legend sometimes is the clothing given by repeated folk word-of-mouth transmission of a fact from father-to-son, from mother-to-daughter until the time of written history evolved; even then, historians were not always un-biased observers, nor schooled in the arts of precise description.

The principal materials of old tapestry were linen thread from the flax plant, wool from sheep, wild and subsequently cultivated cotton, wild and sub-sequently cultivated silk from silkworms. All are the subject of innumerable legends.

There is a story that flax was first grown in the Garden of Eden, for it goes back to the beginning of the world when the gods chose the finest woven linen for raiment. Archaeological discoveries at Robenhausen in Switzerland have shown that flax was grown and processed into linen cloth during the Stone Age when mammoths still roamed through Europe. Discovery of the purple dye, murex, by the mythical Hercules and his dog (*see* Appendix 3) resulted some 5500 years ago in the Phoenicians' (derived from the Greek 'Phoinikis' meaning 'red-skinned') extensive international trade in both the dye and purple cloth from Tyre, and bartering it for wool and spices throughout the Mediterranean and as far away as south-west England, where they traded murex for tin. According to Herodotus (485–425 BC), Xerxes of Persia (510–465 BC) obtained flaxen ropes from the Phoenicians for the bridge he wanted to build over the Hellespont. Long before Rome was much more than a village, a princess of Tyre increased the wealth of that town by constructing branch dyeing factories at Carthage and other Mediterranean coastal towns. And the Roman sheep-breeding expert, Lucius Columalla, resident in Spain, is credited with having crossed the native Spanish sheep with the selectively-bred Roman Tarrentine sheep to produce the merino wool sheep.

Cotton (derived from the Arabic word 'quoton') was, according to some legends, first cultivated in India and spread as the result of Arabic traders' activities to central Asia and China about 5500 years ago. Unless the Brahmin sacrificial thread was of cotton, the Manu Laws of India imposed heavy penalties. Alexander the Great (356–323 BC) is said to have commended the locally printed cotton fabric of India.

The Chinese Empress Hsi-Ling-Chi accidentally dropped silkworm cocoons into a bowl of hot water and, noticing how the fine strands of silk separated from the cocoon, she started intensive cultivation of mulberry trees to feed thousands of silkworms, from the cocoons of which she reeled the silk, and so founded the industry of sericulture, to weave silk into the finest of all cloths. This story of the industry's origins goes back some 4600 years. Another story concerns the attempt of the Roman Pompey, and Marcus Aurelius, to import silk from China. The first was lucky and obtained the silk he wanted; the second was refused and had to obtain his supply from Persia (Iran). The origins of silk puzzled the Western world for long. The geographer Pausanias believed it resulted from the Chinese cramming food into a spider-like insect until its abdomen burst under the pressure of the silk it was growing. A Roman historian claimed that silk was the watered and combed earth of some parts of China. According to a fable, silk production spread to India after a Chinese princess smuggled silkworm eggs to her betrothed, an Indian prince. An alternative version is that two Persian monks of the sixth century smuggled eggs of the silkworm out of China for the Emperor Justinian of Constantinople (Istamboul). The 10 000km (6 200 mile) Silk Road stretching across Asia and Europe from China to Greece and Rome was pioneered 2 100 years ago, and was instrumental in spreading silk and other commodities, as well as becoming a highway in the spread of knowledge—and banditry. Archaeological discoveries in the Chinese province of Sinkiang, dating from 2 000 years ago or earlier, show a strong Greek–Syrian influence in the design of silk fabrics.

A legend suggests the Chinese wove hemp into finer garments than linen could have produced some 4600 years ago (2700 BC). From China, hemp spread to Persia and Central Asia; legends refer to its use in India some 2 500 years ago, and also by the Egyptians, Babylonians and peoples of Arabian countries generally. The Arabic for 'hemp' is 'canvas'. Herodotus wrote that the Greeks regarded hemp as being superior to flax. The Spanish conquerors of Peru are said to have brought to Europe some South American varieties of cannabis, from which hemp is made.

The tutelary goddess of Egyptian weaving was Neith or Pthymais, who is represented with a shuttle-symbol. Alfred the Great's mother is reputed to have been a skilled weaver, who taught her daughters the art. India claims origin of the spinning wheel, but a picture painted in China about 700 years ago shows what appears to be the spinning of wild silk with a spinning wheel. There are contemporary legends of Persian origin attributing the origin of spinning wheels to that country. The earliest European references to the spinning wheel appear in the fourteenth century. The Greeks claimed that the art of spinning was invented by Pallas Athena, who is always represented with a distaff.

The Old Testament contains some of the earliest written mentions of weaving and of material which appears to be tapestry. *Exodus*, xxvi describes tapestry similar to that of ancient Egyptians:

> Moreover, thou shalt make the tabernacle with ten curtains of fine twined linen, and blue, and purple, and scarlet: with cherubim of cunning work shalt thou make them. The length of one curtain shall be eight and twenty cubits, and the breadth of one curtain four cubits: and every one of the curtains shall have one measure. The five curtains shall be coupled together one to another: and other five curtains shall be coupled one to another. And thou shalt make loops of blue upon the edge of the one curtain, from the selvedge in the coupling; and likewise shalt thou make in the uttermost edge of another curtain, in the coupling of the second. Fifty loops shalt thou make in the edge of the curtain that is in the

coupling of the second, that the loops may take hold one of another. And thou shalt make fifty taches of gold, and couple the curtains together with the taches; and it shall be one tabernacle.

This was what the people of Israel were to do when they wandered through the desert in preparation for the Land of Promise. And they were to prepare a veil:

And thou shalt make a veil of blue, and purple, and scarlet, and fine twined linen, of cunning work: with cherubim shall it be made.

And a 'hanging' for the door of the tent was to be made likewise.

Persia's age-long association with the materials of tapestry weaving suggests that tapestry is meant when 'hangings' are referred to in the scene of the feast given by King Ahasuerus in his palace of Shushan:

Where were white, green, and blue, hangings, fastened with cords of fine linen and purple to silver rings and pillars of marble . . .

(*Esther*, i, 6)

The Latin name for tapestry is derived from the Greek, and so it has been assumed the Greeks taught the Romans how to weave tapestries. In Book 2 of the *Odyssey* Homer (*c* 700 BC) describes how Odysseus' wife Penelope had woven a shroud for her father-in-law, Laertes. Odysseus was away and Penelope had kept a crowd of suitors at a distance by promising to marry one of them after the shroud was finished. It was the custom of the Greeks to make a shroud of the finest weaving to use when burying their dead, and to make this covering while the beloved was still alive, for it was a great slight to be buried without

6 *Penelope seated by her warp-weighted loom*; depicted on the Chuisi Vase from 400 BC (A History of Tapestry *by* W.G. Thomson, Hodder & Stoughton)

one. To gain time against the return of Odysseus, Penelope unpicked by night the portion she had woven by day:

> Did not the sun, thro' heav'n's wide azure roll'd
> For three long years, the royal fraud behold?
> While she laborious in delusion spread
> The spacious loom, and mix'd the various thread;
> Where as to life the woundrous figures rise,
> Thus spoke the inventive Queen with artful sighs.
> 'Tho cold in death Ulysses breathes no more,
> Cease yet awhile to urge the bridal hour;
> Cease 'till to great Laertes I bequeath
> A task of grief, his ornaments of death,
> Lest when the Fates his royal ashes claim,
> The Grecian maidens taint my spotless fame;
> When he, whom living mighty realms obeyed,
> Shall want in death a shroud to grace his shade.'
> Thus she: at once the gen'rous train complies,
> Nor fraud mistrusts in virtue's fair disguise.
> The work she ply's but studious of delay,
> By night revers'd the labours of the day.

A Greek vase about 2500 years old (*c* 500 BC) is decorated with a picture of Penelope at her loom (*see* 6).

Andromache was secretly weaving a similar vestment for Hector at the time of his death:

> Pensive she ply's the melancholy loom,
> A growing work employ'd her secret hours,
> Confus'dly gay with intermingled flow'rs.
>
> (*Iliad*, Book 22)

When Helen of Troy is called by Iris to witness the combat between Menelaus and Paris:

> Her in the palace at her loom she found;
> The golden web her own sad story crown'd,
> The Trojan wars she weav'd (herself the prize),
> And the dire triumphs of her fatal eyes.
>
> (*Iliad*, Book 3)

The most comprehensive description of ancient tapestry weaving is given by the Roman poet Ovid (43 BC–AD 17) some 1960 years ago, in his *Metamorphoses*. He describes a duel, fought with looms as weapons, between the goddess Pallas and Arachne. The latter was a famous lady weaver, whose dexterity and pride in her work so aroused the anger of the goddess tutelary of the craft, that she challenged her mortal rival to face defeat in a weaving contest. The poem is too long to print in full; the following are the initial few lines:

> Straight to their Posts appointed both repair,
> And fix their threaded Looms with equal care;
> Around the solid Beam the Web is ty'd,
> While hollow Canes the parting Warp divide;
> Through which with nimble Flight the Shuttles play,
> And for the Woof prepare a ready way;
> The Woof and Warp unite, press'd by the toothy Slay.

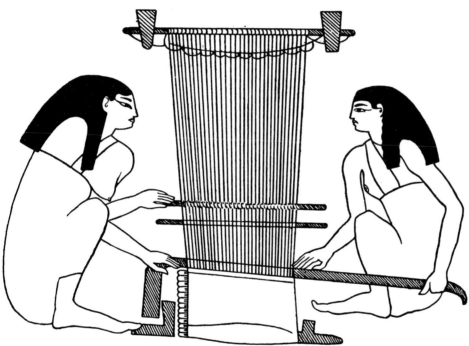

7 These wall paintings done in 3000 BC, from the tomb chambers of Beni-Hassan in Egypt, show the spinning of linen thread, and the preparation of a low-warp loom supported off the ground by stakes. The lower loom – a high-warp loom – is depicted in greater detail in 8. It will be seen that it has many of the features of a modern loom, including heddle loops round alternate warps, shown below the top of the loom. Egyptian spinners appear to have prided themselves on the number of threads they could spin simultaneously and, by climbing on successively higher platforms, the length of thread they could spin before winding spun thread on the spindle (*Upper series of drawings from the Science Museum, London; drawing of loom from* A History of Tapestry *by* W. G. Thomson, Hodder & Stoughton)

Arachne chose for her subject *The Amours of the Gods* and Pallas was so overcome with vexation at the success of a work not inferior to her own, and incensed beyond control at her rival's deliberate insult in selecting for subject *The Amours of the Gods*, that she belaboured her hapless foe with a shuttle and finally changed Arachne to a spider to weave evermore. The description in *Metamorphoses* is so lucid that it is undoubtedly of a tapestry which the poet had seen, and gives an invaluable idea of the subject, style and treatment of these hangings in Roman times.

The high-warp loom with stone-weighted warps and the weaving extending downwards from the top depicted on the Greek vase in 6 and 8 was comparable with a loom used in more recent times in northern Europe, and

Norwegian museums have examples. The *Njal Saga* of Iceland was most probably written about 700 years ago, *c* AD 1280. The following is taken from an early translation. The most recent translation by Magnus Magnusson and Hermann Palsson, published by Penguin Books, gives a slightly different version, but both link Scotland with Iceland and the warp-weighted loom:

> In the north of Caithness, Darad came up to a rock, having seen several figures approach and disappear into it. In this rock there was an opening through which he saw wild women weaving, and singing as they wove. And the weights of the loom he beheld were human heads—the heads of heroes: and of entrails were the warps and woof; swords were the shuttles; and for a comb they had arrows. Now as they sang their awful song, the words dinned in his ears and became understandable. They sang that they were the Valkyries and that the web they were weaving was the web of Darad. As the song ceased they tore in pieces the work they had done, and departed as they had come, some going north and some going south.

In Norse mythology the Valkyries were the chosen handmaidens of the god Odin, and had the special responsibility of riding through the skies at the time of battle, and pointing out the heroes who were to die. Caithness is part of northern Scotland which was under Norwegian influence for several centuries.

The Likely Origins of Tapestry

The first material with tapestry-like characteristics may have been woven by Nature herself among the reeds, rushes and tall grasses of some sea, lake or river-side marsh some 400000 years ago, in the equatorial regions; in fact, in the very places where prehistoric man is thought to have developed, where he first learned to make tools and use resources of his habitat to improve his conditions.

When the winds of autumn swept over rushes fringing a lake or river, the tall leaf blades would bend over to fall between the strong and upright former heads of flower-stalks, inter-twining with them to make a semi-woven mat-like mass which a hunting animal might use as a lair to spring out from on its prey, or to shelter under. Observing the benefits and possibilities of structures like these, prehistoric man may have gathered tall flower-head stalks or cut willowy saplings to make a warp-like framework; and gathered grasses, rushes and long creeper plants to make a weft that he could intertwine about the sapling warps, pressing the strands down over the saplings so as to construct a dense shield, hide, or wattle-like mass that could serve equally as a door to a cave or a defence barrier. Some authorities claim that tapestry-like textiles were the first to be developed because nature provided all the materials long before man learned to spin bast fibres into a strong thread. It was a short step to making a basket, or to choosing certain types of rush or reed, because of such properties as toughness, colour, resistance to rot or to vermin. Weaving should, perhaps, be regarded as man's first true invention, for an artefact was created with properties substantially differing from its constituent parts, and in sum total far greater than them individually. For greater strength lengths of skin, hair and strips of bark are likely to have been used which, in time, might have been plaited to increase length and resistance to strain. Gradually colours would have been introduced for ornament, or to make a camouflaged door for the entrance to a cave, or to cover a pit in the ground baited to ensnare large animals of the hunt. There is evidence that the women of a tribe were responsible for weaving and the men for hunting.

The last ice-cap covering northern Europe started to recede between 25 000 and 15 000 years ago. The ice did not melt progressively; there was a succession of miniature ice-ages, all decreasing in intensity and duration. As the ice melted, the level of the seas was raised and some previously dry land was submerged, such as the land-bridge that had linked Asia to America in the Bering Sea, and that which linked Britain with continental Europe. But before Asia and America were separated by the 85 km (53 mile) wide channel, there was an Asian immigration to the North American continent which spread out to form communities with their own local characteristics and customs. With continuing recession of the ice-cap, Europe's west coast from Spain to Denmark was the first to enjoy an increasingly temperate climate, with the result that plant life started to spread up the valleys in spring and herds of grazing animals found these new pastures to return only when winter approached, to their former haunts. Plants particularly suitable for the making of wickerwork, basket and mat-like or primitive tapestry constructions grew in abundance, and soon were followed by plants like flax, which had been indigenous to the Caucasus region.

Hunters followed the migrating herds into the newly ice-free valleys, making skin-covered wickerwork encampments there for families, and followed the herds southwards again as winter approached. As the climate continued to warm up, the herds moved further north or inland and, in time, the hunters wintered with their families in the new valleys, having found means of making more permanent habitations of wattle and daub or mud-brick, thatched with rushes. The discovery of how to build a home in a place of choice rather than be dependent upon a cave, was the first step in turning a hunter of nomadic habits into a community dweller who could concentrate his efforts in and around one place. Thus developed the need to weave mats, and wickerwork or rush baskets for food storage, or as a shield or shelter. In regions subject to natural disaster or where the climate was inhospitable, the hunter continued as a nomad. The communities tended to form along the herds' migratory routes which, in course of time, turned into trade routes as well. Evolution was not uniform, but was stimulated where climate, food supplies, and man's initiative combined to create optimum conditions.

The simplest basket was woven much as it is today, with a single 'warp' of thin bamboo spiralling round on itself, and stitched in place by raffia (the weft) which covers the bamboo and leaves a typically ribbed surface. London's British Museum has a grass fibre basket buried some 7 000 years ago in a grain storage-pit near to Wady-el-Faiym, Egypt. New York's American Museum of Natural History has the baked mud-impression of a basket that was buried more than 6 000 years ago at Mostagedda, south of Cairo, Egypt.

8 Drawings on an Athenian vase made about 500 BC depict most of the stages in the preparation of weft and its conversion into tapestry on a weighted-warp upright loom, on which the fabric is woven downwards from the top (*Metropolitan Museum of Art, USA*)

Second only to the development of weaving itself was the discovery that fibres could be lengthened into a continuous, long and fairly even thickness thread by the process of spinning, a process that was known to the Swiss lake-dwellers of the Stone Age at Robenhausen. Cultivated flax (*Linum usitatissium*) was grown from the wild variety (*Linum angustifolium*) probably concurrently in the Euphrates and the Tigris river valleys, and on the banks of Egypt's Nile. Flax is thought to have originated in the Caucasus region, from which it spread out as far west as the Canary Islands. The discovery that a long, even thread could be made by teasing out a continuous succession of certain animal and vegetable fibres, and binding them together by spinning, was a development of immense importance. The first method of spinning, dated in Europe and Asia to more than 10000 years ago, was accomplished by holding a bundle of loose fibres in one hand and, with the other hand, teasing out a length which was rubbed against the thigh by the fingers of that hand, to twist the thread. It is of great interest that this method of spinning was used by North American Indian weavers of bags until about 320 years ago; they spun fibres like ramie (from a plant related to the nettle family), and fibres from the bark of the slippery elm, cedar and linden trees. The spinning spindle originated from between 10000 and 11000 years ago and was to remain the principal means of making thread until some 700 years ago, when the spinning wheel (variously attributed to the ingenuity of the Indians, Chinese or Persians) came into use. The spinning spindle was a circular straight stick about 45cm (18in) long with a notch or a hole at the top end and, at the lower end, a circular pancake shaped weight (the 'whorl') of stone, bone or fire-hardened wood or earthenware, through the centre of which the stick was fastened. The spinner teased out a length of fibre and fixed the end in a hole or notch and then set the stick rotating, with the circular weight acting as a flywheel. As each length of fibre was spun into a thread, it was fed through the notch or hole and wound round the spindle for storage. When the spindle was bulging with spun thread, this was reeled off onto a bobbin, and the spinning process started again. The next development was a means of aligning the fibre strands to facilitate pulling them out to form a thread; this was done by drawing the yarn out initially with teazels of the teazel plant, and later on, by wire brushes, the process being known as 'carding'. The carded fibres were then wound round a stick called a 'distaff', which replaced the bundle of loose fibres held by the spinner. These widespread primitive means of spinning produced extraordinarily fine thread that in some instances has never been bettered. Whorls have been found in the deposits of many ancient towns and settlements; in the debris of Jericho of between 9000 and 10000 years ago; in the Mediterranean island of Cyprus, where the whorls were associated with wool-spinning; in the United Soviet Socialist Republic of Turkmen, where archaeologists have uncovered villages with histories extending from 6000 to 3000 years ago; and in Afghanistan, where stone-age farming communities spun sheep and goat wool to make woven fabrics; and in China, India, Persia and the Middle East generally.

It is virtually impossible to determine which early textiles had tapestry characteristics. But if one compares the physical properties of tapestry with those of more loosely woven cloths and studies the probability of a particular civilization or people having materials and equipment needed for making it—as opposed to other types of cloth—there are logical reasons for thinking that tapestry was a preferred textile for certain purposes and circumstances. For example, as a door hanging and as a decorative wall covering (its density minimized draughts and, hung over a damp wall, it did not deteriorate in the same way as paintings might have done); as a bed canopy and covering (it was easier to keep clean than skins, did not smell as skins tended to do, and was healthier for those who suffered allergies from fur); for clothing (principally gloves, tunics, caps and windproof capes); and for saddle-covers (tapestry could easily be woven to particular shapes and showed wear less than wool or fur-covered skins). It is almost certain that the legendary 'flying-carpet' was no carpet or rug, but a tapestry. The techniques of tapestry weaving preceded the arts of rug and carpet-making. When looking at early painted pictures and at mosaics, it is of interest to note whether there is a carpet or rug on the floor. It is not unusual to find the floor is covered with tiles, or the artist has chosen to show flowering plants as the floor or ground, but that the walls of a building or throne are hung with tapestry. This is particularly true of early paintings of the Madonna and Child.

The Foundations of Ancient Tapestry in Europe and Asia

The oldest woven textile yet found is linen cloth made by Swiss lake-dwellers about 14000 years ago (12000 BC). Weaving may have been accomplished by interleaving threads. The first loom dates from some 4000 years later. The spinning and weaving of linen thread on low-warp looms appears to have started in Egypt about 8000 years ago (6000 BC). The thread was so exceedingly fine and the skill of the weavers so remarkably great that they apparently had no great difficulty in weaving linen with a texture of more than a hundred warps per centimetre. Woven for mummy wrappings, the textile was in lengths of many metres. The tomb chambers of Beni-Hassan are about 5000 years old (3000 BC) and have several wall inscriptions representing spinners and weavers at work, as shown in 7. The Egyptians considered wool impure and used garments made of it only for secular purposes. The Museum of Egyptian Antiquities in Cairo has three fragments of tapestry from the tomb of Thoutmôsis IV, which are, by ancient Egyptian standards, of coarse texture. One piece measures about 12 × 3·5cm (4¾ × 1½in) and is of white linen weave with hieroglyphics of the Ká name of Thoutmôsis III, Men-kheper-Rá, a king of the eighth dynasty, of about 3500 years ago (1503–1449 BC), and the father of Amenothes II (Museum Catalogue no. 46528). The second piece is similar, and the third piece, measuring 28·6 × 42·5cm (11¼ × 16¾in), has narrow borders at the right and left sides with incomplete edges at top and bottom. The left border has a repeating pattern of alternate lotus flowers and buds, beautifully rendered in red, blue and green linen threads on a ground that was once white. The pattern is of exquisite delicacy in design and execution. The border at the right has a double row of alternate truncated discs in red and blue. A network of lotus flowers in blue and red, alternating with papyrus inflorescences in blue, red, brown and yellow, outlined in black, lies on a field of white between the borders. At the lower left part of the field the diaper pattern gives place to the praenomen of Amenothes II in a cartouche, supported by uraei worked in blue, brown, black, red and yellow, the one on the left wearing the red crown of Lower Egypt, the other the white crown, red-outlined, denoting the sovereignty of Upper Egypt. Over the cartouche the titles of the king are given in hieroglyphics. Amenothes II of the eighteenth dynasty reigned from about 1449–1423 BC, some 3500 years ago. Texture is 12·6 w/cm (60 w/in) approximately. Warps run vertically to the

9 A pre-Inca loom found in a tomb, in an almost perfect state of preservation (*Trustees of the British Museum, London*)

direction of reading the hieroglyphics in the larger piece, and horizontally in the smaller piece. The weft is appreciably thicker than the warp, and the delicacy with which floral and other forms are rendered leaves no doubt that a vertical loom was used. This is confirmed by the fact that the patterns are exactly the same on both sides of the fabric, there being no 'passings' or ends of threads visible; probably the weaver worked from the face of the tapestry. The warp bears traces of tension changes made to facilitate design execution, as when a vulture's wing on the smaller fragment shows warp relaxation to aid weaving. Warp tension variations were arranged on an upright loom like that shown in 6 and 8, where the warps were held perpendicular by being attached to weights instead of to a roller. The execution of the human forearm in one of the hieroglyphics of the smallest piece resembles needlework but more likely was woven by a technique common in later Coptic work, known as 'ressaut'. Similarly, execution of the semi-circular arch forms of the hieroglyphics is achieved by weaving from a nucleus at the middle of the base with the shape built up by concentric layers of weft threads; this technique also is found in later Coptic work where the weft, ceasing to be at right-angles to the warp, crosses it obliquely to express a curved form. In the spaces between contiguous warps bearing weft threads of different colours there is, at intervals, a crossing stitch which holds the fabric together. With the exception of the particular techniques described there is but little difference in weaving methods between these 3400-year-old fragments and later tapestries. The upright warp-weighted loom appears to have superseded the type of upright loom depicted in 7 and, through Egypt's close links from about 3000 BC or earlier with Crete, north Mesopotamia or Syria, and the Aegean generally, seems to have been adopted widely, as the pictures reproduced from Greek vases show. The Scandinavians and Scots were familiar with this type of loom, as the quotation from the *Njal Saga* has shown. The early Egyptian low-warp loom was crude, comprising four posts driven into the ground on which was mounted a rectangular frame with devices for holding the warp threads with a density of as many as 200 w/cm (508 w/in). Linen as fine as silk was woven in strips up to 150cm (5ft) wide and 55·3m (180ft) long approximately. Tombs dating from about 3400 BC have yielded fragments of plain linen cloth, and also a scrap thought to be at least 7900 years old. Silk and cotton were unknown, and wool little used. The royal spinning mills were at Memphis, Panopolis and Thebes. Dyes were first used about 4000 years ago (2000 BC) and made by an extremely unpleasant process involving urine; in addition to blue from woad and red from madder, red and yellow were obtained from dyer's thistle. Until about 1320 BC the Egyptians' royal and priestly textiles were sent to Tyre for the Phoenicians to dye them purple with murex; the process was so costly that only the powerful and wealthy could afford to be clothed 'in the purple'. Paintings show that tapestry design included stripes, spots and zigzag patterns and decorative weaves. The tomb of Tutankhamen (1360–1350 BC) contained a tapestried robe and glove. Tapestry weaving continued in Egypt until the start of the Christian era.

But it is now desirable to consider the development of tapestry from its earliest beginnings in other regions of the world, to bring them to the same period at which we shall—for a little—leave that of Egypt.

There is archaeological evidence of wool-spinning and weaving at Khirpkitia, in the Mediterranean island of Cyprus, from about 7000 to 8000 years ago (5000 to 6000 BC), but although facilities for the technique existed, it is not clear how early tapestry weaving started to grow there, eventually, into a famous manufactory. In central Germany's Göhlitzsch near the river Elbe, a chamber tomb with wall engravings that appeared to represent textile hangings was dated at about 1900 BC. The Elbe with the rivers Saale and Weser formed parallel alternative routes linking Jutland with the eastern Mediterranean via the Brenner Pass and the Adriatic which, 400 years later, formed the trade route for the bartering of amber for metals, between Danish Jutland and the Greek archipelago during the Baltic states' Bronze Age. This ancient commercial enterprise is of great interest because Danish tombs of the period have yielded evidence that men and women dressed in woven woollen clothes, and suggests that the warp-weighted loom may have been used from the Mediterranean to the Baltic earlier than 1900 BC, although first depicted by the Greeks about a millennium or more later. Earlier than 1900 BC emigrants skilled in farming and metal-working had traversed a route across Europe extending from the Baltic to the Caucasus with a corresponding spread of knowledge and distribution of artefacts of similar types over this route. Except in a few places, specimens of ancient textiles have not survived environmental conditions of several thousands of years as they have done, for example, in the hot dry sands of Egypt and Peru.

Leningrad's Hermitage Museum has specimens of tapestry excavated many years ago from the Tomb of the Seven Brothers at Tembriouck, Kouban, an ancient Greek settlement on the north-east shore of the Black Sea. The fragments are about 2400 years old (300–400 BC) and appear to have been part of a head-covering ornamented with a diamond pattern and a powdering of ducks on a reddish ground that has a border of stags' heads disposed upside-down to the pattern. The pattern is the same on both sides, which suggests that the tapestry was woven from the front on an upright loom with weighted warps.

Both Romans and Greeks treated tapestry as an essential part of the furnishings of a stately home or building, and later as objects of luxurious art. Tapestry weaving does not appear to have been professionally practised to any great extent in Rome; hangings initially were imported from abroad, for example from Babylon, Egypt, Persia, India and even Gaul. Babylon was famous for its embroideries and tapestries and, according to some accounts, decked its walls with the richest hangings on festive occasions. Pliny (died AD 113) wrote that some Babylonian hangings made for Rome during the last years of the Republic were sold a hundred years later to Nero (AD 37–68), and that he ordered a large awning to be woven for one of Rome's theatres, the design of which was to be Apollo driving his chariot; another tapestry was in the shape of a purple curtain adorned with representations of Britons. Some weaving done in Rome was the work of women slaves who were required to make enough for household requirements and to sell at a profit in the public market. The Greeks are said to have made tapestries to cover the Parthenon. Latin writers of 2000 years ago describe the magnificent tapestries they had seen in Babylon and other cities. There is no doubt that for several centuries preceding the Christian era, Persia was a major producer of fine tapestries.

In the Far East the Neolithic inhabitants of Japan, the Jōmon people of Caucasian origins (and ancestors of the more recent Ainu peoples), lived in villages c 2000 BC and wove textiles on horizontal looms with plaited or twisted cord. The loom was staked to the ground at the far end from the woman weaver. The warps fanned out from the stake to a rod which held them equidistant and parallel, beyond which they projected to a similar rod in front of the weaver. This rod was either staked to the ground at its two ends or these were attached to the ends of a strap which encircled the weaver. To vary warp tension the weaver leant either forward or backwards.

The Foundations of Ancient Tapestry in the Americas

Although the main migration of Asian peoples to the Americas may have ended with the submersion of the Bering land-bridge by the melting waters of the ice-age, there is reason to believe that immigration continued by raft or boat. As the immigrants spread out to form isolated communities or nomadic bands, they developed their own traditions, customs, dialects and eventually languages, and modes of self-expression. Those who stayed in northern latitudes encountered a hard life with little time or materials for construction of other things than the essentials. Consequently, for example, Alaska natives have always made baskets and, according to information received recently from the Anchorage Historical and Fine Arts Museum, traditional methods of construction are still being used today. The Aleuts make rye-grass baskets that display their incredible agility, and Eskimo baskets are of beach grass. The only real textile industry in Alaska has been among the Tlingit Indians of the north-west coast, who wove ceremonial Chilkat blankets of cedar bark and mountain goat wool. America's last mini ice-age was from 9000 to 8000 BC, some 10000 years ago; the main initial spread of hunting and husbandry dates from c 8000 to 5000 BC which, by happy coincidence for purposes of comparison, matches closely with the period during which spinning and weaving appears to have started in Europe, Africa, etc.

Archaeological excavation in the Americas has uncovered evidence of spinning and weaving of many kinds from about 5000 BC. In Utah's 'Danger Cave' textile bags and traps woven with twisted flax, bullrushes, hemp and cedar or sagebrush bark were found and dated to between 5000 and 7000 years old. Other and later period objects were found in Nevada, Oregon and

10 Woven on wool warps with a wool weft, this slit-technique, Nazca, south-coast, Classic-Period (AD 250–70) Peruvian tapestry is an excellent example of design of the period. The principal motif is a figure with its main axis parallel to the weft. The elaborate headdress has appendages in the form of heads, possibly intended to be feline, with extended tongues terminating in similar heads. Colours are rust-red with golden shades, blue, green and black outlines (*Burrell Collection, Glasgow Art Gallery*)

other parts of the United States of America. A variety of looms which came into use included the backstrap loom, and also one with a warp frame on which were woven yucca fibre textiles with the weft rammed solidly as in tapestry. North American Indians produced many types of woven fabric but these are scarcely identifiable with tapestry.

During the twentieth century increasing research has been carried out on the incredible textiles—particularly tapestry—produced in ancient Peru. As there is often considerable confusion among people who have not actually visited South America, or who do not have a detailed knowledge of the development of this part of the world, it is appropriate to give a few outline facts. The political boundaries of the Peru of today are not the same as those of the Inca Empire, which stretched in the north from the southern boundary of Columbia to the boundaries of Chile and Argentina in the south, and encompassed an area of almost 91 million hectares (350000 square miles), with a seaboard extending to nearly half the total west coast, and with lands extending into the high Andes. The three principal periods which receive most attention historically are: (1) the pre-Inca period, referring to dates before AD 1250; (2) the pre-Columbian period, referring to dates before 1498 when Christopher Columbus landed in South America; and (3) the pre-Conquest period, referring to dates before 1532, when the Spaniards conquered Peru. Europeans and others with no personal experience of Central and South America sometimes confuse the art of ancient Peru and Mexico, and mistake the former's Tiahuanaco culture of AD 700–1200 for the latter's Teotihuacan, Aztec or Maya cultures, or even think there was a strong link between the two countries. It should be said that apart from a possible slight trade in shells, turquoise and the metals of jewellery, there was no significant link.

Peruvian climatic conditions of old presented the same contrasts as today. The coastal regions were warm and dry, and the mountainous areas were wet and temperate with intense cold in the higher ranges. Historical research has been made difficult by the fact that Peruvians made no records of their history and did not communicate in writing until after the Spanish Conquest. Consequently the accurate dating of artefacts has proved extremely difficult, and has not been helped by the virtual impossibility of associating many items with a particular tomb or place because they were once the spoils of grave-robbers! Textiles bear no weaver's mark or like means of identification. Stylistic and analytical tests do not always prove trustworthy. There has been considerable controversy about the dates of Peruvian cultural development but, by noting certain similarities in a suitably large sample of textiles, it has proved possible to build up an outline of Peruvian textile history.

The main weaving materials were cotton grown on the coast, maguey (a bast fibre derived from the cactus plant), and the wool of llama, alpaca, vicuna and guanaco from the mountain regions. Some of these materials display a variety of natural colours and, in particular, alpaca wool was obtained in bluish or dark grey, and black. Vegetable and animal dyes (including murex) were used to give several shades of red, blue, purple and yellow. Dramatic effects were obtained by the use of vivid shades and neutral colours such as various shades of brown, yellows and greys. Vicuna wool textiles were so fine that they resembled silk, which was unknown in pre-Conquest times. Salt of aluminium was used as the dye mordant.

The Peruvians disposed of their dead in a manner somewhat similar to that of the ancient Egyptians, and it is in these tomb chambers in the coastal areas that so many ancient textiles have been found. The corpse of the deceased was wrapped, or perhaps one should more appropriately say bundled, in great lengths of textiles that included brocade, painted or tie-and-dye cloth, velvet and pile-carpet-like fabrics, and also tapestry. The considerable variety and number of pots, vases and ornaments inhumed with the dead had the effect —as one archaeologist recently remarked—of creating a continuing demand for the production of new objects and may have been a way in antiquity of disposing honourably of outmoded possessions associated with the spirit of the deceased. The hot and dry climate of the coastal areas has favoured the

Plate 5 The design is typical of sixth century Peruvian Chimu tapestry; the fragment depicts a warrior with his right arm terminating in two smaller figures, and with upper and lower borders of zoomorphic figures. Colours are red, mustard, and blue on a red ground (*Art Gallery, University of Notre Dame, USA: Gift of Mrs Ann McNear*)

Plate 6 This Peruvian textile dates from the Classic Period of AD 250–750. It is more of an embroidery than a tapestry and is reproduced to illustrate the condor motif, which was a favourite form of woven decoration. The piece was found in a Paracas tomb (*Burrell Collection, Glasgow Art Gallery*)

preservation of the contents of many tombs.

Recent excavation of deposits dated by the carbon-14 measurement method has produced evidence of fabric weaving without looms from between 5000 and 6000 years ago (4000–3000 BC). Among the finds were wood needles and spinning spindles with stone whorls. On the coast, some thirty settlements have been located. The backstrap loom is likely to have been in use well before 1200 BC (some 3200 years ago) by communities with a mastery of building techniques, and who were agriculturists and farmers. Their total dependence on folk-memory for records, and on speech for communication, is likely to have made their progress slower than that of some other civilizations. The first identifiable culture did not start until about 2000 years ago (400 BC) and was the Paracas Cavernas culture of southern Peru. It continued for about 800 years and was succeeded by the Paracas Necropolis culture, which continued until c AD 1000. In the valleys of Nazca and Ica a separate but parallel culture developed between AD 400–1000. In the north, the Chimu culture flourished from about AD 1300 to 1448 in conditions not as favourable for preservation of textiles. Contemporary with Nazca and Chimu cultures of the coastal settlements, the Tiahuanaco culture developed in the mountain region centred on Lake Titicaca, some 3900m (12645ft) above sea-level, near the boundaries with Bolivia. This culture has been dated variously as extending from AD 700 to 1200, or from AD 600 to 1300, while some authorities split it into two phases. It continued to exert a strong influence right up to the time of the Spanish Conquest.

Despite the primitive weaving equipment, the ancient textiles of Peru, which were brought to light as the burial chambers of the Paracas Cavernas and other cultures were systematically explored, exhibit an incredible mental and manipulative ability in design, colour artistry and mastery of weaving techniques. Tapestry was rare but textiles in many weaves abounded. The majority of mummy wrappings were of plain weave or embroidered in wool with a stem stitch on cotton material. In addition to the natural colours of the materials, red and sapphire dyes were used in designs suggestive of gods and serpents. Clothing of the dead included short tunics, head coverings like a turban and waist-bands. Until weavers of the Cavernas culture traded their cotton for the wool of the highlands, textiles were predominantly of cotton. Some authorities claim the Paracas Cavernas and Necropolis cultures were subservient to the Nazca valley culture ('Paracas' refers to the Paracas Peninsula and 'Cavernas' to the bottle-shaped shaft tombs hewn in the ground; the 'Necropolis' tomb was discovered in the Peninsula in 1920). Cavernas and later weavers used a backstrap loom with heddles to select the warp thread. Extremely fine thread woven on slender spindles often used as bobbins produced a weft density exceeding 60 weft threads per centimetre (150 w/in) in finer tapestries. The variety of weaving techniques was as great as any in Europe and, in fact, tapestries were often more complex in the range of techniques than French or Flemish. Reversible fabrics were woven on two sets of warps; slit, interlocking, dove-tailing, twill and warp-twisting techniques were incorporated. The texture of vicuna wool tapestries was as fine as silk, and the colours used incorporated some twelve tints including material natural colours; despite this limitation, the geometrical and predominant figures were often fearsome or startling in effect. A range of colours incorporating up to 200 tints characterized the Necropolis culture, with repeating patterns and colour inversion to give contrast. Extravagant designs of a semi-human, semi-animal, semi-mythical god or beast character together with fantasies of a fish-, bird-, toad- or cat-like nature formed the subject of many textiles. Despite the seeming practical limitations of the loom, wrappings of 6 × 50m (20 × 162ft) or more have been found. Later tapestries contain fur from chinchillas and bats, and human hair.

Chimu culture textiles are vigorous and often have fish and bird motifs, the latter with fantastic plumage. A variety of zigzag lines and geometrical patterns are common. The Tiahuanaco culture was based on an advanced civilization of the interior of Peru, and was deeply influenced by a religion dominated by a god known to the Incas as Virachoca. Tapestries of the period often display cat-like images. During the reign of the Incas weaving was mostly concentrated on production of magnificent clothing for high officials and mummy wrappings, with wall hangings as a secondary consideration. Output of tapestry was greater, particularly by the Chimu weavers. The Incas brought no innovation to the tapestry arts except perhaps the generation of a greater range of what may be symbology in design. For years a theory has been advanced that the grotesque figures and details of so many textiles are elements of religious symbology to which the key was lost centuries ago, but have been copied and slightly exaggerated by each successive generation. Motifs incorporated in the earliest designs may have been an attempt to establish primitive hieroglyphics; it is almost unbelievable that the extremely gifted people of Greater Peru, who demonstrated their capabilities in so many ways, should have failed to produce any formal method of recording apart from knots on a string as a tally of numbers. But perhaps the very absence of writing placed such emphasis on pictorial arts that it encouraged designers of religious motifs to excel themselves in the production of eye-catching textiles with exuberant textures. The Paracas and Nazca fabrics have abounding multi-coloured symbols and marks, and the latter culture's décor makes repeated use of a spotted cat, which, in some versions, has pawfuls of leaves or seed-pods and suggests a form of fertility symbol. Compared with the latter's benign demeanour there is a part-cat, part-human, part-bird, seemingly carnivorous and complex apparition, which could be a devil-god; motifs based on a complex version of a fish and of a bird—with devil-like characteristics—are recurring symbols. A careful study of tapestry design leaves one with the impression that tapissiers carried the main responsibility for priestly recording and visual communication with the people, much in the same way as the nuns of medieval convents wove tapestries of sacred subjects, or the monks of contemporary monasteries excelled in the artistry and calligraphy of illuminated texts. The vigour, originality, and magnificent execution of Peruvian tapestries should provide inspiration for modern tapissiers who are good technicians but short on design ideas.

In the wake of the Spanish Conquest of Peru, tapestries were influenced by the design requirements of the invaders, and the craft showed increasing Hispano, or Hispano-Moresque influences, and largely withered as a discrete expression of native people. Since the beginning of this century Peruvian tapestry has been subjected to increasingly intense study.

The Foundations of Tapestry in Coptic Egypt

Compared with its former glory, Egypt had deteriorated almost out of recognition by the year 30 BC, and was incorporated into the Roman Empire with the status of a colonial possession. The population was predominantly Egyptian.

11 The design of a woman's head emphasized by what looks like a halo suggests that this second or third century tapestry fragment was woven by Copts of Aegean origins, influenced by Christianity. Materials are wool and linen (*Detroit Institute of Arts; gift of Octavia W. Bates Fund*)

The governing power regarded Egypt as a wealthy land and imposed crippling taxes on the peasantry. In this climate of widespread and grinding misery Christianity took root, as the result, it is said, of the preachings of St Mark. Towards the end of AD 200 the Church was centred in Alexandria, which became the focal point both for pilgrimage by Christians and for persecution by their Roman overlords. The conversion of Constantine to Christianity resulted, in AD 313, in the proclamation of Constantine and Licinius and formal recognition of the Church, although this proclamation was not really effective until the edict of Theodosius I in AD 379. Religious freedom lasted until AD 641 when, led by the general—Amr—of the Kaliph Omar, the Persians descended on Egypt and overpowered it in a short time. Thus, in a period of barely 700 years the art of the Copts—the direct descendants of the Egyptians of pharaonic times—was under the influence of Greece, Rome, Byzantium and Muslim Persia.

'Copt' is an abbreviation of the Greek 'Aigyptios' for the pharaonic 'Het-Ka-

Ptah', meaning the 'house of the Ka (soul) of Ptah' or shrine of Memphis, a name given to all Egyptian Christians in the Nile valley by the seventh century Muslim conquerors. This brief history is necessary to explain some of the strange contrasts in Coptic tapestry design, as, for instance, when a pagan god is given a Christian halo.

Whether pagan or converted to Christianity, the Egyptians continued the age-old burial customs for the dead. In the last quarter of the nineteenth century an Egyptologist, Gaston Maspero of the Cairo Museum, announced the discovery of innumerable relics of art work in the ancient necropolis of Akhmin-Panapolis in Upper Egypt. These finds were followed by the uncovering of other burial grounds at Denderah, Antinoë, Fayoum and Erment. The art was that of Graeco-Roman, Byzantium and Muslim Egypt in the form of clothes and articles buried with the dead in the hot dry sand, which had inhibited decay throughout the centuries. The dead were buried in the clothes they had worn in life; in a shirt or tunic woven in one piece with an aperture in the middle through which the head and neck of the wearer were passed. The material was usually fine linen with bands and panels of tapestry woven in wool and, very occasionally, silk. Symbols of Christianity were few in the earliest deposits, many of which were pre-Christian; the Christian symbols were mixed with pagan motifs during the early years of Christianity but became dominant in burials during the Byzantium period, although repulsive in the latter period of the style, and were gradually lost after the seventh century when the Muslim conquerors swept through the land and everywhere set their impression on art. A few centuries later, tapestry ornamentation was eclipsed by embroidery and the use of brocades, and so on.

The districts where the burial grounds were discovered had been the sites of ancient Hellenic settlements. When the power of Greece waned, Rome claimed the provinces for her own. As the lineal descendants of the pharaonic Egyptians, the Copts had practised the ancient crafts almost as an hereditary instinct. They had in the past woven garments for their Persian and Greek conquerors, and they did the same for their Roman masters, adopting freely that distinctive national style, for there is but little of recognizable Egyptian design in these weavings. Occasionally in the Roman and Christian ornamentation there are examples of atavism in the reversion to some ancient Egyptian symbol used as an element in design; but in general the work is carried out to the letter and in the spirit of the art of the ruling power. In the last Christian period, when that influence became weakened and debased, a characteristic Coptic style took its place, a style in which natural forms are outraged, and the only palliatives are bright colouring and fine texture.

But if the design in the best period of Coptic weaving is exclusively foreign, the technique of the finished work is unmistakably national, and there are few examples that do not bear the impress of the Copt. The tunics are for the greater part woven in the simplest shuttlework fashion, but are ornamented by tapestried bands, panels or diamond reticulations. This treatment is not exclusively Coptic, it is to be found in tapestry-woven clothes of Greater Peru. The fabric was begun in ordinary shuttle-weaving and carried on until the weaver desired to introduce a tapestry panel. At that point he changed the weft or threads in the shuttle and, working with two or more of the warp threads combined as one, he proceeded with his tapestry-weaving, beating down this new weft with the comb. The ordinary shuttle-weaving was continued to right and left of the insertion, and when the tapestry panel was completed the warp threads were divided into their original number, the plain weaving being proceeded with along the width of the loom. Such a method was delightfully simple and effective, for the in-woven panel or band being generally of wool or silk is slightly raised above the surface of the shuttle-woven linen that surrounds it. A simple upright loom or frame was used, and the workman seated in front might dispense with the heddles normally fitted to pull the distant warps towards him. This would produce a very pliant fabric, the warps being kept loose enough to permit the passing of the shuttle. Some of the later specimens of these inserted panels have been executed by another method, that of draw-thread work, a tambour-frame taking the place of the loom. But whatever the method of production was, the result was the same.

The chief characteristic feature in Coptic weaving is the extreme development of the principle of the free shuttle or spindle, or, as the French call it, the 'ressaut' or 'crapaud'. Tapestry weavers of western countries customarily keep their weft threads fairly perpendicular to the warps. Occasionally in rounding a leaf, etc., the weft to a slight extent takes the direction of the outline, but generally a rounded form is indicated in part by a series of step or ladder-like formations. The Copt did not bind himself by these formal methods, and carried the opposite principle to the extreme. He made his weft wander in any direction he wished, diagonally to the warp if he willed it, till sometimes weft and warp became almost parallel. He built up his mass form first, then his flying shuttle jumped from point to point, quite indifferent to the relative positions of warp and weft. This is the method pursued in those intricate geometric patterns traced in white outline on a dark purple ground, which at first glance give the impression of a needlework execution to anyone who is unacquainted with the capacity of the weaver's tools. The curious procedure is carried to such excess that the outlining weft forms almost a framing to the mass it encloses. This free shuttlework had been a heritage from the ancient Egyptians, for in one of the Cairo Museum's specimens there is an example where two of these shuttles have been used, and in the semi-circular forms the weft travels round the shapes. Apart from the above-cited peculiarities, Coptic tapestry-weaving is similar to medieval and some modern weaves. There are the slits in the fabric where a change of colour comes parallel to the warp, and the inter-crossing stitches when it is of considerable extent. In general the texture is finer than that met with in most of the medieval tapestries, but sometimes it is as coarse as 7·7 w/cm (19 w/in) or less. In some specimens, in all the periods of Coptic weaving, the fineness of texture is unrivalled. This is the case with linen or wool weaving, as well as silk, for the Egyptian linen and wool were spun as fine as silk. The 'byssus' weavings held in such repute among the Greeks may well have been something akin to the finest weaving in the ornamentations of these faded grave-clothes.

Very rarely a piece with purely Greek designs is found. There is one particularly fine specimen in London's Victoria and Albert Museum, which is a collar for a tunic. The design is carried out in dark purple wool and ecru linen thread on a linen warp. The anthemion ornament is depicted with all the spirit and free rendering of such detail in Greek art. The checker pattern in the upper part has a certain barbarous richness in pleasing contrast to the almost fragile elegance and grace of the honeysuckle below, and this effect is emphasized by the plain dark band that separates them. So faithfully has the Copt followed the letter, and especially the spirit of his model that, had the collar been found elsewhere in Egypt, it would have been attributed to Greek workmanship. But the technique of the weaving gives a clue to the maker; the needlework effect caused by the free shuttle is here too. The white outlines of the bands, instead of having their curves indicated by series of 'stair-steps', are boldly executed with the 'crapaud'. The white veins in the interior of the anthemion pattern are done by the same agency, so upon this collar the Copt has set his mark. The owner of the garment had been laid to rest in it between AD 200 and 300 which makes it one of the earliest Coptic tapestries.

The Copts served their Roman masters in the same faithful spirit. The Roman tunic was in the first period very simple, being in most cases ornamented with plain bands in one colour, either red-brown, brownish-purple, or black. When a little ornamentation was attempted, it was merely an outline of ecru threads that traced geometric forms—spirals and zigzags—on a dark ground. Some of the works of the Roman period are splendidly decorative. Sometimes, instead of an in-woven decoration of tapestry, the makers used an appliqué, which gives an impression of clumsiness. There are examples of tapestry panels having been cut from original garments and sewn on to other clothes as a means of providing tapestry decoration economically. There are also woven portraits from the Roman period.

In addition to dress ornaments and decorative panels of uncertain use, fragments of mural tapestries have been unearthed. These, when entire, must have been of fairly large dimensions, but as the fragments are somewhat rare and mostly naturalistic in treatment, classification is difficult.

In many garments woven before the fifth century, Christian symbols, such as the cross, are found, but as these were also pagan elements, they cannot be regarded as proof that the wearer was a Christian. Some may have been used as tokens by which one believer might privily recognize another in times of persecution, and the garment being buried with him would bear witness to his religion. Under Christian influence a change took place: the Copt increasingly designed tapestries and was less beholden to the wishes of others. At first the change was but slight; the design motifs were still spirited but the drawing was less free and accurate, and any animals shown tend to appear as if restrained by surrounding bands or branches of trees. The pagan hunter is turned into a saint, such as St George, who slays a crocodile-like dragon, and trees or plants throw off a greater number of branches, twigs, leaves or flower-heads.

Then a cramping tendency begins to be felt, and symbolism is evident everywhere. Subjects such as the basket with loaves, the fishes, the dove as the soul incarnate rising to heaven or drinking from a cup (the water of eternal life), the eagle meaning courage or the lion power are to be found everywhere, even in the borders enclosed in a framework of stems. The purple panels, upon which were traced, as by a spider, simple geometric or ornamental forms, become over-patterned and design is of bewildering complexity. Crosses are found in every pattern, and are formed by floriated lines, interlacing octagons or by rosettes. The Copt was especially fond of polygonal forms, as the intersections gave the form of a cross. The figure drawing has lost all the strength and grace of the Roman period, malproportion is the rule, knowledge of detail is lost, and drapery becomes rigid. Colour becomes more assertive as drawing deteriorates and, symbolism developing, nature grows less and less important. At length individual form is lost in religious pre-occupation

and the human figure, animal form and even architecture become grotesque.

Coptic tapestry did not benefit much by the use of silk. It is rarely met with in early specimens, and its general introduction did not take place until the sixth century, when art was in decadence, and imitation of weaving by means of printed cotton and embroidery had begun to supplant it. The latter is specially applicable to the ornamentation of rich, storiated dresses, such as those fashionable in fourth century Rome; gorgeous beyond comparison those garments must have been! The venerable Austerius, Bishop of Amasia, denounced the dresses of his time; he censured 'the frivolous and haughty people who bear the gospels on their mantles instead of in their hearts'.

12 A Coptic tunic ornament said to be Eros, but more suggestive of a winged Mercury, and to date from AD 500–600. The white lines giving detail to the central figure, the outer edge of the black ring surrounding it and some animals, are examples of flying-shuttle weaving whereby a white or coloured line of thread may be laid across a woven part (*Detroit Institute of Arts; City Purchase*)

The seventh century brought great changes in Egyptian art-work. The Muslim rulers of Egypt attempted to impose a ban on the representation of natural things and on the use of silk in articles of dress. The latter precept was cleverly evaded: it applied only to garments, and by weaving silk upon a linen or wool warp the follower of the Prophet considered that as these entered into the composition of the fabric, it could not be denounced as silken, no matter how rich the silk weft might be. Silk alone may have been used for the many hangings decorated with portraits, human figures, animals, flowers and landscapes in silk, silver and gold that were documented as belonging to the early Muslim potentates. The penalty for portraying the likeness of natural objects was imposed on the maker of the offending work, not upon the owner or user, so the faithful permitted themselves to acquire unholy things, provided they were made by the infidel. Special privileges were given by the Muslims to the 'people of the Book' as they are called in the Koran, which enabled the Christians, Jews, Magians and Sabians to continue weaving unholy patterns upon payment of tribute and by rendering other marks of humiliation and servitude. It is most probable, therefore, that the Copts were the weavers of the magnificent robes of Saracenic pattern, fragments of which are plentiful in some Egyptian cemeteries; many bear debased Coptic renderings of animal form. Egypt appears to have been a gigantic manufactory for woven tapestry and textiles in general, with Alexandria, Tunis, Damietta, Sehata, Touneh and Misr as the centres of this industry, which continued into the eleventh century under El Hakim El Mansur, one of the Fatimy Kaliphs and founder of the curious sect known as the Druses. It was customary to maintain a weaving establishment within the ruler's palace. This institution was called the 'Tiraz' and gave its name to the rich fabrics woven there, into which the name of the sultan or sovereign was woven and which were made available only for his use and that of his chosen officials. A writer of the Saracenic period described in glowing terms the wonderful 'Tiraz' fabrics woven on the 800 looms of the Almeria workshops. During a rebellion at the end of the eleventh century the palace of the Kaliph Al Mustansir B'illah was looted and found to contain silken textiles of every kind and colour and of inestimable value. About 1000 gold-wrought silk tapestries of all sizes and colours represented the various dynasties with portraits of the king and notables. Above each figure was an inscription giving his name, the time he lived, and his principal actions; surely the first pictorial *Who's Who*! The heyday of Coptic art occurred in the thirteenth century, by which time it had profoundly influenced textile arts throughout the world. Like Peruvian tapestries, those produced by the Copts should offer design inspiration to modern tapissiers, for these ancient pieces demonstrate so well what can be achieved on a plane surface by a master of design and weaving.

The Foundations of Tapestry in China

Extremely fine texture reversible all-silk tapestries were being woven in China before AD 700, at about the time the Chinese are known to have used an early type of spinning wheel. The earliest extant tapestries date from the eighth century and, contrary to European custom, have warps vertical with respect to the pattern, which is composed of climbing plants, flowers, ducks, lions, and so on. The extremely fine texture gives the impression that the tapestries are paintings on silk. These early examples were discovered in remote parts of Central Asia near to the ancient Silk Road linking China with the Mediterranean, in the Sinkiang Uighur Region. Later eighth century pieces

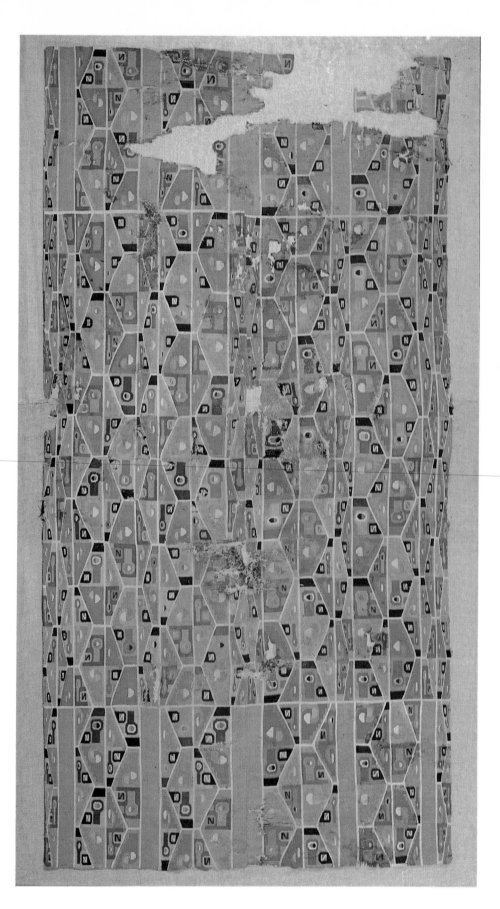

Plate 7 This Peruvian Tiahuanaco ninth century poncho comprises two tapestry strips joined vertically with an overcast stitch. The warp is cotton and weft is wool; measurements are 212 × 104·8cm (7ft × 3ft 6in). Despite burial for a millennium or longer, the material is in good condition (*Art Gallery, University of Notre Dame, USA: gift of Mrs Ann McNear*)

Plate 8 This is part of a tapestry woven in Peru in the sixteenth or early seventeenth century, after the Spanish Conquest. Inca period figures are in the border. At the centre (not shown) is a Spanish armorial. Measurements are 244 × 216cm (8ft × 7ft 1in) for the complete hanging (*Trustees of the British Museum, London*)

Plate 9 This is part of a large tapestry woven with wool and linen by fourth century Copts in Egypt, and depicts two Erotes (lovers) in a boat. The piece was found in the burial grounds of Ahmin, Egypt (*Trustees of the British Museum, London*)

Plate 10 This extraordinarily complex Coptic wool and linen tapestry roundel is from AD 400–500. It was a decorative feature of an undyed linen cloth in plain weave. Almost the only sign of ageing is change in the wool colour from purple to near-black. With all the aids and facilities available to help today's amateur weavers, it would be of interest to find how many of today's weavers could weave as perfectly this geometric pattern (*Trustees of the British Museum, London*)

Plate 11 A Coptic tapestry roundel dating from about AD 500 and measuring 19·1 × 18cm (7·375 × 7·125 in) which is part of a larger linen-woven piece, suggesting that the roundel is one of several ornamental devices on, for example, a tunic (*Burrell Collection, Glasgow Art Gallery*)

Plate 12 A colourfully cheerful Coptic square tapestry panel woven integrally with a linen cloth, and dating from between AD 500 to 800. The basket of flowers surrounded by a border of animals and boys is woven in coloured wools (*Trustees of the British Museum, London*)

Plate 13 This Hispano-Moresque carpet design is typical of the artichoke pattern woven by the Moorish invaders of Spain, whose religion forbade them to depict animals. Quite a number of fifteenth or sixteenth century tapestries have background patterns similar to this, which suggests Sassanian or Islamic design influence, and it is found even in Flemish tapestries or those woven in Alsace in the early fifteenth century. Other Hispano-Moresque designs are based on octagonal patterns of great complexity. Some of these carpets have a woollen pile composed of fibre ends knotted into the base with a density of a hundred or more hand-made knots per square centimetre (*Author's copyright reserved*)

(called 'k'o-ssu' or 'k'o-sseu' meaning cut-silk) were discovered in the Caves of the Thousand Buddhas in Kansu Province, and have a more complex and fanciful design; one of the largest specimens of this art exceeds 4·75 square metres (43 square feet) in size and is displayed in Japan's Taimadera Temple, near Nara; the motif is the *History of the Priest Shan-tao* of the T''ang dynasty of AD 628–907. Successive Chinese dynasties encouraged the art of tapestry and Ting-chou in the province of Hopeh became an important manufacturing centre, and was followed by an official manufactory sponsored by the Yüan dynasty (1279–1368) at Hangchow, in Chekiang. The typically oriental style k'o-ssu tapestry approached its peak of perfection during the Kang-hsi period (1661–1722), with gold and silver metal thread interposed with the silk. Tapestries were made for clothing, furnishings, wall hangings and so on, the tints and texture being carefully selected and regulated according to the purpose of the piece; for example, large hangings display brighter colours and a coarser texture; in some designs there is evidence of Syrian, Persian or Egyptian influence. The subject is often a visionary impression of heroes or legendary figures against a delicate rendering of a Chinese landscape, with small groups of figures disposed in groups, each engaged in some activity. The texture is so fine that the uninformed observer would scarcely call the piece tapestry—unless aided by a magnifying-glass. When chinoiserie became fashionable in Europe and the subject of western ateliers, the true and original Chinese k'o-ssu tapestry was often copied, and its importance as a discrete art in the history of tapestry all but forgotten. Native production of k'o-ssu tapestries continued until recent times. Fine examples of this magnificent type of tapestry are to be found in most major museums with a textiles department.

The Foundations of Tapestry in Japan

The Japanese learned the secrets of k'o-ssu during the early part of the sixteenth century. They put their seal on it by using more cotton than silk for the weft, and by making a weft thread like that used when gold or silver is to be used; on a core of cotton they twisted a thread-covering of silk, and used this as weft which, used with the bare cotton weft, emphasized highlights but gave a coarser total texture. Established during Japan's Muromachi or Ashikaga period, the weaving of 'tsuzure-nishiki' or multi-colour tapestries continued until recent times, and had the same sort of period-motif designs as the Chinese.

13 This is an all-silk, tapestry-woven, k'o-ssu (cut-silk) Ming Dynasty (1368–1644), Chinese chair-cover made, probably, during the early part of the seventeenth century. Some of the weft is gold-foil-wrapped thread. Measurements are 158·1 × 47·6cm (5ft 2¼in × 1ft 6¾in) (*St Louis Art Museum, Missouri; gift of Mrs Samuel C. Davis*)

Bibliography

Abbabe, F. *Precolumbian Art.* Octopus Books, London (1972)

Bacon, E. *Vanished Civilizations.* Thames & Hudson, London (1963)

Beutlich, T. *The Technique of Woven Tapestry.* Batsford, London (1967)

The Bible. The Book of 'Exodus' and of 'Esther'

Bourguet, S. J. du. *Coptic Art.* Methuen, London (1971)

David, H. *Recent Peruvian Acquisitions.* Dayton Art Institute, USA (1974)

Disselheff, H. D. *Ancient America.* Methuen, London (1972)

Gallagher, S. *Medieval Art.* Tudor Press Pub. Co., USA (1969)

Gervers, V. (editor). *Studies in Textile History.* Royal Ontario Museum, Canada (1978)

d'Harcourt, R. *Textiles of Ancient Peru and Their Techniques.* University of Washington Press, USA (1962)

Hoffman, M. *The Warp-Weighted Loom.* Oslo (1974)

Marillier, H. C. *History of the Merton Abbey Tapestry Works.* Constable & Co., London (1927)

Piggott, S. (editor). *The Dawn of Civilization.* Thames & Hudson, London (1962)

2 The Founding of Western Tapestry Industries

Following the Islamic conquest of Egypt in AD 640, Coptic tapestry lost its earlier pristine vigour as the tapissiers increasingly conformed to the requirements of the invaders, whose beliefs forbade representation of the human form. Between 850 and 1170 silk was used increasingly with wool, and metal was wound on thin strands of silk to be used as weft also. There was a colour bias towards brilliant red, scarlet and golden yellow hues. Patterns were often geometric with the addition of small birds and animals and inscriptions in plain or over-stylized Kufic characters proclaiming religious dogmas or the names of men of high estate. Tapestries of a somewhat similar nature were produced in Persia (Iran) until about the end of the eleventh century, and in Syria, where, until about the thirteenth century, the best and most complex pieces were of fine texture in silk and gold thread. Eleventh century Persia developed a tapestry-weave carpet: a carpet without the familiar 'pile' formed by masses of upright thread ends. This tapestry-weave carpet in modern times is called a 'kilim' or 'kelim'.

The inhabitants of western Europe were renowned for their woven fabrics from very early times. In Book VIII of *Historiae Naturalis*, Pliny states that the weavers of Gaul rivalled those of Babylon and Alexandria. Of the Gallic people, the Atrebates were the most famous weavers and their speciality was the production of saies, a material from which robes were made. The red saies of Atrebatum were in great demand in Rome and the main decoration of these consisted of stripes, chequers or lozenge patterns. 'Atrebatum' is the Latin cognomen for Arras, a town that has changed hands several times, being variously in Flanders or northern France. In other parts of Gaul there is scant evidence of organized manufacture. The women of the family spun the wool and wove the cloth for the chieftain or king; the rich man's household included artisans in the necessary industries. There are reports of workshops in Marseilles and other maritime towns in the south of France; towns likely to have been involved with the Phoenicians in their murex dye and cloth trade of olden times; professional craftsmen working under organized corporations do not appear to have existed elsewhere. In the early years of Christian Rome, the churches and basilicas were decorated with the same zeal as that evinced by the pagan Romans in decorating the imperial palaces, and the fashion embraced the provincial churches and monasteries. But after a while Rome degenerated and in western Europe her grip slackened. The inevitable catastrophe followed. Towards the end of the fifth century western civilization was virtually annihilated by the warlike nations of northern Europe. Vandals, Suevi, Visigoths, Burgundians and Ostrogoths swept down upon the Roman possessions and the enfeebled power of Rome was engulfed by the barbaric wave. The devastation, plundering and internecine wars among the northern invaders played havoc with the already decaying arts of the Romans. Glorying in their manly valour and strength, the Goths regarded with contempt luxurious and intel-

GE...M:- hIC:PORTA...TVR:CORPVS:EADWARDI:REGIS:AD:ECCLESIA PETRI

the earliest surviving European tapestries (apart from the fragments found in Swiss lake-dwellers' deposits) are a small piece of pronounced Byzntine design portraying Bishop Gunther of Bamberg, dating from the eleventh century, in Bamberg Cathedral, Germany, and a fragment of contemporary date found in old St Gereon's Church, in Cologne (*see* 14). The chief feature of this latter piece is a circular band enclosing animals—a bull, a griffin and a bird. The background has a foundation pattern of triangles upon which is placed ornament of Byzantine inspiration. A border encloses the whole and consists of floriated bands issuing from grotesque masks. The animals show a certain oriental influence, rather strongly marked; but otherwise the style is distinctly western; this is particularly so with regard to the border which has a design like a leaded window, and suggests that the designer found inspiration for the medallions in some fabric brought from the East, surrounding these with a background and border of his own making. Another early German product is a set of twelfth century or earlier (the design may be much earlier) long and narrow hangings for the choir stalls of Halberstadt Cathedral. The subjects are taken from the Old and the New Testaments and include the life of Abraham and of Jacob, Christ and the Apostles, and also St George and the Dragon. Colours are rather sombre and made to appear more so by intensity of the highlights. The Textile Museum in Washington, DC has a complex and ornate woven hanging of wool said to date from the fourth or fifth century.

Commerce between western Europe and the East was fitful and inconsiderable before the eleventh century. Venice traded with Constantinople, which was at the western end of the old Silk Road to China. In general, each country's needs could be satisfied within its borders and only luxuries were the subject of international trade. Then came the Crusades, carrying a surging mass of Europeans eastward, with continuous going and returning starting in 1096 and continuing for more than a century. The effect was to introduce eastern ideas and materials to the West and, paradoxically, a gradual freeing of craftsmen from dependence on the church for protection or patronage. Kings and nobles demanded tapestries with a lighter and more exotic design style which, in turn, influenced the nature of production. As there was an almost concurrent

15 An embroidery called the *Bayeux Tapestry* is probably the best known 'tapestry' of all, and is composed of coloured woollen stitches on a long linen cloth. It is supposed to have been ordered by Bishop Odo of Bayeux, France, who was the half-brother of William the Conqueror, and made between 1066–8 in England, perhaps in the monastery of Westminster. The cloth depicts a series of episodes surrounding the Norman invasion of England in 1066. The part shown here portrays the funeral of Edward the Confessor (*c*1004–66), the Anglo-Saxon king who founded Westminster Abbey, the first representation of which appears in the 'tapestry' (*Mayor of Bayeux; Phaidon Press; Victoria and Albert Museum; Crown Copyright*)

16 This fragment of German woollen tapestry dates from about 1300–25 and may have been woven at the Dominican Convent of Adelhausen. It may be part of a larger piece which is in the Freiburg-im-Breisgau Museum. The bird motif is taken from Arabic silk-woven textiles of the thirteenth century (*Burrell Collection, Glasgow Art Gallery*)

reduction in demand for tapestries for church hangings, the shift in patronage to the royal and noble houses was beneficial for tapissiers. The churches were starting to give more wall space to windows and to tombs and there was a correspondingly smaller area for hangings. Mythology began to compete with sacred history as a source of subjects for design, and the formal and impressive Romanesque style began to give way to semi-naturalistic Gothic. This change was more rapid in France and England than in Germany, despite the fact that German weavers were free craftsmen before the tenth century.

Without some slight reminder of the history of France and the Low Countries, any reference to Flanders is likely to be confusing. Originally inhabited by Celtic tribes subjugated by Julius Caesar just over 2000 years ago in 52 BC, Flanders at the end of the tenth century extended from near Calais to the outflow of the river Scheldte into the North Sea and included the Pas de Calais, parts of Picardy and much of modern Belgium; it was a major power north of France. The Treaty of Verdun made Flanders autonomous and gave the Carolingian king of the western Franks, Charles the Bald, suzerainty over the territory as it was then. Charles, a grandson of Charlemagne, made his son-in-law the first Count of Flanders; this was Baldwin I Bras-de-Fer, or Iron-Arm

(840–79). Flanders expanded territorially to the east under successive counts: Baldwin II (879–918), Arnulf (918–63), Baldwin III (died 962), Arnulf II (965–88), Baldwin IV (988–1035), Baldwin V (1036–67), Baldwin VI (1067–70), Robert Frison (1071–93), Thierry of Alsace (1128–68) and Philip (1169–91). Baldwin III established weavers at Ghent, with indoor cloth halls also at Bruges and Ypres. Baldwin IV added Valenciennes and worked hard to promote the cloth industry, which was starting to rely heavily on imports of wool from England. Baldwin V added Alost (or Aalst), Tournai and Hainault, and encouraged commerce and industry. The prominent part played by Baldwin IX (1194–1204) in eastern politics (he founded the Latin empire of Constantinople) must have rendered great service in making eastern arts and crafts known with greater effect and advantage to the cloth workers of Flanders than elsewhere in Europe. The dress and decorative fabrics such as those that were woven in the eastern Mediterranean region, and in Egypt under the Kaliphs, would have excited the interest of Flemish designers and influenced their tapestries and other fabrics. Philip the Fair (1268–1314) invaded Flanders and tried to make it a French dependency, but in 1302 his army was ejected at Courtrai. Philip the Bold (or Hardy), Duke of Burgundy (1364–1404), was a son of King John the Good of France, and in 1369 married Marguerite, daughter of the last Count of Flanders, Louis de Male. On the death of Louis in 1384, Artois became a possession of the powerful house of Burgundy. On the death of the Duke's brother, Charles V of France, in 1380, Philip was to all intents and purposes the king while acting as regent for his nephew, Charles VI, during the latter's minority and mental instability. Philip the Bold kept this influential position until his death in 1404. Succeeding dukes of Burgundy were: John the Fearless (1404–18), Philip the Good (1418–67), and Charles the Rash or Bold—'Charles-le-Téméraire'—(1467–77). The latter's army was defeated at Grandson in 1476 by the Germans and Swiss. Following a further defeat by the Swiss at Morat in the same year, Charles was killed at Nancy in 1477. His daughter, Marie of Burgundy, was powerless to prevent Flanders and Artois from falling into the hands of Louis XI of France. Since 1472 Tournai had been a French enclave in Burgundian possessions to which tribute was paid in return for peace. In 1479, Louis ordered the inhabitants of Arras to distribute themselves among various French towns and, in reverse, he ordered various French citizens to move to Arras, which was to be called Franchise. The better class of Frenchman was reluctant to move with his family to live in a foreign town and consequently Arras was populated with the scum of France and the weaving industries decayed. In 1484, Charles VIII of France tried to reverse the process and encouraged the original inhabitants to return to their homes. But events proved it was too late to invoke the ancient genius of Arras.

The Treaty of Troyes (1420) declared the Dauphin of France to be illegitimate and nominated Henry V of England heir to the French throne; he was to marry the French king Charles VI's daughter and act as regent until his father-in-law's death. Consequently, while the power of the Burgundian dukedom held, the English ruled the whole of northern France. The Hundred Years' War between England and France, during which the former tried to dominate the latter from 1339, came to an end in 1453. The marriage of Charles VII of France to Margaret of York in 1468 renewed the connection between the countries.

Until about the end of the eleventh century tapestry was woven mostly in monasteries and convents but, as workshops outside monastic walls were set up, there was a move for craftsmen to form themselves into corporations or guilds both to maintain standards of quality and for self-protection. Paris had three 'Tapissiers' trade corporations, the first formed in 1254, and that of Tapissiers de la haute lisse in 1302; London, 1331; Tournai, 1423, and Brussels, 1448. Up to the end of the sixteenth century, tapestry workshops (some with only one or two weavers) are recorded as having been in existence at the following places during the year quoted.

Flanders including Artois

Alost: 1564. *Amiens:* 1329. *Antwerp:* 1411. *Arras:* A mandate of 2 July 1313 from the Countess of Flanders is the first positive record of a tapestry, 'de faire faire six tapis à Arras'. Her son, Robert, had the first positively recorded high-loom tapestry: 'five draps worked in a high-loom fashion'. *Ath:* 1564. *Audenarde: see* Oudenarde. *Binche:* 1521. *Bruges:* had a corporation of weavers in 1302. *Brussels* (Brabant): 1417. *Cambrai:* 1440. *Courtrai* (Kortrijk): 1539. *Douai:* 1360. *Enghien:* 1410. *Geeraadsbergen:* 1519 (tapestries may be marked GAB in border or selvedge). *Ghent:* 1419. *Grammont:* 1564. *Lessines:* 1564. *Lille:* 1398. *Louvain:* 1491. *Middelburg:* 1450. *Mons:* 1398. *Oudenarde:* 1450. *St Omer:* 1315. *St Trond:* 1491. *Tournai* (a French enclave in Burgundy): 1352 (in

Plate 14 The brightly coloured and well preserved thirteenth century Baldishol (Norway) fragment of tapestry of *The Months*, of which the part depicting April and May survives, has design features reflecting both Eastern influences and those found in the *Bayeux tapestry*. The knight signifies the renewed courtly pleasures of spring (*Kunstindustrimuseet, Oslo*)

Plate 15 The *Wild Men and Moors* tapestry, of which part is shown, is typical of other fourteenth and fifteenth century allegorical pieces woven in south Germany. The armorials in the lower border are those of Zorn von Bulach or Zorn von Plobsheim and Blümel or Blümlein, which were all powerful Strasbourg families at that time (*Boston Museum of Fine Arts, Charles Potter Kling Fund, Boston*)

18 *The Camp of the Gypsies* is a wool and silk panel measuring 386 × 343cm (12ft 8in × 11ft 3in) forming part of the series *The History of Carrabarra, so-called of the Egyptians*, woven in the Tournai workshop of Arnold Poissonnier, probably soon after 1421. The rectangular insertions at the upper left and right may have been taken from another tapestry in the same set, or be missing parts of the same tapestry (*Burrell Collection, Glasgow Art Gallery*)

1398 the weavers received statutes as a corporation). *Valenciennes*: 1364. *Ypres*: 1539 (in the early fifteenth century mainly a centre for designers, e.g., François de Wechter).

France

Alsace: workshops in the region of Strasbourg 1390. *Aubusson*: AD 732 (legendary). *Beauvais*: 1500. *Felletin*: 1456. *Fontainebleau*: 1535. *Le Mans*: 1509. *Limoges*: 1502. *Lyons*: 1358. *Marseilles*: pre-Roman. *Montpellier*: 1458. *Navarre*: 1413. *Paris*: 1385 (weaver Jacques Dourdin); 1503 (Archbishop of Sens' Residence: weaver Alardin de Souhyn); 1551 (Hospital of the Trinity); 1597 (Jesuits' House, Faubourg St Antoine; moved to Louvre 1606; Fontainebleau 1535). *Perpignan*: 1410. *Poitiers*: 732. *Quievrain*: pre-1364. *Reims*: 1328. *Rennes*: 1477. *Tournai*: 1332. *Tours*: 1519. *Troyes*: 1519. *Vitré*: 1476. *Saumur*: 985 (Monastery of St Florent); 1524 (Manufactory).

From about 1410, nomadic French and Flemish tapissiers established temporary workshops in Auvergne and provinces of the Marche; the modern departments of Charente, La Creuse, Haut-Vienne, Indre and Vienne. When the court and nobility moved to make the river Loire valley their home and chateaux were built there increasingly, semi-nomadic workshops were set up

Plate 16 (*opposite*) This is one of the miniatures from the illuminated pages of the *Book of Hours* of King Alfonso the Fifth of Aragon, Spain, which was written about 1450. The King is shown kneeling on a rug, which displays his armorials and lies on a tiled floor. Beside him, an ecclesiastic supports a book of devotions. In the background are a window, a canopied bed and, hanging from hooks fixed to the stone walls, there is a hunting tapestry of the style and period of the late fourteenth century. This miniature painting is especially interesting because it shows a tapestry of the period used to line the walls of a mid-fifteenth century bedchamber, and the design appears to be more European than Hispano-Moresque (*British Library Board, London; add. 28962, f 14v*)

19 Like a strip cartoon, this mid-fifteenth century *Labours of the Months* Rhenish tapestry indicates typical agricultural tasks for the months starting with July: scything the long grass in the field, raking it up and turning it to dry into hay; August: cutting the corn with a sickle and binding it into sheaves; September: ploughing the ground and breaking the earth down into fine tilth, and then sowing seeds for the next crop; October: grape-picking and wine-making preparations; November: animal slaughter for winter meat stocking; December: feasting on the fruits of monthly labours. (For illustrative convenience the tapestry – which is in one long length – is shown in two sections with an overlap at the end of the September scene) (*Victoria and Albert Museum; Crown Copyright*)

at Bourges under Charles VII, at Tours under Louis XI, at Angers under Charles VIII and at Blois under Louis XII, and had the omnibus name of 'Loire Workshops'. These nomads often found lodgings in castles while producing hangings to the order of a nobleman. Known as 'tapissiers de passage' they worked from headquarters where commissions were accepted. After the contract was signed, the tapissier took his dismantled loom to the premises allocated by his client, set it up and, with the help of assistants and apprentices, wove the tapestry under the eyes of the patron. In France the craft did not entirely die out from the earliest times. All over the land, in the most remote districts, and irrespective of political and frontier changes, in the large towns, farmhouses and hamlets, weavers plied their calling. They were insignificant in numbers compared with the Flemish workshops, but, as in more modern times, a single weaver or two could produce a prodigious quantity of tapestried materials. Invasion by the Norsemen, followed some two hundred years later by the incursion of Saracens from the south, and the continuous movement along east–west trade routes straddling the country gave much stimulus to design and France—a predominantly agricultural country—had plenty of raw materials for textile weaving.

England, Scotland and Ireland

England

Barcheston: 1565–9. Canterbury: 1563. Colchester: 1563. Faversham: 1302. Kendal: 1331. London: 1316 (Great Wardrobe: 1236. Westminster: 1175). Norwich: 1563. Oxford: 1317. Ramsey, Monastery of: 1316. Sandwich: 1561. Winchester: 1294. York: 1336.

Scotland

Berwick: pre-1467. Dunblane: 1497. Edinburgh: 1467.

Ireland

Kilkenny: 1339.

Throughout the thirteenth century the surname 'd'Arras' or 'd'Araz' is frequently encountered in records. Other surnames link the owner with the craft of weaving and the place where he learned his craft—e.g., Philip le Tapiter d'Arras. The export of English wool to Flanders and its return in the form of tapestries or woollen cloth produced a continuous movement of

60

20 It is important to remember when considering old tapestries that until the Lancashire-born mechanic, James Hargreaves (1720–78), invented the spinning jenny all fibres were spun by hand. The spindle wheel, which originated in China about AD 1200–1250, was turned by hand, just as the ancient spindle and whorl was worked by hand (*see* 7). Towards the end of the sixteenth century a foot-operated treadle, like that seen fitted to this Saxony spinning wheel, came into use to speed thread production. The inset traces the path of the fibres, to which a twisting movement is given by the rotating spindle that is the equivalent of the old hand-operated spindle and, like it, has the finished thread wound round it. The length of spun thread enters the hollow shaft and is then fed on to the spindle (*Science Museum, London (inset), and Wheatley Park School, Oxford whose scholars made the Saxony Wheel from their own designs*)

merchants and, towards the latter part of the fifteenth century, a flow of Flemish refugees seeking employment abroad. A great many Flemish workmen came to England in the time of Henry I (1068–1135) and migrated later to Scotland, where they received every encouragement as Scotland always enjoyed closer relations with the Low Countries than England.

Italy

Ferrara : 1464. Florence : 1455. Genoa : 1395. Mantua : 1419. Milan : 1460. Modena : 1488. Perugia : 1463. Rome : 1455. Siena : 1438. Venice : 1421. Vigevano : 1501.

The fifteenth century marks the beginning of tapestry manufacture in Italy. The gifts of the Dukes of Burgundy to the Popes and others, and possibly the purchases of tapestries by Italian noblemen, had made the products of Arras so famous in Italy that the finest tapestries became known as 'Arrazzi'. Noblemen and town authorities in some parts of Italy started to offer subsidies to foreign weavers who would agree to establish workshops in Italy, which led to the emigration of a considerable number of French and Flemish weavers.

Spain

Aragon : 1388. Barcelona : 1462. Cordoba : 976. Madrid : 1590. Salamanca : 1579.

It is impossible to determine precisely where the Moorish invaders of Spain started to weave tapestries, from AD 756.

Holland

Delft : 1587. Middelburg : 1562.

Scandinavian Countries

Denmark
Copenhagen : 1522. Elsinore : 1581.
Sweden
Stockholm : 1523.
Norway
Gudbrandsdalen : 1600.

Germany and Switzerland

Bamberg, Convent at: 1495. *Frankenthal* and *Lauingen : 1530. Hamburg : 1589. Munich : 1557. Nuremberg : 1530. Stettin* or *Szczecinek* (German pre-1945): 1551. *Wesel : 1599. Basle : 1453.*

The Americas

New Mexico
Pueblo Indian post-conquest tapestry-woven textiles from imported Spanish churro sheep wool: 1540–98 e.g., Rio Grande Spanish Colonial tapestries.
Peru
Spanish Colonial tapestries from *c*1550.

The Medieval Period, extending up to about AD 1400, and the Gothic Period extending from 1400 to about 1510, comprise the two periods when tapestry design and weaving were regarded as being of the highest order of perfection in the opinion of the pre-Raphaelite William Morris and the mid-twentieth century tapestry reformer Jean Lurçat (1891–1966) of France. The illustrations associated with this chapter therefore have been selected to show as wide a range of design and subject as space permits.

Medieval art was largely that which developed in Europe during the Middle Ages and was nurtured by the Church after the collapse of the Roman Empire. When Charlemagne inherited the kingdom of the Franks in AD 768 and in 800 was crowned Emperor of the Holy Roman Empire by Pope Leo III,

21 Details from a fourteenth century south German tapestry (above), and a fifteenth century west German tapestry (below). The former is from *Scenes from a Romance*, a 73·7 × 366cm (2ft 5in × 12ft) piece. The latter is from *Taking the Veil*, an 89 × 348cm (2ft 11in × 11ft) piece depicting steps in a woman's religious life. Both have linen warps and a weft of wool and silver-gilt threads (*Victoria and Albert Museum; Crown Copyright*)

he attempted to create the foundations of a new civilization by convincing the Frankish people that there was strength in culture and learning. He faced the task of uniting a great conglomerate of largely illiterate peoples of barbarian origins that were the raw material of a Christian empire he hoped to mould into a cultured entity while at the same time warding off attacks by Viking and Magyar raiders. Towards this aim he recruited intellectuals from as far away as Ireland and stimulated religious foundations to revive the arts and letters in terms of their own inspirational genius. Despite this, self-expression was often deeply influenced by a background of Byzantium, early Christian, Oriental, Roman or Muslim art and symbology. In the churches, mosaics were replaced by wall paintings and, in course of time, by painted fabrics and then tapestries. In particular, the art of Byzantium remained strong and influenced the art of Russia, Greece and Italy, via Ravenna and Venice, for a far longer time than it influenced western Europe after destruction of Constantinople by the Turks in 1453. But, by the time the popes and Italian noblemen were taking an active interest in the tapestry of Arras, the principles of Byzantine art in Italy were fading to be replaced by an amalgam of design principles and techniques called 'Gothic'.

From the fourteenth century tapestry was regarded as a major form of decorative art and workshops in Brussels, Arras and Tournai, and to a lesser extent in other towns, were fully occupied in meeting the demand for fabrics designed for various purposes. Following the decline in demand for church hangings as the desire for more windows and tomb spaces in these buildings increased, there was a steady demand for made-to-measure wall hangings for castles, palaces and stately homes. The demand was for wall hangings of immense size as well as small strips to hang between windows (entre-fenêtres) and to hang over doorways or doors (portières) to reduce draughts. It was not

22 Four large and magnificent fifteenth century tapestries with hunting scenes provide a faithful record, paralleled by contemporary accounts of the Dukes of Burgundy and Orleans, of the changing fashions of courtiers of the period. *The Boar and Bear Hunt* shows the fashions of the early 1430s; the high-waisted gowns of the women have collars wider than their shoulders, and their headdresses are heart shaped; the men wear bulky garments with large drooping sleeves and low-slung belts. This hanging measures 405 × 1021cm (13ft 3½in × 33ft 6in) (*Victoria and Albert Museum; Crown Copyright*)

uncommon to order a 'chamber' of tapestries to equip a particular room, perhaps a bed-chamber. A chamber would consist of a canopy, head-board covering, curtains and perhaps a coverlet for a four-poster bed, chair and sofa covers, made-to-measure wall and doorway hangings, curtains and accessories like a *Bible* cover, cushion covers and, if the room had an altar, a cover for that as well. The design might be a fanciful portrayal—often almost like a strip cartoon—of some great historic exploit or story involving the lord of the house, or represent a mythological or a religious episode. Not uncommonly a monarch or a nobleman carried in his baggage a chamber or a suite of tapestries to decorate the place to which he was travelling. If the shape of his hangings did not fit the new walls it was easy enough to cut a tapestry! The tent or lodging of battlefield commanders was often decorated with costly hangings for reasons of prestige and comfort. Consequently a victorious army often came into possession of priceless hangings found in the quarters or baggage of a vanquished foe. When Charles the Rash, Duke of Burgundy, was defeated by the Swiss at Grandson in 1476, they seized a great quantity of Burgundian tapestries he had brought with him. Many of these tapestries eventually arrived in Berne, where they may be seen in the Historisches Museum. A document surviving from the reign of Edward I of England (1272–1307) requires the royal chamberlain to ensure the king's apartments are properly adorned with tapestry: 'Ut camerae tapis et banqueriis ornentur.'

Records of tapestries made to order include references in the Wardrobe Papers of Henry III for 1236–7, which give Friar Geoffrey's accounts for four cloths of Arras for the espousals of the Countesses of Chester, Pembroke and Roogie, and Richard de Clare. But the greatest surviving early tapestry made to order is an almost complete set ordered in about 1375 by Louis I, Duke of Anjou. The set represent St John's vision of the *Apocalypse* and was intended for the Chapel walls of Angers Castle, to which it has returned after many years of rough treatment and dispersal. The tapestries were woven in Paris and the set comprised a total of seven hangings, of which five had the same plan. Each of these five was to display two horizontal sequences of seven scenes, each scene alternately with a blue or a red field. At the left end of each of these five tapestries there is a canopied Gothic structure surmounted by angels and

23 Probably woven in or near Basel about 1450–75, *The Wandering Housewife* is a satirical cartoon of the over-active housewife. This tapestry was possibly a cushion cover and shows a woman riding on a donkey loaded with various possessions including a baby tucked under her chin and a spinning staff with which she is busy as she goes along. The inscription has been translated as: 'I have household articles enough, otherwise I would not be so important.' Made of wool, the piece measures 80 × 103·5cm (2ft 7½in × 3ft 4in) (*Burrell Collection, Glasgow Art Gallery*)

flanked by standards bearing the arms of Lorraine and Anjou, extending to the full height of the hanging. Seated under the canopy a patriarchal figure—identified as Louis I, Duke of Anjou—is reading from a scroll or book, and meditating on the visions of the Apocalypse extending in scenes to his left. Probably his posture refers to the third verse of the first chapter of *Revelation*: 'Blessed is he that readeth, and they that hear the words of this prophecy, and keep those things that are written therein: for the time is at hand' (*see* 17). Two of the seven tapestries had a total of only fifteen scenes to fit into a space adjacent to the chapel altar. Inspiration for the design of this set was derived from an illuminated manuscript (now in the Bibliothèque Nationale, Paris) lent to the Duke of Anjou by his brother, Charles V of France. The cartoon artist was Hennequin or Jehan of Bruges, the painter-in-ordinary and valet-de-chambre to the king; the cartoons were probably painted on linen. The original sketches made by an artist are still called 'portraiteurs et patrons' or, by the weavers, 'petits patrons'. The Duke commissioned the tapestry merchant and weaver Nicolas Bataille (a leading member of the corporation of Tapissiers of Paris, and described as a 'tapissier sarazinois' when he wove six tapestries of 'arras work' for the Duke of Burgundy in 1373) to weave the set of seven hangings which, when complete, had a height of 553cm (18ft) and a total length of 145.2m (472ft). They were woven in Paris on high-warp looms entirely in wool with a palette of between fifteen and twenty colours (seemingly there is still controversy about the exact number). Bataille must have been a superb organizer and manager; he could scarcely have been bettered by any modern tapissier. Between January 1378 and December 1379, three tapestries totalling in length some 24m (78ft) were completed despite the fact that he had on his other looms a number of similarly intricate and important tapestries. And the complete set of seven hangings was completed within six years or less (the final records are incomplete; in the last entry Bataille is styled 'tapissier de Paris').

25 This amusing Swiss cushion cover dating from 1450–75 is of a wolf or fox preaching to four geese with rosaries in their beaks while a fox eyes them hungrily from below the latticed pulpit, and is presumably an allegory or memento of a folk story. The preacher holds an open book and seemingly has two captive geese at his back. Size is 54·6 × 59cm (1ft 9½in × 1ft 11¼in) and texture 4·9 w/cm (12·5 w/in) (*Burrell Collection, Glasgow Art Gallery*)

26 *The Loving Couple Under the Elder Tree* stand against an ornate red background suggestive of Eastern influence. The girl, at the left, is dressed in blue and has a circlet of forget-me-not flowers in her saffron-yellow hair. The young man, dressed in a blue jacket edged with ermine, carries a sword in his left hand and, with his right hand, points to the inscription; pointed shoes are on his feet. This wool, silk and linen tapestry dates from about 1465–70 and was probably woven in the Basel region. Size is 89 × 98cm (2ft 11¾in × 3ft 2½in) and texture is 6 w/cm (15·2 w/in) (*Swiss National Museum, Zurich*)

27 (*far right*) This is a detail from one of the *War of Troy* tapestries woven in 1475 by Pasquier Grenier's Tournai workshop. Execution of the design and weaving is fantastic. The set was made for the magistrates of Bruges, who later presented the tapestries to Charles the Bold of Burgundy (*Victoria and Albert Museum*; *Crown Copyright*)

the finest woven pictures of sacred subjects, for presentation to the representative of St Peter. Was it desirable to influence the English to come to a peaceful arrangement and close the sanguinary conflict with the French? Straightway with his overtures and suggestions went hangings woven in gold and the finest materials, to render complaisant the mind of the English king and councillors. Was an opponent to be gained over, or a friend to be rewarded for service rendered? A gift of hangings would be the best instrument in accomplishing either aim.

By this practice the tapestries of Arras found a home in the palaces and castles of Europe, and the fame of the manufactory grew worldwide. Some of the earliest surviving tapestries are of *St Piat and St Eleuthère*. They were woven in 1404 in the Arras atelier of Pierre Feré. Toussaint Prier, the chaplain to Philip the Good, gave them to Tournai Cathedral, where they are still. John the Fearless used the gift of tapestry principally for attainment of political advantage; for example, the Earl of Warwick was presented with a hanging representing *Persons and Birds* at Lille when acting as an envoy for Henry IV of England. During the dukedom of Philip the Good the prosperity of Arras reached its zenith and started to decline. The (still existing) inventory of the tapestries that Philip inherited list close on a hundred hangings and other pieces made with metallic threads, wool and silk. The Duke was a king in all but name and in 1440 he had a special building made adjacent to his residence at Arras, for the storage of tapestries; like his grandfather, Philip the Bold, he was a great patron of the arts, and he continued to order tapestries from the workshops of Arras, Bruges, Tournai, and Brussels. One of the most important sets was the *History of Gideon* designed by the Duke's court painter, Bauduin de Bailleul. For the new Pope, Eugenius IV, Philip ordered from a Lombard merchant living in Bruges the *Three Moral Histories of the Pope, the Emperor and Nobility*. Philip the Good was succeeded by his son Charles the Rash in 1467. The latter appears to have done little to arrest the declining fortunes of Arras, which his military adventures finally doomed to extinction in 1477. At his marriage in Bruges in 1468 to the English Princess Margaret of York there was a grand display of Burgundy's richest tapestries, including (according to contemporary accounts) *The History of Gideon, The Golden Fleece, The History of the Battle of Liège, The Coronation of King Clovis, The first Christian King of France, The Renewal of the Alliance between Him and Gondebaut, King of Burgundy* and *The Passion of Our Lord*.

The fall of Arras marks the end of the first period in the history of European tapestry. As the influence of Arras waned the tapestry workshops in smaller Flemish towns and also in France, Germany, Italy and Spain gained increasing recognition. The Flemish towns of Bruges, Lille and Valenciennes came to prominence and, despite its chequered allegiance to France, England and the Netherlands, Tournai outshone them all. By 1423 the Tournai corporation of high-loom weavers was of such a strength as to form an independent company in the civic muster. The most notable tapissier was Pasquier Grenier, or Garnier (died 1493), who was, in effect, the appointed merchant-tapissier to the house of Burgundy. Among the tapestries he sold to the dukes were a chamber depicting a *History of Ahasuerus and Esther*, the *Story of the Knight of China*, *Wood-cutter's*, *Orange Trees* and the *Destruction of Troy*. In 1486 Pasquier and John Grenier were accorded protection in their export trade to England. Nearly two years later Henry VII of England bought from them a *History of*

28 The *Lachener Hortus Conclusus Teppich* (*Lachener Closed Garden Tapestry*) was woven about 1480 for the Chapel of the Holy Cross of the parish church at Lachen and it is the largest altar frontal in the collection of the Swiss State Museum; it measures 105 × 379cm (3ft 7in × 12ft 5¼in). The part shown symbolizes the Annunciation and Mary's Immaculate Conception. She is seated in a wall-surrounded garden with David's shield-covered tower at her back, and wears a white dress with a blue mantle; in her halo are the words 'ecce ancilla domini'. Above her a dove symbolizes the Holy Ghost, and above, the Christ Child approaches with a cross. Mary grasps the horn of the Unicorn and a young man beside her – symbolizing Adam – spears the Unicorn while Eve collects its blood. Three small figures with their armorials at the bottom edge represent the donors – the family, Von Irmensee – with the date MCCCCLXXX (1480) under the middle figure. This colourful and rich hanging is made of wool, silk, gold and silver threads, with a texture of 5–6 w/cm (12–15 w/in) (*Swiss National Museum, Zurich*)

Troy consisting of eleven hangings (*see* 27), and two altar pieces. Antoine Grenier is mentioned in 1495 as being at Tournai, and at Paris in the early sixteenth century. Pierre Grenier, merchant, is listed in 1579 at Oudenarde.

It is often impossible to distinguish between tapestries made at Arras and Tournai, but one of the distinctions is found in the arrangement of flowers or plants when these are included in the design. Tournai tapestries tend to display herbage that is less formalized or schematized; this is particularly true with respect to verdures and to 'mille-fleur' tapestries, which appear to have been woven mainly in Tournai. Some authorities claim mille-fleur pieces are principally the work of Loire workshops where the warmer climate of Touraine is likely to have produced a greater profusion than in the north of flowers, birds and animals to draw upon as models for design. Arras workshops probably were the first to weave with a finer wool thread than other manufacturing towns, or to make weft with a combination of fine wool and silk which, when the *Jousts of St Denis* was woven, resulted in it being recorded as '... figured with gold and of fine Arras thread'. Frequently mentioned as something quite special, 'Arras thread' is sometimes written 'of Arras thread with gold'.

Tournai and Arras lie close together and it was common for weavers to move from one town to the other, or for ideas and methods of workshops to be exchanged. Weavers of the Gothic and Renaissance periods seem to have been mobile by nature and prepared to offer their services where conditions suited them provided they were acceptable to local corporations. Quite a number of Flemish tapissiers emigrated to work at, or to help establish, workshops in Italy and other countries and appear to have had no difficulty in adapting to a new language or customs. Typical of intermingling of Arras expertise with that of Tournai was production of the *History of Gideon*, a tapestry designed by Bailleul of Arras and woven at Tournai. Gothic tapestries average 5 or 6 w/cm (13 or 15 w/in) with a few rich pieces of 7 w/cm (18 w/in) or more. Towards the end of the fifteenth century the design subject veered away from the religious type to the secular. Military subjects appeared and also a combination of mythical with other themes. In the early fifteenth century Arras produced, for example, the altarpiece, *Descent from the Cross, the Entombment and the Resurrection*, now in the Victoria and Albert Museum; also the *Resurrection* (Musée de Cluny, Paris) and the *Entombment* (Toledo Museum, Spain). Brussels produced the allegorical *Triumphs*, inspired by the fourteenth century Italian poet Francis Petrarch (*see* 30), and Pasquier Grenier of Tournai wove the literary-inspired *Story of the Swan Knight* for Philip the Good. The mystical and semi-religious unicorn appears in several Gothic tapestries; for example in the *Lady with the Unicorn* set in Musée de Cluny (*see* 34, woven perhaps about 1444, and 28). The Cloister Museum, New York, has a magnificent and well researched set that depicts *Hunting the Unicorn*. Another carefully researched set of tapestries of the hunt is the so-called *Devonshire Hunting Tapestries* formerly at Hardwick Hall and now in London's Victoria and Albert Museum (*see* 22). Woven at Arras during the first half of the fifteenth century, this set of four large and magnificently detailed hangings is not merely of importance as a superb example of decoration of the period; it also impinges on the world of study of the social scientist, textile technologist, naturalist, botanist, anthropologist, designer and artist. Scenically these tapestries faithfully record a fraction of the world of the wealthy and the leisured in typical surroundings of the period.

Britain and some other countries have Gothic tapestries which are an historical mystery. Two of these are illustrated in this book (*see* Plates 17 and 22) A third hanging, *The Coventry Tapestry*, which has been in St Mary's Hall, Coventry, Warwickshire, since before 1519, unfortunately could not be illustrated because it is undergoing extensive renovation. It measures about 305 × 915cm (10 × 30ft) and is composed of an upper and a lower row of three scenes each, filled with an abundance of figures and detail. In the middle of the lower part the Virgin stands supported by angels and the Apostles; to the left a king kneels, accompanied by nobles and an ecclesiastic, in front of an openwork grille; to the right is a queen, followed by ladies. Pillars stretching to the top separate the secular and sacred subjects. Saintly men are depicted to the left, saintly women to the right. The original subject between these groups in the upper scenes has been removed and a later piece, 'Justitia', put in its place. In the narrow floral borders are scrolls with isolated Gothic letters.

Concurrently with the increasing popularity of Tournai following the downfall of Arras, Brussels developed as a weaving town. In 1477 a London merchant, John Pasmer, ordered Gilles van der Putte of Brussels to supply a hanging of four *Evangelists* and some ecclesiastics with a richly ornamented tabernacle, for Brussels was famous for its excellence in producing painting-like tapestries of religious subjects, such as *The Adoration of the Magi* (Sens Cathedral, France), *The Glorification of Christ* (National Gallery of Art, Washington, DC), *The Life of Mary* (Museo del Tapices La Seo, Zaragoza, Spain) and *The Feast of St Gregory* (Patrimonio Nacional, Madrid).

Up to the end of the fifteenth century workshops in Germany, Switzerland and Alsace produced a wide range of pieces including many with religious motifs (*see* 21) In Alsace a number of rather mysterious pieces depicting wild men and women with animals were woven (*see* Plate 15 and jacket), the symbolic or allegorical meanings of which are not yet fully understood. In addition to the collections mentioned earlier, the following establishments have examples of these earlier tapestries: *Austria*: Museum für angewandte Kunst, Vienna. *Belgium*: Musées Royaux d'Art et d'Histoire, Brussels. *France*: Louvre, Paris; Musée Historique, Orleans; Musée, Besançon; Petit Séminaire, Strasbourg. *Germany*: German National Museum, Nuremberg; Kunstgewerbemuseum, Cologne, and Berlin; Museum für Kunsthandwerk, Frankfurt; Rathaus, Regensburg; Martin von Wagner Museum der Universität, Würzburg; Kapitelsaal, Mainz. (In Germany, Nuremberg was a major centre of weaving.) *Switzerland*: Historisches Museum, Basel; Schweizerisches Landesmuseum, Zurich.

In about 1436 the house of Mantua in Italy placed a workshop in Ferrara under the direction of a Flemish immigrant, Giacomo d'Angelo. In 1438 the town of Siena recruited from Brussels the master-weaver Boteram, who was charged with the task of giving instruction in his craft in the town. In the mid-fifteenth century the Duke of Mantua encouraged the emigration of Flemish weavers to Italy to man workshops in Ferrara and Mantua, so that he would no longer have to rely entirely on hangings woven abroad. In 1444 Luigi Gonzaga of Mantua appointed Boteram the director of weaving in Ferrara. The greatest benefactor of the workshops was Borso of the d'Este family, who employed Italian artists such as Cosimo Tura, Gerardo de Vicenza, Battista Dosso, Giovanni Pordenone, Benuvenuto Tisi, Jules Romain and Ugolino, to design cartoons both for tapestries to be woven in Italy and Flanders. Known to his employers as 'Rinaldi di Gualteri', Boteram eventually was joined by other gifted tapissiers such as Liévin Gillisz of Bruges (he established the first workshop in Florence) and by Rinaldo Grue and Giovanni Mille of Tournai. The development of the Ferrara workshop slowed down with the death in 1478 of Luigi de Gonzaga and the effect of Italy's civil wars towards the end of the century. The workshop's highest achievements came between 1534 and 1559. The Siena workshop, under the ex-Arras weaver Jacquet Benoit, is remembered for his six-piece set of the *History of St Peter* for Pope Nicholas V, in 1451. The workshop in Milan established by Francesco Sforza in 1455 achieved notoriety in the sixteenth century with its *Life of the Virgin*. The Medici workshop at Florence founded during the first half of the fifteenth century was second in importance to Ferrara but achieved little of note under Lorenzo the Magnificent. Its main activity developed in the sixteenth century when its

73

Plate 17 (*opposite above*) Winchester College possesses most interesting fragments of a large hanging of ecclesiastical character, which, when completed, measured about 305 × 366cm (10 × 12ft). The design consists of a series of eight vertical strips or 'pales' of alternate blue and red; these were ornamented with a fifteenth century pattern of diamond shapes. Upon this field are disposed three horizontal series of eight emblems. In the top row white roses alternate with the sacred monogram 'I.H.S.' in golden colour. On the second and seventh devices, shields of arms are superimposed – the ground azure, with three golden crowns one above another – the traditional arms of Belinus, King of Britain and reputed ancestor of the Tudor family. The second row of devices consists of the same monogram, alternating with red and white roses. In the centre of this series is the *Agnus Dei,* with two sprays of roses springing almost horizontally to the left and right, while the Lamb rests on a red rose. The lowest series of devices is similar to that at the top, but of the third series only one of the monograms has been preserved. The groundwork pattern is Italian in origin, and the devices are those of King Henry VII. This tapestry was woven during the last quarter of the fifteenth century and has been attributed to a workshop in the Low Countries, or in England (*By permission of the Warden and Fellows of Winchester College*)

twenty-odd looms carried out work for the Medici and others. Between 1455 and the end of the century the Pope sponsored a manufactory in Rome managed by the Parisian weaver Renaud de Raincourt. A set of the *History of Creation* is said to have been completed. The succeeding pontiff, Pope Calixtus III, closed the workshop. Tapestry-weaving in Italy during the fifteenth century is little more than a list of workshops supported by towns or noblemen. Initially much of the activity was to do with importing tapestries from Flanders and elsewhere, repairing of existing tapestries. Only towards the last third of the century did a solid foundation for tapestry production start to emerge.

Tapestry-weaving in England, Scotland, Spain and other countries was on a minor scale compared with the activities of Flanders and France and mostly concerned meeting home needs. The end of the fifteenth century marks the threshold between the Gothic and Renaissance periods, with a great difference in design values, and aspirations.

Bibliography
Alexander, E. J. and Woodward, C. H. 'The Flora of the Unicorn Tapestries'. *J. of the New York Botanical Garden*, pp. 17–26. Spring 1957. Boston, USA
Arts Council of Great Britain. *Treasures from the Burrell Collection.* London (1975)
Belle-Jouffray, M. *The Art of the Tapestry* (tr. from French). London (1965)
The Bible; the Old and the New Testament
de Boyer de Sainte-Suzanne, Baron. *Notes d'un Curieux sur les Tapisseries tissues de haute ou basse lisse.* Paris (nineteenth century)
Digby, G. W. and Hefford, W. *The Devonshire Hunting Tapestries.* HMSO, London (1971)
Glysin, F. *Swiss Medieval Tapestries.* Batsford, London (1947)
d'Hulst, R. A. *Flemish Tapestries from the 15th to the 18th Century.* Editions Arcade, Brussels (1967)
Jubinal, M. *Recherches sur l'Usage et l'Origine des Tapisseries à Personnages.* Paris (1840)
Marillier, H. C. *The Tapestries at Hampton Court Palace.* HMSO, London (1962)
Müntz, E. *La Tapisserie.* Paris (1880)
Rorimer, J. *Unicorn Tapestries at the Cloisters.* New York (1962)
Sevensma, W. *Tapestries* (tr. from Dutch). Merlin Press, London (1965)
Thomson, W. G. and Berberyan, O. S. *Carpets of Spain and the Orient in the Collection of Charles Deering Esq.* London (1924)
Turner, A. and Brown, C. *Burgundy.* Batsford, London (1977)
Van Drival, Le C. *Les Tapisseries d'Arras.* Paris
Weigert, R. A. *French Tapestry* (tr. from French). Faber, London (1958)

Plate 18 (*opposite below*) The home of the Marquess of Bath at Longleat House, near Warminster in Wiltshire, has a long saloon with walls lined with tapestries which do much to create an atmosphere of quiet elegance. These Flemish sixteenth century hangings depict scenes from *The Life of Cyrus, King of Persia* (*The Marquess of Bath*)

Plate 19 (*opposite above*) This beautiful piece depicts *The Descent from the Cross* (according to Luke xxiii 53). This small but magnificent framed hanging is in Westminster Abbey's Henry the Seventh Chapel over the altar in the south aisle and is the jewel of the Abbey's collection. It was given in 1929 by the Duke of Westminster in memory of the Countess Grosvenor. The central scene depicts the Body of Christ being taken from the cross. At the corners are the Four Evangelists with their distinctive emblems. At the top, St John with an eagle and St Matthew with an angel; at the bottom, St Mark with a lion and St Luke with a Unicorn (instead of an ox). A rich but delicate pattern of flowers and fruit fill the borders surrounding the central field, with a Fountain of Life at the centre of the top and bottom borders. The workshop that wove this 118 × 145cm (3ft 10½in × 4ft 9in) panel has not been identified, but may have been in the Netherlands (note the windmill in the upper left central part). The style is that of the first third of the sixteenth century. The gilt frame is decorated with armorials (*Dean and Chapter of Westminster, London*)

Plate 20 (*opposite below*) Following defeat of the Spanish Armada in 1588, the war between England and Spain dragged on for nearly 16 years. Soon after coming to the throne, King James I of England (James VI of Scotland) decided to negotiate an end to hostilities. Spanish and Flemish plenipotentiaries were invited to London in May 1604 to attend a conference in a magnificently tapestried room of old Somerset House. The Hispano-Flemish noblemen are seated on the left side of the tapestry-covered table with the English Commissioners on the right side of it. The hanging behind each group dates from 1560 and has been identified. The table tapestry may have been woven by the Barcheston workshop. The picture was probably painted by a Flemish artist (*National Portrait Gallery, London*)

3 The Renaissance of the Sixteenth Century

The Gothic period, which had followed the Medieval from about AD 1400, and during which the brash glitter of a continuously moving court surrounding the ambitious but art-loving dukes of Burgundy had encouraged each duke in turn to exert ever greater effort to achieve the ultimate in tapestry possession, in turn influenced fashions in design. Not for them were the pious or simple allegorical pictorial tapestries of the Medieval period. They demanded colourful, lively or obviously beautiful hangings which matched their own exuberance and exploits. They directed Flemish designers to produce cartoons which depicted in a single hanging a variety of impressions, narratives and personages, and with rich detail conveyed a stunning impact to the eye of the beholder. With adequate resources to promote this new art, the house of Burgundy successfully imposed this new-look tapestry on Europe, to its great benefit. But, like all new trends in art, it had its day and started to show signs of change in style from about 1475 and to be eclipsed towards the end of the fifteenth century. From about the third quarter of the fifteenth century the composition becomes more orderly, and consists of groups of figures, separated more or less by foliage or landscape. The groups are generally arranged so as to be read in two horizontal series, one above the other, as in the hangings depicted by 33 and, to a lesser extent, by 29; compare these with the jumble of figures

30 *The Triumph of Fame over Death* is one of a set of tapestries depicting *The Triumphs of Petrarch* and, like 29, is one of the most magnificent of all surviving sixteenth century Flemish hangings. More than 8m (26ft) long, it has a texture of 6.7 w/cm (17 w/in). The car of 'Fame' is drawn by four ornately bedecked elephants and that of 'Fate' is drawn by four bulls. The scene is one of action, like a cartoon, and tells a story

31 *The Open-Air meal in the Garden of Love* is associated with four tapestries in the Corcoram Gallery of Art, Washington DC. It is part of an allegory of events that culminated on 22 May 1506 with the signing of a marriage contract between the French King Louis XII's daughter, Claude, and his cousin and successor, Francis I. The royal couple toast one another across the table, attended by a jester and others who symbolize the nuptial celebrations of Louis XII and his second queen, Anne, when they met at the Castle of Nantes in January 1499. The embracing couple in the foreground signify that Claude and Francis are marrying for love as much as for stately reasons. Woven in Tournai *c* 1510, this wool and silk piece measures 292 x 361cm (9ft 7in x 11ft 10in) (*Burrell Collection, Glasgow Art Gallery*)

32 Tapestries depicting *Scenes from the Life of St Lawrence* or *The Martyrdom of St Lawrence* were popular among sixteenth century German and French weavers; there is evidence that some of those who wove tapestries like these may have been amateurs or apprentices, possibly cloistered nuns or monks, or gentlewomen in their castles; the long and narrow dimensions suggest that looms were of small and simple construction. This part of a larger tapestry formerly in Nuremberg's Lorenzkirche (which also exhibited *The Martyrdom of St Lawrence*) measures 99 × 196cm (3ft 3in × 6ft 5in) and comprises *Scenes from the Life of St Lawrence*. Nuremburg's German National Museum has fragments of these tapestries (*Burrell Collection, Glasgow Art Gallery*)

in 22, 24, 27 and 30. The groups are of nearly equal importance although, in some cases, their relative hierarchical position or status may be shown by making some figures smaller. The foliage changes in character from about 1475 with outlines used more and emphasis on individual leaves heightened or lessened, according to contextual emphasis requirements for tonal balance. The treatment of flesh has lost its painter-like method and is of browner tint throughout. The flowery meadows of earlier periods have developed into beds of exquisite flowers, rendered with unexampled freedom and delicacy and true to natural growth. A new decorative feature makes its appearance: this is a surrounding band or border, generally of naturally disposed flowers, with little difference between them and those of the foreground. Typical of this developing style is the mille-fleur tapestry of the *Armorials of Charles the Rash* woven by Jan de Haze in Brussels in about 1470, and now in the Historisches Museum, Berne, Switzerland. Other examples are depicted in 29, 33, 34 and 35.

Although English tapestry workshops were not on anything like the same scale as those of continental Europe during the fifteenth century, the importance of tapestry to the English and Scottish is impossible to overestimate. It was used for furnishings in everyday life, and for indoor and outdoor decoration on occasions of festivity, pomp or ceremony. The entrance into London of Queen Elizabeth, wife of Henry VII (reign 1485–1509), was a brilliant spectacle, as the old historian describes it:

> Al the strets ther, whiche she shulde passe bye wer clenly dressed and besene with cloth of Tappestrye and Arras; and some streetes as Chepe, hanged with riche clothes of golde, velvettes and silkes.

Among the last great examples of tapestries of the Gothic period is *The Story of Caesar*, woven at Tournai *c*1465–70 (Historisches Museum, Berne), and *The Adoration of the Eternal Father*, Brussels 1485 (Metropolitan Museum of Art, NY, USA).

After 1500 a new element comes into design. The composition tends more to general effect and a straining towards dramatic force begins to be felt. This is most apparent in the set representing the *Triumphs of Petrarch*, one of which is dated 1507 (*see* 30). It gives a foretaste of the radical change of style from 1515, when a complete revolution in design took hold, aided in some respects by various political developments. From 1490 the Spanish wool and textile industries had been severely disrupted by the banishment of almost 800 000 workers of Moorish and foreign origin. Some restrictions had been placed on the export of wool from England to help home industries.

Belgium

Although the demand for tapestries from Tournai continued unabated until well into the sixteenth century, the cumulative effect of the town's political and other misfortunes doomed its workshops to extinction by the mid-century. Many deaths from pestilence in 1513, military sieges and transfer of allegiance in 1517 from England to France, and to the Netherlands in 1521, followed by religious persecution when Tournai became one of the centres of the Reformed faith, resulted in many weavers and artisans leaving the town as refugees to seek work in countries more settled and tolerant. These were the highly skilled Flemish tapissiers who changed weaving from being a closely guarded semi-secret art, based on a few closely knit regions or towns, into an industry of an almost international nature. Among Tournai's later tapestries of note are a set of *The Conquest of India* of which *The Camel Caravan* is in the Burrell Collection in Glasgow, Scotland, and a series of the *Months*, of which one tapestry is in the Bowes Museum, Barnard Castle, Durham, and probably was the work of John Grenier. In 1513 the magistrates of Tournai ordered a hanging depicting the *City of Ladies* for presentation to Marguerite of Austria, Governess-General of the Low Countries, when she visited Henry VIII of England, who had captured Tournai. The English Governor of the town received a *History of Hercules* and the Earl Suffolk a *History of Judith*. Tournai weavers are supposed to have woven seventeen large tapestries between 1509 and 1531 representing the *History of the Virgin* for Reims Cathedral. The figures in the tapestry are Gothic, while the architecture is early Renaissance. Some of the last existing tapestries woven at Tournai were *A History of Joseph and Jacob* for the Bishop of Croy, about 1554 (two hangings and fragments are in Tournai Cathedral).

Marguerite of Austria bought many tapestries from the weavers of Enghien, a town which, during the early sixteenth century, was associated with two famous tapissiers, Laurent Flaschoen and Peter van Aelst. John Mustan of Enghien was the appointed tapestry merchant to Henry VIII of England, who seems to have had a mania for acquiring tapestries by any means. One of the most notable features in the political history of Henry VIII's reign, when attention was concentrated on the Netherlands, was the despatching of agents to Antwerp and elsewhere in the Low Countries on pretence of purchasing tapestries, but really to acquire political intelligence, and Henry by his agents was well advised of happenings. Thus, in the 'News from Antwerp, 26 May 1539' he is informed that 'Jerome Sanese is yet there and has spent 3 000 crowns on tapestry'. On 20 October 1539 there is the first political intelligence: 'the treasurer Babo Frenchman [Philibert Babou de la Bourdaissière, treasurer of France and superintendent of royal buildings] has been here five or six days under cover of buying tapestries, but he is no man to be here for things of little importance . . .'. These 'under cover' activities continued until the end of

33 It is likely that this tapestry, woven in Brussels in about 1510 was designed for a cathedral. It depicts *The Creation and Fall of Man* and is part of a set on the subject of *Man's Redemption* that was very popular; other tapestries in the set include *The Vices Attack Man, The Combat of the Virtues and Vices,* and *The Resurrection.* Made of wool and silk, the piece is 416·5 × 813cm (13ft 8in × 26ft 8in) in size. In the days before books were in every home or the mass of people could read, instruction was aided by sketches and pictures. As religious themes were thought to be the most important to teach the common people, the walls of churches were covered with frescoes easily understood by the illiterate. Miracle, paternoster and morality plays were reinforced by magnificent tapestries brought out and hung near the altar on feast days and other great occasions (*Fine Arts Museums of San Francisco*)

the century and are illustrated by an account in the *Calendar of State Papers, Domestic Series,* 'Addenda' for 1589–1625. The uncle of Lord Paget wrote to the agent, Barnes: 'I am promised a passport for you by the Cardinal under cover that you desire to come to Antwerp to buy tapestry and pictures for the Earl of Essex or some other of account, so when you come you must allege that cause.'

One of the main activities of sixteenth century Antwerp was to act as a market place and clearing house for tapestry; another was to provide through its various workshops some special services, such as adding to or changing existing tapestries, undertaking repairs and renovations, weaving borders, verdures or other special decorative parts for tapestries woven in the main in Brussels or elsewhere. There appears to have been a continuous movement of weavers between Antwerp, Brussels and Oudenarde, and some Brussels workshops had a branch in Antwerp. A method of producing a tapestry quickly is indicated by a document dated 1595 which details a bipartite Brussels–Antwerp arrangement. An Antwerp tapestry merchant, Carlier, received an order from the Sieur de Rhosane. Carlier employed Jacques Geubels of Brussels to weave several parts representing a gallery with pillars. To Chretian van Visch went an order to weave another part of the tapestry, and to his workman was given the task of weaving the verdure.

Unless there is an unambiguous town, weaver's or merchant's mark it is often difficult to distinguish between tapestries made in Brussels and those made in Bruges; the mark of the latter town is a weaver's spindle and a Gothic B surmounted by a crown. One of the most beautiful sixteenth century tapestries from Bruges is the *Adoration of the Infant Jesus* in London's Victoria and Albert Museum. Whilst producing some of the finest hangings made in the first quarter of the century, Bruges acted in some respects like Antwerp as a centre for tapestry fairs and marketing.

34 *The Lady with the Unicorn* mille-fleur tapestries are deservedly among the most famous in the world for their delicacy, colour, beauty and mystery. The set of six hangings formerly in the Auvergne Castle of Boussac are now in the Cluny Museum, Paris. Woven in the Loire valley region about 1500, they exhibit the best of the late medieval style coupled with the ornateness that started to develop with the onset of the Renaissance, when tapestry had to hold its own in an integrated scheme of décor or furnishing for palace or castle. The total of colours is small and effect is produced by skilful contrasts. The delicately drawn flowers and animals of the background are picked out against a warm red field. The tent is in royal blue and its shape emphasized by a scattering of small gold or golden-brown ornaments laid on a fine tracery of thin dark lines. The lady, and the servant holding the open jewel-box, are clothed in powder-red garments; the tent lining is cream. The armorials are those of the Le Viste family of Lyons and may refer to Claude Le Viste who married Chabannes-Vande-nesse about 1510. Five tapestries of this set are thought to represent the five senses of hearing, feeling, smelling, seeing and tasting. This sixth piece may be a subtle dedication to the recipient of the set. The inscription above the tent entrance, '*à mon seul désir*', translates as 'to my only desire' (*Cluny Museum and Musées Nationaux, Paris*)

Oudenarde, like Enghien, is famous for its verdure tapestries and had as great a strength of tapissiers as Bruges or Enghien. An immense number of tapestries was produced and at one time every tapestried house or collector seemed to have at least one Oudenarde verdure. Many unauthenticated 'greenery' tapestries and fragments surviving in British stately homes and country houses are optimistically attributed by owners to Oudenarde. The Austrian State collection has several pieces of the set, the *History of David*, and the Bowes Museum has the *Return of Jacob* and several verdures. Oudenarde tapestries have few vigorous reds; most reds are a soft shade—a strange characteristic!

The origins of tapestry weaving in Brussels cannot be precisely dated, but there were certainly looms there in the fourteenth century. A corporation of tapissiers was formed in 1448 and regulations published in 1451. Sixteenth

Plate 21 (*opposite above*) Among the many fine tapestries woven at Barcheston were a series of pictorial maps of English counties projected on a scale as large as 4·73cm:1km (3in:1 mile) using the engraved maps of Christian Saxton's *Surveys of the Counties of England* (published in 1579) as cartoons. *The Sheldon Tapestry of Warwickshire* measures 396·5 × 526cm (13ft × 17ft 3in) excluding a border 48cm (17in) wide. In addition to Warwickshire, the map shows parts of the shires of Derby, Gloucester and Stafford, and is dated 1588. Other views of England include maps of Warwick and Worcester, the valley of the river Thames and the counties of Oxfordshire and Berkshire. The maps were made to adorn the Sheldon mansions at Weston Park and elsewhere (*Warwickshire Museum Collection, Warwick*)

Plate 22 (*opposite below*) Said to have been discovered under wall-plaster in the room of an old house in south-west England, this tapestry hung in Lyme Regis Parish Church from 1886–1977 and is now in the care of the National Trust. Some authorities claim the scene is the *Marriage of Prince Arthur to Katherine of Aragon*. If this was so, the Prince should appear short and dark and the marriage surely should be in the presence of his father, King Henry the Seventh of England, and the interior should resemble old St Paul's in London. But there is not a male crowned head anywhere, the bridegroom is tall and fair, and the view seen at the upper left of the tapestry is of a distant town with open country between. Authorities who claim this is the *Marriage of King Henry the Eighth to Katherine of Aragon* have much evidence in their favour. Shortly after the death of Henry VII, the future Henry VIII married his deceased brother's widow at Greenwich before his own coronation, and he was tall and fair. There can be little doubt that the bride depicted is Katherine. The pomegranate symbol of Granada and Aragon decorates a pillar, and the carpet on the floor has a Hispano-Moresque design. The hanging is about 183 × 447cm (6 × 14ft) in size, and was most likely woven in Flanders early in the sixteenth century (*National Trust for Places of Historic Interest or Natural Beauty*)

Plate 23 (*overleaf above*) Although not in the best condition, these fragments of sixteenth century Ferrara tapestry are of interest because they depict episodes from *The Life of the Virgin* taken from the pre-1511 drawings of Albrecht Dürer. Made with a wool and silk weft on a linen warp with a texture of 6·6 w/cm (17 w/in) and measuring in total 191·7 × 305·2cm (6ft 3½in × 9ft 6½in), these two tapestries represent the *Presentation of the Virgin* and the *Annunciation*. The piece at the left has the top and bottom borders missing, and that at the right has no borders. The scene at the left is of the Virgin ascending the steps of the Temple with a group waiting to follow, while the high priest and other ecclesiastics await her above. On the left are sellers of doves and fruit; a lamb is tied by its legs below. Through an arched doorway there is a vista of landscape, and the ceiling appears to be decorated with an armoured man holding a flaming cresset, and a horse. The vertical borders are decorated with a formal ornament of a Moorish variety. A red medallion on the left carries an inscription, and that on the right, the date MDX (1510). The companion panel has a scene framed by an archway with a cameo head in either corner, probably of Augustus and the oracle he consulted. Beyond is a lofty room with a ceiling painting, or a picture on the far wall, depicting at its centre a representation of Judith with the head of Holofernes. At the centre of the room an angel holding a sceptre approaches the Virgin, who is seated beneath a canopy with her arms crossed, at the right. A glimpse of landscape is seen through an arch in the background and, above it, there is a vision of God the Father. The perspective of the upper part of both tapestries is a little difficult to follow; one authority has suggested, for example, that the armoured man in the first tapestry is standing on the roof (*The Bowes Museum, Barnard Castle, England*)

Plate 24 (*overleaf below*) These are Brussels hangings from the *Months* or *Seasons* series from the Wainscot Room at Hopetoun House Edinburgh, that were probably specially commissioned for this room. It is likely that these pieces were woven in the workshop of Jos de Vos who, with Jerome le Clerck and Jan Cobus, produced a great quantity of prized tapestries from about 1703 onwards, including panels of *Marlborough's Victories*, and copies of the *Conquest of Tunis by Charles V* from cartoons painted by Jan Vermayen in 1535. The Hopetoun House *Months* or *Seasons* tapestries are said to be after cartoons by Bernard van Orley (1471–1541), a student of Raphael's, but may be from cartoons by Jan van Orley. With the exception of a few specially woven modern ones, tapestries were not made to be put in museums. The best place to view a tapestry is in a building for which it was designed, surrounded by at least some of the furnishings of its period. The Scottish home of the Marquess of Linlithgow at Hopetoun House, near Edinburgh and the famous Forth Bridge, is a magnificently designed late seventeenth century mansion set in a stately park. The House has been likened to Versailles and on its walls has a wide variety of seventeenth to nineteenth century tapestries which the public may see (*Hopetoun House Preservation Trust, print from the Pilgrim Press Ltd, Derby*)

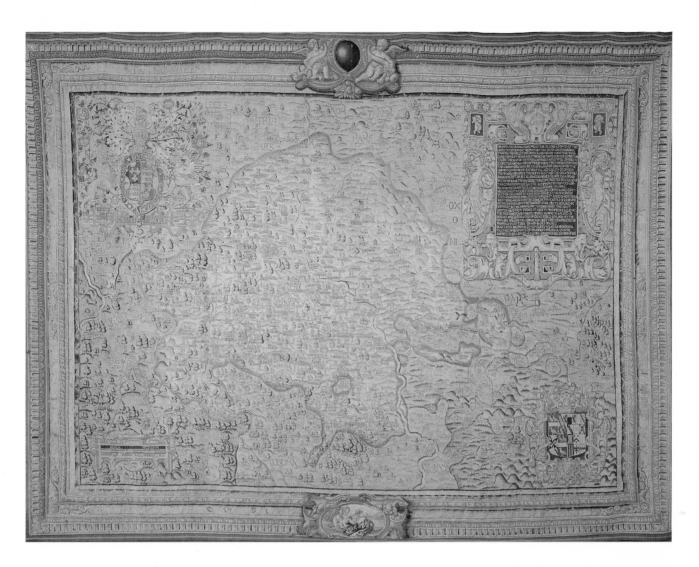

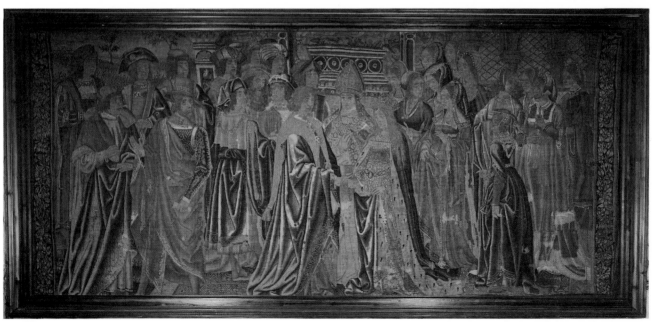

Plate 25 (*previous page, above left*) This, a *Tapestry Portrait of Pope Innocent XIII*, was woven at the Atelier of the Ospizio di San Michele about 1721, and is made of wool with a little silk and silvered thread on what appears to be a silk warp. The Pope stands half turned to the left with his right hand partly raised in the act of blessing; he has a scroll in his left hand and appears to be dressed informally in robes of red and white with fur and lace trimming. Pope Clement XI founded this Atelier and it is supposed that Pope Innocent XIII had his portrait made soon after his accession. The texture of this hanging is very fine, with an average of 8·6 w/cm (22 w/in); the tapestry measures 104·3 × 77·5cm (3ft 5in × 2ft 6½in). The Vatican is said to have a replica of this portrait, which may have hung until the troubles of 1848 either in the Atelier or in the Villa Albani (*The Bowes Museum, Barnard Castle, England*)

Plate 26 (*previous page, above right*) Another magnificent house where tapestries may be seen in a contemporary setting is in the home of the Duke of Richmond and Gordon, at Goodwood, near Chichester, in Sussex. The Tapestry Drawing Room was redesigned to accommodate the tapestries purchased by the third Duke in Paris while he was Ambassador there in 1765. This is a set of four Louis the Fifteenth tapestries by Michel Audran and Pierre François Cozette, illustrating episodes from Cervantes' *Don Quixote*, after the original designs of Charles Coypel. Three are signed 'Cozette' and dated 1762–4 and are *Dom Quichotte suspendu à la grille*, *Les Filles de l'Hotellerie*, and *L'Armet de Mambrin*; the fourth, by Michel Audran, is *La Tête Enchantée*. This set forms part of the fifth series of weavings of the original design by Coypel, and are usually referred to as 'Marly' tapestries since 12 of the 24 were ordered by the King for the Chateau de Marly; later, six were taken by the Empress Eugenie. Of the remaining 12, four were purchased by the Duke of Richmond (*The Trustees of the Goodwood Collection*)

Plate 27 (*previous page, below*) There are a few privileged people in every country who, at some time in their lives, will have seen this tapestry. It is one of two Gobelin panels from the series *Jason and the Golden Fleece* which were designed in the 1740s by Detry. Both were woven between 1777 and 1780 by Cozette. This magnificent tapestry hangs on the wall of the Ballroom in Buckingham Palace, the place where investitures are held. The two panels form part of a set of six; the others are at Windsor Castle. They were purchased for King George the Fourth in 1826 (*By Gracious Permission of Her Majesty the Queen*)

Plate 28 (*opposite above*) Part of W.G. Thomson's early twentieth century cartoon for *The Lord of the Hunt* tapestry (*Author's copyright reserved*)

Plate 29 (*opposite below*) *The Wine Press* designed by Sir Frank Brangwyn RA and woven in 1947 by the Dovecot Studios, was one of the small and colourfully cheerful tapestries produced in the immediate post-war period. It is noteworthy that Brangwyn worked with William Morris and this tapestry is typical of the 'new look' which Jean Lurçat was promoting in France concurrently. Texture is 4·7 w/cm (12 w/in) and measurements 206 × 251·6cm (6ft 9in × 8ft 3in) (*Edinburgh Tapestry Co*)

century chroniclers claim that every court of Europe had hangings of Brussels make. Pieces of no great size, but finely woven with gold and silver thread, silk and the finest wools, have been attributed to the workshops of Brussels, such as *St Luke Painting the Virgin*, in the Louvre, Paris.

The most significant evidence of the superiority of craftsmen in Brussels is that the designs of the greatest artist of his time were entrusted to weavers of that town to be reproduced in tapestry. The Medici Pope, Leo X, commissioned Raphael to design a set of cartoons depicting the *Acts of the Apostles*, to be woven in gold, silver, the finest silks and wools. The subjects were chosen from themes connected with the dynamic history of the early church, and were: the *Miraculous Draught of Fishes*, *The Healing of the Lame Man by St Peter and St John at the Beautiful Gate of the Temple*, *The Death of Ananias*, *The Blinding of Elymas*, *Christ's Charge to Peter*, *The Sacrifice at Lystra*, *St Paul Preaching at Athens*, *The Stoning of St Stephen*, *The Conversion of St Paul* and *St Paul in Prison*. They varied in length, but the majority were about 457·5 × 1281cm (15 × 42ft). Raphael was assisted by Giovanno da Udine and Francesco Penni, and the cartoons were ready in 1515. The Pope selected Peter van Aelst, a Brussels master weaver, as being best fitted to translate Raphael's works into tapestry. The cartoons, now only seven of the original ten, are in London's Victoria and

35 *The Seignorial Life (Courtly Life)* is another set of magnificent French tapestries contemporary with the *Unicorn* set, and illustrates the customs and habits of the aristocracy of the period. Although probably allegorical, the scene depicted – *The Bath* – of a noble lady, appears not to suggest anything outrageous or unusual; there is no suggestion of disapproval in this beautiful scene (*Cluny Museum and Musées Nationaux, Paris*)

Albert Museum (*see* 37). Van Aelst had been tapissier to Philip the Handsome (son of the Holy Roman Emperor Maximilian I (1493–1519) of Habsburg and his wife Marie of Burgundy, daughter of Charles the Rash), and to Philip's son, Holy Roman Emperor Charles V of Spain. In weaving the *Acts of the Apostles* van Aelst had the artistic advice of the Flemish painter Bernard van Orley (1471–1541) who, if he had not actually worked in Raphael's studio, was a close follower of that master. In 1519, less than four years from delivery of the cartoons, van Aelst presented the tapestries to his papal master. Their reception in Rome was almost wildly enthusiastic and Raphael, nearing the end of his short life, was able to behold them. In accordance with Flemish custom, the cartoons became the property of van Aelst and remained in Brussels until by circuitous means they came under the notice of the artist Rubens, who persuaded Charles I of England to buy them, whereafter they became the property of the English crown, as they are today. The tapestries were intended to be hung in the Sistine Chapel—the Pope's private chapel—only on important ceremonial occasions. The widespread attention the cartoons and tapestries received, coupled with Raphael's dedication to the art of the ancient world of Greece and Rome and to the emphasis on portrayal of a few well chosen muscular or, as in the representation of the lame man, unaffected figures or groups, promoted rapidly a new school of tapestry design, which banished the over-crowded compositions of the Medieval and Gothic periods with their prettiness, mysticism and fairy tale qualities. The year 1515 was the watershed between pre-Raphael art and the Renaissance—an art-form that took hold with such commitment that weavers were forbidden on pain of unpleasant consequences to diverge from the cartoon prepared by the artist, and also an art-form that eventually produced expensive tapestries so much like the painted picture that it was cheaper to purchase the picture.

But in sixteenth century Brussels the impact of the *Acts of the Apostles* was to make the tapissiers and workshops of that city the most sought after in the world, and many requests were received for copies of the set to be made for other clients. With prosperity came the use of methods not in accordance with the best traditions of the craft; for example, the colouring by liquid dyes of such features as the lips, cheeks and flesh parts. Within five years of Raphael's tapestries being completed these degenerate methods had so debased the reputation of Brussels that an ordinance promulgated in 1525 prohibited the touching-up by means of liquid substances of any tapestry worth more than 12 pence per ell and the copying or imitation of models already executed by another. This was followed in 1528 by an edict promulgated in the interests of trade in Brussels; all tapestries greater in size than six ells were to be marked

36 'Astronomy' is the allegorical female figure at the right, who is one of the Seven Liberal Arts. With her are two scholars and two shepherds, all studying the stars. 'Astronomy' and the man facing her, said to represent the famous fifteenth century scientist, Regiomontanus, are clothed in the fashion of the reign of Louis XII of France. Colours are made from a restricted palette of dark blues and reds, sombre browns and yellows, highlighted with silk. Measurements are 240 × 340cm (7ft 10½in × 11ft 2in). The texture is rather coarse although the weaver has skilfully attempted to compensate for this. Most likely the product of an early sixteenth century workshop in northern France, this tapestry may be associated with the Liberal Arts *Music* piece in the Boston Museum of Fine Arts, USA (*Röhsska Konstslöjds-museet, Gothenburg, Sweden*)

91

37 As far as tapestry is concerned, the Renaissance Period started when the Medici Pope Leo X commissioned Raffaello Sanzio (1483–1520), popularly known as Raphael, to design ten tapestries for the Sistine Chapel, the Pope's personal Chapel in the Vatican. The meaning of 'Renaissance' was the re-discovery in Italy of the elegance and grandeur of the ancient art of Greece and Rome, and especially the high degree of visual illusion and human emotion which could be conveyed through facial expression and bodily posture. The cartoons for the tapestries were painted by Raphael between 1515 and 1516; all related to episodes in the life of St Peter or St Paul. This cartoon depicts *The Healing of the Lame Man by St Peter and St John at the Beautiful Gate of the Temple.* Raphael's palette consisted mainly of inorganic pigments that have aged or faded little during the 450 years since he painted the cartoons, despite exposure and rough treatment. The other surviving cartoons, seven in all, are in London's Victoria and Albert Museum (*By gracious permission of Her Majesty the Queen*)

with a red shield supported by two letters 'B', the letters to be lighter in tone than that of the selvedge into which they and the shield were woven. Neither of these bye-laws eradicated the degenerate practices and so, in 1544, Charles V enacted laws to govern the industry throughout the Low Countries. Tapestries were to be made only in accordance with the regulations of the corporation of tapestry weavers as in Louvain, Brussels, Antwerp, Bruges, Oudenarde, Alost, Enghien, Binche, Lille and Tournai, and the quality of materials was to be specified when the material exceeded a certain price. Warp was to be woollen thread of Lyons, Spain or Aragon or similar, thoroughly clean and coloured with a fast dye; each tapestry was to be woven in one piece only. All tapestries were to have the woven mark or ensign of the master-weaver or manufacturer at one of the lower corners as well as the town mark required under the edict of 1528. Some of the requirements of this ordinance were got round by tapissiers who made a tapestry in several, seemingly complete, parts and then sewed these together. This practice encouraged the adoption of low-warp looms which, in turn, hastened further deterioration in the standards of Brussels which, by 1560, was also suffering the effects of ferment with the emigration of persecuted artists and weavers to England and elsewhere.

The encouragement and patronage of the Emperor Maximilian and Philip of Spain were strong factors in the early prosperity of Brussels which also owed much to the master weavers van Aelst and William (weaving 1548–54), the son of Pierre Pannemaker; the ten rich tapestries depicting the *History of Abraham*, hanging in England's Hampton Court Palace, bear the mark of William Pannemaker (*see* 39). One of his most magnificent sets was designed by Jan Vermeyen of Haarlem, who accompanied his patron—Charles V of Spain —to the battlefield to make sketches for the *Conquest of Tunis* now in Madrid (Patrimonio Nacional); Pannemaker was given a great quantity of gold and silver thread and about 248kg (559lb) of silk dyed in 19 colours of from three to five shades each, spun in Granada. By 1554 weaving was completed and approved by the jurors of Brussels. François Geubels was another master-weaver of Brussels whose work was much admired; his *Hunts of Maximilian* is

38 *The Luttrell Armorial Tapestry* is one of the earliest surviving textiles of this nature. It may have been hung on a wall, or laid on a table on special occasions. During the Middle Ages a table tapestry was customary when men of high rank met for a conference (*see* Plate 20). In sixteenth century Europe a document 'laid on the tapis' meant a paper put on the agenda for consideration; 'tapis' was derived from the fifteenth century use of 'tappetium' for 'tapestry'. *The Luttrell Armorial Tapestry*, woven with wool, silk and metal thread, measures 193 x 551.5cm (6ft 4in x 18ft 1in), and may be the work of either an English or a Netherlands manufactory. The central shield with the arms of Luttrell impaling Wyndham above the initials AL refer to Sir Andrew Luttrell of Dunster (Somersetshire) whose marriage with Margaret, daughter of Sir Thomas Wyndham of Felbrigg in Norfolk, took place in 1514 when they were both minors. The central field is an interlocking complex of squares, circles, and quatrefoils enclosing daisies, roses and honeysuckle; two armorials flank the central one. Scattered in the running plant border pattern are 12 armorials of different shapes. Sir Andrew died in 1538 and was survived by his widow for more than 40 years; she may have ordered this tapestry in memory of her husband, for she bequeathed it to her daughter Margaret Edgecumbe, from whom it descended to Lord Mount Edgecumbe of Cothele House, Cornwall (*Burrell Collection, Glasgow Art Gallery*)

in the Louvre, Paris. The output of tapestries by Brussels workshops was vast. The crowned heads of Europe and lesser mortals placed many orders, with the result that Raphael—although credited with being responsible for the Renaissance—was not the only foreigner whose designs created a vogue.

France

The main development in France was the establishment by Francis I, in about 1535, of a royal manufactory at Fontainebleau near Paris. He recruited Flemish and Italian weavers to work with native tapissiers and placed the workshops under the direction of Philibert Babou de la Bourdaissière, who shortly before had endeavoured to consolidate and strengthen the manufactories at Tours by installing there a Flemish weaver, Jean Duval (died 1552), and his sons, Marc, Hector and Étienne. The Duval workshop is best known for the extant hangings of the *Life of St William*. The Italian architect Sebastian Serlio and artist Primaticcio joined with artists living at Fontainebleau to design tapestries for the king's châteaux; six hangings of unorthodox design survive in Vienna's Kunsthistorisches Museum. The Fontainebleau high-warp looms survived for only 12 years, but the establishment served as a proving-ground for the far more successful manufactory sponsored by Henri II of France and based on the orphanage at the Hôpital de la Trinité, Paris, where there were 150 or more children who could be instructed in the useful craft of tapissier. Inaugurated in 1551, this manufactory eventually produced the orphan tapissier, du

39 This is one of ten magnificent tapestries depicting *The History of Abraham* woven about 1540 by William Pannemaker of Brussels, whose mark appears in the selvedges. The tapestry illustrated, *The Meeting of Abraham and Melchizedek*, refers to Genesis xxiv 18–20. The set formed part of the vast purchases of hanging made by King Henry the Eighth for the decoration of his palace at Hampton Court, near London, where they still hang. The cartoons were probably the work of the Flemish artist Bernard van Orley (1485–1542). This hanging is 480 × 762·5cm (15ft 9in × 25ft 7in) in size and has a texture of 7 w/cm (18 w/in) with a weft of wool, silk and gold threads (*By gracious permission of Her Majesty the Queen*)

Bourg, who made his name by weaving a set depicting *Scenes from the Life of Christ,* and was ordered by the king to join with another weaver, Giraud Laurent, to establish another workshop in the Faubourg St Antoine, in a house vacated by the Jesuits when they were expelled from Paris. When the Jesuits were allowed to return in 1607, this workshop was transferred to the Louvre. The Trinité workshop lasted until about 1650.

The Parisian workshops appear to have woven a motley selection of pieces ranging from small pieces of a religious nature such as choir stall hangings, priests' robes, altar hangings, palls and secular fabrics such as saddle-covers, gloves and bed hangings; armorial hangings were produced by Laurents' son, Henri. In the mid-sixteenth century the designer Jean Coussine designed a set of eight hangings in the new Renaissance style of the *Life of St Mammes*. In provincial France the Marche manufactories of Felletin and Aubusson were starting to be widely known with the continuing production of pre-Renaissance religious motif and verdure pieces. Tapestries produced in the Tours workshops in general were superior and enjoyed greater patronage than those of Felletin and Aubusson. The attempt made six years before he was crowned, by the future Henri IV, to start a manufactory at Béarne was abortive but may have served as a useful exercise in advance of his founding the Saint-Marcel establishment in Paris later. The many workshops elsewhere appear to have woven pieces principally for their local patrons.

Italy

In the early sixteenth century manufactories in Italy were in a state of collapse following military activities. When peace came a splendid rejuvenation of the craft took place and this was spurred on by the international reputation earned by Raphael's *Acts of the Apostles* for the Vatican. Almost every tapestry seems to have been woven by an immigrant from Flanders or France, but designed by a native artist with the exception of Vigevano, where the weavers, under the aegis of Benedetto da Milano, seem to have been entirely native. The Italian workshops were conducted on different lines from those of Flanders, being founded by, and dependent on, one of the noblemen or families who headed one or other of Italy's independent states. The principal workshops

94

during the sixteenth century were at: (1) Ferrara (sponsored by the d'Este family); (2) Florence (sponsored by the Medicis); (3) Rome where Pope Nicholas V (1447–55) tried to sustain an atelier which produced a *Creation* set, and where in 1558 Jan Rost of Florence tried to sustain an atelier on behalf of Pope Paul IV (1555–9); (4) Venice, which was more a marketing than a manufacturing city, and there is some suggestion that the Medicis had an extension of their Florentine workshops there. From about 1473 Cosimo Tura had supplied cartoons to local weavers. From the mid-sixteenth century a host of tapissiers are listed, including Ambrose Spireletti (1562), the Flemish Francesco and Caspar Carnes (1564–72) and Van der Goes (1586). Tapestries attributed to Venetian looms include *Four Theological Virtues* (designed by Titian) in 1562, *Descent of the Holy Spirit, Doge L Loredam receiving his ducal cap* and *History of Semale*; the latter three are in Venetian churches or museums; and (5) Milan, where production continued from the fifteenth century, with attribution of some panels of *Caesar*. No definite list exists of production by the Bologna, Corregio, Udine and smaller workshops.

Ferrara was at its most brilliant between 1534 and 1559, when Duke Ercole II of Mantua died, and the workshops came to a close. In the 1530s the Duke appointed a group of eight highly experienced Flemish weavers including

40 Tapestry sets representing the story of Esther and Ahasuerus (from Esther ii) were popular with designers and weavers before the fifteenth century, one of the earliest sets surviving being of Burgundian origins. The hanging here is of *Esther before Ahasuerus*. It was woven in Brussels in about 1500–25 (*Victoria and Albert Museum; Crown Copyright*)

95

41 In about 1509, a wealthy wool merchant, William Willington purchased the manor of Barcheston, Warwickshire. In 1534 William Sheldon of Beoley, Worcestershire, purchased land nearby and made Weston Park, where he built a great mansion; his family originated at Sheldon in Warwickshire. He married Mary, the daughter of William Willington, and was elected one of two members of parliament representing Worcestershire in 1547 and 1554–5. Realizing the advantages of turning Cotswold sheeps' wool into tapestries, he sent Richard Hyckes (or Hicks) of Barcheston to Flanders to study. Hyckes learned the art of tapestry-weaving and returned to Barcheston about 1569 with some Flemish weavers. Sheldon had purchased Barcheston Manor House about 1561, and installed Hyckes and the Flemish weavers there with looms. The manufactory he established at Beoley shortly after was burned down during the mid-seventeenth century. Weaving continued at Barcheston until about 1647. The Manor House has undergone few external changes since it was the site of England's first major tapestry manufactory in 1569 or earlier (*With acknowledgement to Mr and Mrs Morris of Barcheston, and the artist of the sketch, S.C.Spencer*)

Jean (van der) Rost (or Roost) with Nicolas (Niccolò) and Hans (Jan or Giovanni) Karcher as co-directors of weaving. Despite the popularity of the Renaissance style pioneered by Raphael (all Christendom must have been talking of it by the 1540s), Hans Karcher adhered to the pre-Raphaelite style in the limited palette *Ovid's Metamorphoses* designed by Battista Dossi and completed in 1545 (now in the Louvre, Paris). The tapestry-is-a-painting Renaissance style is far more marked in the *Life of the Virgin* (1562–70) hanging (now in Como Cathedral), and other later Ferrara pieces (*see* 44 and Plate 23). It is impossible to be sure which tapestries were woven at Ferrara. The *Putti* series may have been woven at Mantua (examples are in Milan Cathedral). The workshops in Florence were reinforced in 1546 when Jan Rost and co-director Niccolò Karcher transferred their allegiance from Ferrara and Mantua, to make the Florentine manufactory one of the finest in Europe with a huge output up to the death of Cosimo I de Medici (1537–74), who had promoted it as a means of reducing dependence on Flanders. In its later years the main criticism was that the weaver was increasingly turned into a skilful

Plate 30 *The Cycle of Life* is an undenominational design expressing the theme of birth, growth, fruition and death commissioned by Edinburgh's Warriston Crematorium. Designed and woven by Sax Shaw at the Dovecot Studios of the Edinburgh Tapestry Company, this tapestry has attracted much attention and been highly commended. It was woven in 1958 and measures 289·7 × 274·5cm (9ft 6in × 9ft) and has a texture of 3·1 w/cm (8 w/in) (*Sax Shaw*)

Plate 31 Hans Tisdall designed a pair of tapestries on the theme of 'Time' and 'Space' for the former headquarters in London of the English Electric Company. These tapestries were woven during 1959–60 at the Dovecot Studios of the Edinburgh Tapestry Company, and have been described as 'the finest textiles to have been produced in this country for many centuries'. In recent years they were presented by the Lord Nelson of Stafford, the Chairman of the English Electric Company and of the General Electric Company, to the University of Aston at Birmingham. Each tapestry has a texture of 4·7 w/cm (12 w/in) and measures 465 × 249cm (15ft 3in × 8ft 2in). Here is depicted 'Time', in which scientific achievement is linked with man's basic needs: health and warmth derived from the sun and bread from the wheatsheaf, and his concern with matter (*Court of the University of Aston at Birmingham*)

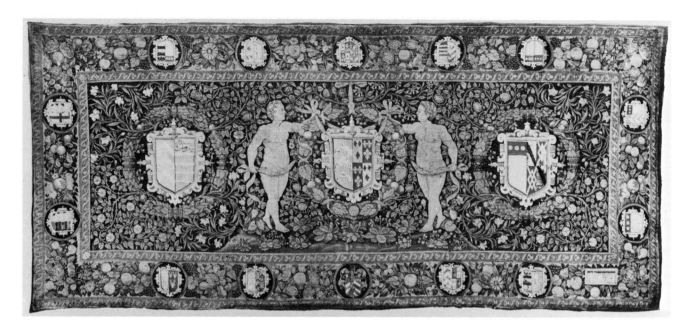

42 This tapestry, probably made at Barcheston in 1564, carries the arms and alliances of the Lewkenor family. The central armorial is enclosed by a wreath, with boy supporters who stand on a mound covered by cowslips, wild strawberries, heartsease and other flowers, against a dark background almost covered by less natural sprays of flowers like lilies, roses and honeysuckle. The border is composed of bunches of flowers and fruit among which are arranged 14 armorials of family alliances. The purpose of this tapestry was explained in a memorandum of 1662 written by Sir John Lewkenor: 'Remember to keep safe the carpet of arms, now aged about 100 years, which in the failure of the older house totalie consuming itself by daughters and heires and passing into other names, was sent hither by Constance Glemham of Trotton, who was one of those heires, for record to the younger house and whole name.' The *Lewkenor Armorial Table Carpet* is woven with wool and silver-gilt threads; it measures 228·8 × 488·6cm (7ft 6in × 16ft ¼in) (*Metropolitan Museum of Art; Fletcher Fund* 1958, *USA*)

slave whose sole duty it was to turn the artist's picture into a faithful reproduction in tapestry. Jean Rost was succeeded on his death in 1574 by his son, Giovanni Rost (or Roost). Production recovered from the death of Cosimo I to reach a further high peak between 1585–96, after which it declined until Ferdinand II (1621–70) appointed a French tapissier, Pierre Lefèvre, and his sons to the workshop. Outstanding hangings of the Florentine workshop include the *Story of Joseph,* designed by Agnolo Bronzino (in Quirinale Palace, Rome), and the *Months,* designed by Francesco Bacchiacca, 1552 (in Florence).

Germany, Switzerland and the Netherlands

Refugees from persecution in Flanders either joined or established workshops in these countries. From the time of Emperor Frederick III (1440–93) refugee weavers had been welcomed in the Palatinate. A workshop was founded at Frankenthal with Everand van Orley as painter and Pierre de Wayere as master weaver. Prince Othon-Henri of Neuburg had a workshop at Lauingen, Bavaria, in 1540. Wesel's workshop founded about 1530 was directed by Jean le Blas. Nuremberg weavers included Anthoni Passa and John Mandekins from the Netherlands. Notable tapestries from these workshops include *Electors and Coats-of-Arms* (Metropolitan Museum of Art, NY) and *Pyramus and Thisbe* (Victoria and Albert Museum, London). Many pieces attributed to fifteenth and sixteenth century Rhineland looms may have been woven in

99

43 This throne canopy was woven by Hans Knieper for the Great Hall at Elsinore Castle in Denmark and was his greatest masterpiece. Tapestry-weaving is supposed to have started in Denmark about 1522. In 1578 King Frederik the Second appointed Hans Knieper of Antwerp the court painter. When the massive fortress guarding the entrance to Elsinore harbour was to be decorated, the King gave Knieper the responsibility for designing tapestries for Kronborg Castle's Great Hall. The King established a tapestry workshop at Elsinore and appointed Anthonis de Corte to direct weaving and to train eight apprentices. Within a year Corte was dead and Knieper took over direction of the manufactory. Between 1581–6 a set of 42 hangings depicting Danish kings in various settings was woven for the Great Hall; only 14 of them have survived, of which seven are still at the Castle. (*Nationalmuseum, Stockholm*)

44 This tapestry, *Children Playing*, was very likely designed by Raphael's assistant, Giulio Romano, when he was working with the Ferrara workshop established under the patronage of the d'Este family in about 1436. By the mid-fifteenth century this manufactory, which had been founded with the help of Flemish weavers, was attracting more of them to work there. During the first third of the sixteenth century, production was re-organized by Duke Hercules (Ercole) the Second with a virtually all-Italian panel of designers, of which Romano was one. This mid-sixteenth century tapestry is similar to one in the Great Hall of Compton Wynates House near Tysoe, in Warwickshire, and to one in the Calouste Gulbenkian Collection in Lisbon, Portugal. The last two bear armorials linking them with the Gonzaga family of Mantua. The Wynates' hanging was probably woven for Sigismondo Gonzaga, Cardinal (1505) and then Bishop of Mantua (1511–20). In addition to the tapestry shown here, the Victoria and Albert Museum has a drawing by Romano likely to have been the design for the Gulbenkian tapestry of *Children Playing and Fishing* (*Victoria and Albert Museum; Crown Copyright*)

Burgundy, Alsace or Switzerland. During the latter part of the sixteenth and the early seventeenth century, Delft in The Netherlands grew to be one of Europe's main centres for tapestry. Registered in Flanders in 1576, François Spierinck was working there, as was Josse Lanckaert of Brussels, by 1587 (*see* 38). A magnificent *Cloth of Estate with the Royal Arms of Edward VI* woven for the Tolhouse in Great Yarmouth, England, is in Glasgow's Burrell Collection. Middelburg is recorded as having had workshops from 1562.

4 The Seventeenth Century

By the end of the sixteenth century the impact of Raphael's reversion to the art of ancient Rome and Greece had influenced the design philosophy of most European tapestry workshops. Gone was the easy partnership between designer and weaver whose mutual interplay during the Medieval and Gothic periods had produced so many beautiful or arresting hangings. Instead of informal collaboration with the designer the weaver was increasingly disciplined to concentrate his skill solely on imitating or interpreting what the designer decreed. The result was that tapestry grew more and more to resemble a woollen or a silk copy of a painting and, often enough, a pretty pretentious one with a wide border heavily ornamented with items bearing little relationship to the subjects in the central, deep and projected, field. The weaver's prime duty was to weave perfectly. Not until the last quarter of the nineteenth century, when William Morris forcibly questioned the merits of Raphaelesque tapestry, was there any fundamental divergence from the Renaissance style, although its retention obviously was all but stifling the tapissier's art.

England

Following the death of Henry VIII in 1547, England was without an enthusiastic royal patron of tapestry until James I (1603–25) (James VI of Scotland) came to the throne. Elizabeth I (1558–1603) did not share her father's passion for tapestry. In 1607, Henri IV of France (1598–1610) established a royal tapestry workshop in Paris at Faubourg St Marcel. King James very soon decided that the success of the French venture laid an obligation on him to found a comparable manufactory. In about 1619 he appointed a board of commissioners to examine the financial and artistic aspects, and for guidance he gave them an abstract of the French king's contract with the Flemish weavers Marc de Comans and François de la Planche, who had been charged with establishing the Parisian workshop. The commissioners' report being in favour of an English manufactory, James made an arrangement under which Sir Francis Crane would finance and manage the manufactory in return for the privilege of receiving fees from his distribution of three or four baronetcies, a tapestry-producing monopoly lasting 21 years, help with recruitment of Flemish weavers and their British naturalization, and duty-free export of the workshop's products. Crane was a man of refined taste, consummate ability and a prominent member of the courts of Elizabeth I, James I and Charles I. With his usual energy he lost no time in carrying out his part of the engagement, and brick-built, three-storey workshops were soon ready at Mortlake, on the south bank of the river Thames, a few miles south-west of London. For his part, the King procured through his agents the immigration of capable tapestry-weavers from the Low Countries, including the master weaver and eventual director of weaving at Mortlake, Philip de Maecht, who had worked under de Comans in Paris. Other notable tapissiers included Pierre Foquentin, Simon Heyns of Oudenarde, Jacques Hendricx, Peter de

45 Evidence of Norwegian weighted-warp loom use, from early times, indicates that rural knowledge of tapestry-weaving techniques never completely died out. Apart from the *Baldishol Tapestry* (*see* Plate 14), the most notable surviving tapestries of old were woven in Gudbrandsdalen from about 1600. Many depict religious subjects such as *The Wise and Foolish Virgins* and *The Adoration of the Magi*. A subject repeated often was *The Beheading of St John and Herod's Feast* shown here. There are several versions of the design and the oldest is probably that appearing in Oslo's Kunstindustrimuseet, said to have been woven in 1613. A third version, probably more recent than that shown, is in a New York collection. All three are split into three main parts, with the Oslo hanging and this one being the most alike in the top and middle parts; the bugler at the bottom right appears in all three, but his instrument is least complex in the New York version. Colours are decisive but sombre and a palette with about 12 colours and shadings is indicated (*Victoria and Albert Museum; Crown Copyright*)

46 *The Cordoba Armorial Tapestry* was possibly woven in the Salamanca workshop of Pedro Gutierrez. He was renowned as a weaver of armorial tapestries and in 1579 Anne of Austria, queen of Philip the Second of Spain, appointed him her tapissier. Alternatively, this tapestry could have been woven at St Isabel in Madrid where, a few years later, Gutierrez established another workshop. The measurements of this hanging are 251 × 239cm (8ft 3in × 7ft 10in); warp is undyed wool with a texture of 4·5 w/cm (11·4 w/in) and the weft is dyed wool. The central shield is that of the first Marqués de Huétor de Santillán, Don Diego Fernandez de Córdoba, who married Doña Maria de la Cueva Bazán y Benavides; her family arms form the right part of the shield. The motto above the shield reads (in translation) 'Without Himself nothing is accomplished'. Four small family crests are in the corners. Looking clockwise from the upper left, these are: Cordoba, Santillán, Carrillo and Mendoza de la Vega. The Mendoza de la Vega crest at the lower left represents the union of the Mendoza and de la Vega families. The 'Ave Maria' has been woven as AVEM ARIA (*Fine Arts Museum of San Francisco*)

47 (*opposite above*) This tapestry hangs on the south side of the Sanctuary in Westminster Abbey, not far from the High Altar. It is one of the three similar pieces given by Sir Paul Pindar (1565?–1650), sometime English ambassador to Turkey and a strong supporter of King Charles the First. One of the three tapestries was destroyed in the Second World War and this, the largest, exhibits the mastery of the designer. Hung from the windowless wall of a church, this tapestry imparts a sense of spaciousness, and there can be little doubt that it was designed for a church: the massive columns are almost identical with those of the *Beautiful Gate of the Temple* cartoon by Raphael (*see* 37). Pindar's regard for Charles the First suggests that the designer may have been Peter Paul Rubens (1577–1640). The date of this tapestry falls probably between 1625–40. Measurements are 330 × 508cm (10ft 10in × 16ft 8in), texture is 6·7 w/cm (17 w/in) and wefts are of wool and silk. (*Dean and Chapter of Westminster, London*)

48 This is a drawing by John Pine of a tapestry from the series on *The Defeat of the Spanish Armada* by the English in 1588. The Admiral Lord Howard and Henry Cornelius Van Vroom, a painter of Haarlem in the Netherlands, drew up designs based on *Expeditionis Hispanorum in Angliam vera descriptio* AD 1588. The contract to weave went to François Spierincx of Antwerp and Delft. The set of 10 was completed in 1617 and placed in the Royal Wardrobe of the Tower of London. Cromwell later had six hung in the House of Lords, but they were destroyed when the Houses of Parliament burned down in 1834. Fortunately, John Pine had made engravings about 1789 and this is his drawing of the engagement off the Isle of Portland, after the English had set the Spanish ship 'Guypuscoan' on fire (*National Maritime Museum, London*)

49 Shown here is *The Entry of Louis XIV into Dunkirk on its capture from the English* in 1662. The fourteen tapestries depicting the *History of the King* (Louis the Fourteeth of France) woven by the Gobelins are regarded as that manufactory's finest mid-seventeenth century set. Depicted were the main events from Louis' Consecration in the church of Our Lady at Reims, to his capture of Lille. Designed by Charles le Brun, the professional director of the Gobelins, the tapestries detailed with great accuracy the elaborate court ceremonials, the rich dress of the period, dramatic elements in national functions and the physical appearance of notable figures. The set of hangings were, in fact, a grand historical document (*Author's copyright reserved*)

Craeght who specialized in naked figures, Louis Vermoulen who specialized in faces, and Josse Ampe of Bruges.

The Mortlake workshops commenced operations under brilliant auspices; the King, the Prince of Wales—later Charles I, the Duke of Buckingham and other nobles were its clientele. The greatest interest nationally was manifested in its progress, but, despite his brilliant directorship and business ability, Sir Francis Crane appears not to have realized fully the financial problems he might have to resolve. He had not appreciated that the finer a tapestry is the longer it takes to weave and that, unless progress-payments were made regularly, the heavy burden of wages and overheads would fall on the director of the workshops. By 1623, Crane was compelled to inform the King that the manufactory could not continue for more than a month unless financial resources were made available; debts vastly exceeded income and all his private fortune had been spent. The King agreed to a financial arrangement out of State funds, which went some way towards helping Crane. James I died in 1625 and was succeeded by Charles I (1625–49), who immediately gave Crane far greater help. The next ten years formed the golden period of the Mortlake manufactory. There was no rival and the Parisian workshops lacked the combination which was essential to attempt competition with Mortlake, which owed its popularity in no small measure to the exceedingly able official designer and draughtsman, Francis Clein, or Cleyn (died 1658). Formerly of Rostock in

108

Mecklenburg, Clein had worked as court painter to Christian IV of Denmark (1588–1648), and—most importantly in view of the Raphaelesque vogue—had studied in Italy. One of his early successes at Mortlake was the series of *Hero and Leander* hangings in gold, silver, silk and finest English wool. Five of the set given by Count Axel Oxenstierna to Karl X Gustaf are in the Swedish Royal Collection; copies are in the Victoria and Albert and the Bowes museums. The designs were the best in use at the period and included the *History of Vulcan and Venus (see 52)*, the *Twelve Months*, the *Four Seasons, Diana and Callisto*,

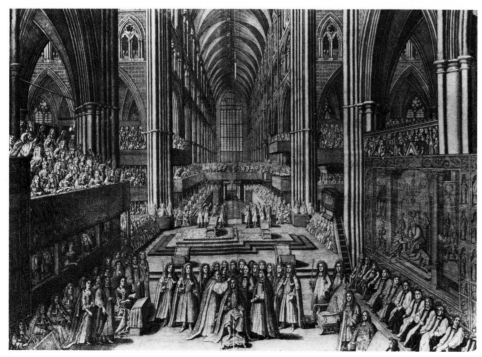

50 On great occasions some English abbeys and cathedrals were decorated with tapestries. At the Coronation of King James II in Westminster Abbey, in 1685, the walls around the the High Altar were draped with hangings from the set of ten depicting *The Life of Abraham,* (*see* 39 and 40). Drawn at, or soon after the Coronation and not by the same hand, these two engravings exhibit some artistic licence, but are accurate enough to reconcile tapestries with those still at Hampton Court Palace. (Above, from left to right) *God appears to Abraham*; beyond pulpit *The Sacrifice of Isaac*; left corner, behind High Altar, and right corner, respectively, *The Purchase of the Field of Ephron*; *The Meeting of Abraham and Melchizedek*; *The Departure of Abraham*. (Below, dimly at left, and right near pulpit, respectively) *The Separation of Abraham and Lot*; *The Circumcision of Isaac and the Expulsion of Hagar*. (*Dean and Chapter of Westminster, London*)

and the *Horses* (Clein). After Sir Anthony Van Dyck (1599–1641) had designed borders, copies were woven of the *Acts of the Apostles* from the Raphael cartoons purchased in Genoa for less than the equivalent of about £2 000 by Sir Francis Crane, on behalf of Charles when he was the Prince of Wales. The Flemish painter from Antwerp, Peter Paul Rubens (1577–1640), knighted by Charles I in 1629 and employed by him to design cartoons for Mortlake, provided the weavers with the *Story of Achilles* and may have designed the hanging at the right of the High Altar in Westminster Abbey (*see* 47).

Under so liberal a patron of the fine arts as Charles I money was literally showered on Mortlake. By the end of the 1620s it had been established long enough to yield handsome profits for its promoter. To show his appreciation, the King gave vast estates under mortgage to Crane, including ten manors, of which one was Grafton in Northamptonshire; the attempt to turn it into a tapestry apprentice training establishment came to nothing. Crane's eventual success stimulated considerable envy, however, and in about 1630 Dru Barton presented a petition to the King alleging what amounted to fraud by Crane; but the only result was that retribution was imposed on Barton who was dismissed from the office of Auditor-General. Sir Francis Crane's health started to fail and, in March 1636, he went to Paris to undergo an operation but died soon after. He was succeeded at Mortlake by his brother, Captain Richard Crane, Gentleman of the Privy Council, who found that at the time of Sir Francis' death the King owed £2 872 for three pieces of tapestry: *Hector and Leander, St Paul and Elymas the Sorcerer* and *Diana and Calisto*. Captain Crane was not successful with his 140 workmen, soon got deeply in difficulty and eventually sold Mortlake to Charles I who put it under new management and changed this (now) royal manufactory's name to the 'King's Works'. The new Governor, Sir James Palmer, was fairly successful until the unfurling of the royal standard at Nottingham in 1642 gave the signal for the outbreak of civil war between Royalists and Roundheads. Royal support for the weavers ceased and they nearly starved; the King owed them £3 937 by 1643. They struggled and were successful in keeping the workshops going only by seeking foreign commissions, since England had no call for luxuries like tapestry in the midst of civil strife. They offered the Dutch Church in London the *Acts of the Apostles*. Seemingly the Church authorities were sympathetic, for many of the weavers were of Low Countries' origin, so an order was given for a set of the *Hunter's Chase*. Contrary to popular belief, Cromwell's regime did not systematically destroy works of art, although many objects including tapestries were confiscated or sold; a great number turned up somewhere else or were used to decorate the official premises of Cromwell's lieutenants. The Council of State mounted an inquiry into conditions at Mortlake, decided it was a project that should be encouraged, appointed Sir Gilbert Pickering to direct operations and John Hollenberche as chief workman, and sent Mantegna's *Triumph of Julius Caesar* from Hampton Court Palace in 1653 as a model for cartoons and new tapestries; meanwhile other plans were being made for new designs.

The demise of the Commonwealth and the accession of Charles II (1660–85) did not produce marked encouragement for the men of Mortlake despite the efforts of Sir Sackville Crow and others to persuade the King to take urgent action. Eventually Crow was appointed to take over control of Mortlake in 1662, tapestry imports were discouraged, an annual subsidy of £1 000 was granted, and the court painter Antonio Verrio was charged with the task of

51 This is a tapestry commemorating the *Battle of Öland* in the Swedish-Danish War of 1675–9, which comprised sea-battles off the islands of Bornholm and Öland in the Baltic and invasion of southern Sweden by the Danes. The sea engagement was won by the Danes and was commemorated by a magnificent, monumental tapestry – one of several documenting the Scania War – woven in Copenhagen a few years later for the banquet hall of Rosenborg Palace, where it is still. The conquest of the Swedes over the Danes is commemorated in another tapestry that hangs in the Royal Castle, Stockholm. The Copenhagen workshop was established in 1604 and conducted by Jean de Wych, who employed 26 weavers on high-warp looms; Isaac Barraband of Aubusson joined the manufactory in 1660 (*De danske Kongers kronologiske Samling på Rosenborg*)

providing suitable new designs. Within five years these arrangements proved unsatisfactory, Crow resigned and by 1670 was imprisoned for his debts. In his place the Earl of Craven and others, including Henry Brouncker (later Viscount Brouncker), took over control and agreed to maintain Mortlake as a tapestry manufactory without subsidy from the King. From this group the establishment passed into the hands of Lady Harvey and her agent Henry Baker, who initially were successful in marketing tapestries including five pieces of the *Triumps of Julius Caesar* (after Mantegna), five pieces of the *Acts of the Apostles,* all now the property of the Duke of Buccleuch at Bowhill House, and in 1673 Baker again sold to the Crown five pieces of *Children Playing.* Despite seeming outward changes in ownership, Lady Harvey apparently exercised control of Mortlake until her death shortly before the industry was closed down in 1703. She was the daughter of the second Lord Montagu of Boughton and sister of Ralph Montagu, later the Earl and Duke of Montagu and Master of the Great Wardrobe. He is recorded as having taken over Mortlake about 1674 when Lady Harvey and her agent failed to repeat their earlier success, the inference being that the Mortlake weavers would provide a valuable back-up resource for the arras activities of the Great Wardrobe. The products of the manufactories at Beauvais, Aubusson, Brussels and the Gobelins had developed rapidly during Sir Richard Crow's time at Mortlake which, growing increasingly uncompetitive, was likely to have continual survival problems unless linked with the Royal Wardrobe. Moreover, weavers originally at Mortlake had branched out on their own. One final effort was made to save the Mortlake workshops as a going concern in 1691. The Earl of Montagu assigned his interest to a corporation of 'Tapestry-makers of England', which had lofty ideals but failed to make headway and was closed in 1703. The activity of the Mortlake workers in the first half of the seventeenth century was intense and an enormous quantity of fine hangings was made, many of which survive in museums and private collections throughout the world.

The early success of Mortlake tends to cast a shadow over other English manufactories, such as Barcheston, which was weaving tapestries well into the seventeenth century. A series of the *Seasons* at Hatfield House, the Hertfordshire home of the Marquis of Salisbury, was woven at Barcheston in 1611. Calculated with respect to the recorded output, weaving must have continued until the 1640s. It seems reasonable that Barcheston was inhibited by the same circumstances which depressed demand for Mortlake tapestries towards the end of the reign of Charles I.

The Lambeth manufactory in London was established either by a former Mortlake weaver or the son of one; his name, William Benood, had early associations with the Flemish community there. A document mentions William and John Benood in 1641 and another paper lists them as resident in 1651 at the Tapestry House at Mortlake. In 1663 John appears as a merchant in London while another was an arras-maker in the Great Wardrobe. In 1670 William Benood competed with Mortlake for a commission, which he was awarded by the Countess of Rutland, and went on to weave six panels of *Vulcan and Venus* to sixteenth century designs. Other Lambeth hangings include *Horses* after Clein, and a set of the *Wars of Troy*—the *Capture of Cassandra* is in the Victoria and Albert Museum. Another workshop was in the neighbourhood of Hatton Garden, which is close to the modern watch and diamond merchants' district of Clerkenwell in east central London. The establishment was conducted by Thomas Poyntz during the late seventeenth century. He had worked at Mortlake and his signature with the Mortlake mark appears on panels representing *November* and *December* (*see* 54). Two sets of hangings representing a naval engagement off the east coast English town of Southwold or Solebay on 28 May 1672, between the English and French fleets under the Duke of York and the Comte d'Estrées on the one side, and the Dutch fleet under de Ruyter on the other, were woven by Francis and Thomas Poyntz. It appears that Thomas Poyntz had a loose arrangement with the Great Wardrobe where Francis Poyntz was employed as a weaver, so there is controversy as to whether the first set, with its imposing border of tritons, shells, dolphins and amorini, was woven at Mortlake or the Great Wardrobe, or even partly at Hatton Garden, for Mortlake had come under control of the Earl of Montagu by 1685, the approximate date the six panels were woven. Three of the first set are at Hampton Court Palace and are signed by Francis Poyntz. The other three have the arms of Sir Robert Walpole added and were signed by Thomas Poyntz. The second set was ordered in 1688 by James II (1685–8) from Thomas Poyntz, for presentation to the first Earl of Dartmouth but were not finished before the king was deposed; they bear the king's cipher and the Dartmouth armorials. Two of the set were in the Iveagh Collection, and three were sold by Christie's on 12 July 1923 to G. H. Lorimer of Philadelphia. The design of the panels is attributed to the Dutch painter, Willem van de Velde.

Britain is fortunate in having several fairly detailed inventories of tapestries in royal ownership, of which the two most important comprise the 'List of Tapestries from the Inventory of King Henry VIII' made soon after 1547 with dimensions of every piece, and the 'Inventory of the Household Goods . . . etc. Belonging to the Late King. Sold by Order of the Council of State, from ye severall Places and Palaces', made soon after the execution of Charles I in 1649. One can gain an impression of how well tapestries in royal use survive a century during a period when they were regarded as essential decor. A further inventory, drawn up in 1695 on the death of Mary, Queen of William III and daughter of James II, acts almost as a check-list for the 1649 inventory, although it is not as detailed.

Until the Great Fire of London in 1666, the Great Wardrobe was situated in a house built by Sir Thomas Beauchamp (died 1359) near the present Mermaid Theatre at Puddle Wharf, Blackfriars, in the City of London. The Crown used it as a depository for royal clothes and furniture, and it provided services such as renovations, but gradually assumed the status—as far as tapestry was concerned—of a manufactory. After the Great Fire the premises were located near the present Savoy Hotel. When Ralph Montagu took over as Master of the Wardrobe the chief arras worker was Francis Poyntz and under him were three ex-Mortlake men: the two John Olphalfens (probably father and son) and David de Maecht, de May, or Demay; also John Paris. Francis Poyntz drew his daily Wardrobe pay with unfailing regularity, and yet in 1668 he sold to the Crown two sets of tapestry for the King's New Lodging in Whitehall, *The Bacchinalls* and *Polidore,* and in 1675 he sold 'a new Suite of hangings of the *Kings and Queens*', at which point there is documentary evidence that Francis was 'His Majesty's Chief Arras Maker'; from about 1678 the 'Arras-makers' office in Hatton Garden' is regarded as part of the premises of the Royal Wardrobe. (The source is *The Lord Chamberlain's Books,* in the Public Records Office, London.) After the death of Francis Poyntz the arras makers of the Great Wardrobe working at Hatton Garden moved under the direction of Thomas Axton, in January 1686, to premises in Great Queen Street, near the present-day Holborn Underground station, off Kingsway.

The function of the Royal Wardrobe as a tapestry manufactory was further confirmed by the appointment of the Belgian tapissier John Vanderbank, or Vandrebanc, in place of Axton. One of his first tasks was to design and weave, for installation in 1693, two fine silk tapestries representing the *Customs House* to fit the end wall of the long room of the Port of London's Customs House, for which he was paid £286 10s. He next wove the first of a series of tapestries with which his name has been associated—*chinoisieries* for the Queen's withdrawing-room at Kensington Palace. The general composition consisted of many groups of figures and details more or less isolated on a dark ground— the scheme of a lacquer screen. The grounds are brown, dark blue or black; the motives are generally creamy white, with shading in vivid mother-of-pearl tints; the figures are sometimes Indian, sometimes Chinese; the architecture is nearly always of Chinese character. An unsigned set, once the property of Elihu Yale (1648–1720), founder of Yale University, USA, now decorates a room at that University. Vanderbank also undertook alterations and repairs to tapestries. In 1706–7 he is recorded as having repaired and lengthened a set of Teniers or *Dutch Boor* pieces in Kensington Palace, and to have woven the portrait of Edmundus de Dummer (*see* 55). A hitherto unpublished fact that strongly contributed to the increasing failure of Mortlake towards the end of the seventeenth century, was that it was too remote from the business and social world of London. Possibly the Earl of Montagu was the first to realize that the facilities required for the efficient operation of the Great Wardrobe were fundamentally the same as those required by a tapestry manufactury and both used the same materials in large measure, the former for repairs and renovation, the latter for weaving, and that both required plentiful supplies of clean water for cleaning fabric and dyeing materials. Close by the various

52 The royal set of tapestries depicting 'Vulcan and Venus' were the first to be woven at the royal Tapestry Manufactory at Mortlake, England, when it was established in AD 1611 by James the First. Shown here is *Neptune interceding for the lovers,* woven at Mortlake between 1650 and 1675. The designer was Francis Clein or Cleyn, a native of Rostock in Mecklenburg, who had studied in Italy before appointment to Mortlake. In 1630 a scandal broke out when a petition was presented to James' successor, Charles the First, alleging the royal purse had been overcharged for the tapestries, described as 'The first suits of tapestrie of the storie of "Vulcan and Venus", which is the foundation of all good Tapestries made in England. Wherein there were but 16 ounces of gold. . .'. This magnificent and popular set was copied several times (*Victoria and Albert Museum; Crown Copyright*)

places where the Great Wardrobe was sited there were small rivers emptying their waters into the Thames and capable of providing copious clean supplies for the needs of a Wardrobe with a tapestry manufactory. The weaving of tapestry at the Great Wardrobe continued well into the eighteenth century, with Moses Vanderbank taking over in 1727 when John Vanderbank retired.

One of the principal provincial seventeenth century tapestry manufactories was at Norwich which, according to the 1655 Committee of Council of the 'Walloon congregation there' was 'the first place that received Protestant strangers, who taught the English various woollen manufactures, which formerly were imported, and that they pray that the privileges granted them by Edward VI may be confirmed for free exercise of their religion in their own language, and of their trades . . .' which included '. . . making of baize, arras, says, tapestry, mockadoes, stames, kersies, and other outlandish commodities not usually made in England'.

Scotland

Except in Scotland's equivalent of the Great Wardrobe, little weaving appears to have been done during the seventeenth century. In 1633 the Scottish Wardrobe had an inventory of about 400 pieces which, of course, had to be repaired, cleaned or modified when not hanging in Holyrood House, Edinburgh Castle, Linlithgow, Dunfermline, Stirling or St Johnston's. After the execution of Charles I, the keeper of the high wardrobe in London's Whitehall, Clement Kinnersley, apparently had some difficulty in persuading his Scottish counterpart, Sir John Achmountie, to send tapestries from Dunottar Castle and

Plate 32 This magnificent reredos screen tapestry was woven by Pinton Frères of France to the design of John H.C. Piper, for Chichester Cathedral in Sussex. The three central panels symbolize the Trinity as an equilateral triangle among flames. Related to this, a white light symbolizes the Father, a Tau Cross symbolizes the Son and a flaming wing, the Holy Ghost. The two flanking panels on either side have, in the upper parts (from left to right) symbols representing the Elements (earth, air, fire, water), and in the lower parts, the Evangelists: St Matthew (winged man), St Mark (winged lion), St Luke (winged ox) and St John (winged eagle) (*Dean and Chapter of Chichester Cathedral; Pitkin Pictorials Ltd*)

Plate 33 Ronald Cruickshank was working on this tapestry in his American home at the time of his death; the weaving was completed by his widow and the tapestry now hangs in St Joseph's Cathedral, Louisiana. Cruickshank was apprenticed at Edinburgh's Dovecot Tapestry Workshops and then opened the Golden Targe Studio in that city before going to America (*Mrs Beatrice Cruickshank, Louisiana, USA*)

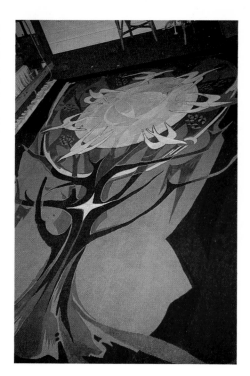

Plate 34 *Sailing* was designed and woven by Swedish-born Helena Hernmarck in her New York City atelier. This lively piece now hangs in the Federal Reserve Bank at Boston. It is one of Miss Hernmarck's most famous tapestries (*Helena Hernmarck, New York*)

Plate 35 Woven in 1977 by Teresa Sagel of New Mexico, *October Leaves* exemplifies the continuing Spanish Colonial weaving tradition. The stripes with Saltillo leaf pattern and elaborate ticking was inspired by Rio Grande blanket tapestries. Materials were undyed commercial yarn and natural dyes including cota (*Thelesperma* sp., Navajo tea) mordanted with alum, chrome, tin and iron (*Museum of New Mexico Collection at the Museum of International Folk Art. Purchased with the aid of funds from the National Endowment for the Arts and International Folk Art Foundation*)

elsewhere in accordance with the orders of the Council of State's edict of 15 November 1655.

Ireland

In contrast to his lukewarm interest in English tapestry manufacture, Charles II gave considerable support to an alderman and linen manufacturer of Dublin. Christopher Lovett obtained letters patent in July 1677 from the King, granting him the use of premises at Chapelizod, looms, yarns, and a loan of £1200 to be returned at the end of a 21 year lease. Despite this aid, the enterprise foundered following the death of Christopher and its management by his widow and executrix, Frances, and John Lovett (presumably her son). By November 1689 they were Protestant refugees in England, petitioning for release of their 38 (unspecified) tapestries from the London customs-house, which was granted, together with annulment of their debt to the King.

A certain Jan van Beaver, employed as a Flemish weaver at Mortlake in 1678, was yet to make his mark in Irish history. The 'Inventory of the Duke and Duchess of Ormonde's goods at Kilkenny, Dunmore and Clonmell' dated 25 August 1675 lists 120 tapestries, of which 34 may have been woven on the sixteenth century Kilkenny looms.

France

Before concentrating on the development of the Gobelins manufactory in Paris it is as well to consider the provincial background of France against which it took shape. In the district of La Marche, comprising Aubusson, Felletin and Bellegarde, considerable progress had been made, with the result that by 1637 Aubusson had almost 2000 weavers. A sign of the times was that a decrease to about 1600 workmen came in 1664, which prompted Louis XIV (1643–1715) to mount an inquiry. The tapissiers reported their urgent need of a good painter to provide suitable cartoons and an able dyer, and that they suffered from coarse wool and bad dyes with a corresponding deterioration in standards. The King authorized the manufactory to use the title 'Royal Manufactory of Aubusson' and promised to supply, at his expense, the painter and dyer. But none was forthcoming and in 1685, on the revocation of the Edict of Nantes, 200 of the best workmen had to leave the town, whose industry was practically destroyed for the rest of the century. Felletin and Bellegarde fared no better.

The industry at Beauvais, however, forms a striking contrast. In 1664 Louis XIV authorized Louis Hinart, a merchant-weaver of tapestry living in Paris, to establish a low-loom manufactory at Beauvais, his native town. Hinart was given a monopoly with great pecuniary advantages including some 50000 livres to establish the premises and purchase materials, with an obligation to pay back 20000 livres without interest within six years. He received a bonus for every foreign workman imported and planned to employ 100 of them during the first year. But it seems that Hinart was too occupied with his Paris business and left the running of the manufactory to others, and in 1684 he was replaced by Philippe Béhagle, a most capable tapissier. Even so, Beauvais produced a considerable output during Hinart's nominal directorship. The list includes verdures and birds, verdures and brooks, verdures and beasts, verdures and landscapes, fine verdures and coarse verdures. Two show *Views in the Gardens of St Cloud*. Other pieces or sets include a *History of Psyche* and *The Village Wedding*. Béhagle was resourceful and energetic. He provided the manufactory with a school of drawing and reorganized it so successfully that a royal visit was made in 1686. Production included a set of *Acts of the Apostles* for Beauvais Cathedral, signed P. BEHAGLE; a set in gold of *The Battle of Landskrona, The Siege of Malmö* and *The Battle of Lund* for the King of Sweden, woven in 1698; *The Conquests of Louis the Great* after Martin; *The Grotesque Chinois* in Bérainesque style and Teniers subjects. Béhagle directed Beauvais until his death in 1704. The Amiens manufactory used two tapestry marks, a double S entwined or the letter A with a fleur-de-lis; the workshop was active from the 1670s in particular.

The Duke d'Epernon's high-loom manufactory in his Château de Cadillac

was operated by the former Parisian weaver Claude de Lapierre between 1632–9. Production included the *History of King Henri the Third,* and the *Battle of Jurac 1569,* now in the Louvre. Lapierre moved to Bordeaux where he set up high-looms and worked with his brother, Joseph, and son, Antoine (died 1666). Stephen and Jacques Deschazault started a Bordeaux manufactory in 1661. Tapestries woven at Caen include *Scenes from the Life of St Ursula,* signed by the royal tapissier Jean Colpaert and dated 1659, and *The Embarkation and the Martyrdom of St Ursula.* Tapestries woven at Felletin in the seventeenth century are often remarkable for their deep colour, simple technique and coarse texture, suggesting—in general effect—a continuation of Gothic traditions. In 1689 the town had 500 workmen and it was said that the majority had worked at the Gobelins and were perfect in their craft. Output included several copies of *The Story of Gombaud and Macée,* sets of *Pots, Flowers and Porticos, Illustrious Ladies* and *The Martyrdom of St Barbara.*

Lille's industry was revived in 1625 by Vincent van Quickelberghe of Oudenarde, who settled there with his sons Jean and Emmanuel; about 1630 the latter went to work at Mortlake and the former returned to Oudenarde.

A high-loom workshop was established in Lille in 1687 by Jean de Melter of Brussels (died 1698), who wove religious subjects after Rubens, and motifs after Teniers. The workshop continued into the eighteenth century under his daughter and her husband, Guillaume Wernier. The Lille low-loom workshop founded by the Brussels tapissiers François and André Pannemaker, after they left the Gobelins, survived for 35 years. François died in 1700 and his son, André, carried on the business with his relative Jacques Destombes. At his Maincy Castle near Vaux, Fouquet established a workshop in 1658. It was directed by Louis Blommaert of Oudenarde and the chief artist was Charles le Brun. Sets of the *History of Constantine, Hunts of Meleager, Landscapes* after Fouquières, *Virtues and Trophies* by le Brun and others were seized by the King when Superintendent Fouquet was disgraced. At Nancy in 1612 the Duke of Lorraine inaugurated workshops directed by the Brussels tapissier Herman l'Abbe. Notable productions included *Battles Against Louis XIV*, designed by the Duke's painter, Charles Herbel. The craft in Tours was much progressed early in the century under Alexander Motheron (died 1639), who obtained state and municipal aid for improved organization of workshops and management and apprentice training. The first new workshop was in La Petite Bourdaisière in 1612; it moved to Logis Chamboisseau in 1625. From the time of his father's death until his own death, Sebastian Motheron directed the enterprise, which closed thereafter. Tapestries included a *History of Coriolanus*, items after Teniers, and religious subjects woven in about 1650 for Tours Cathedral. A letter from the papal legate in France to Cardinal Barberini indicates that in about 1636 Cardinal Richelieu negotiated for several very high pieces to be made in Tours.

The royal workshops in Paris were a continuation of those inaugurated in the sixteenth century, mentioned in the previous chapter, and comprised:

1. the manufactory and apprentice training school at the Hôpital de la Trinité;

2. the workshops directed at the Faubourg St Antoine by du Bourg and Girard Laurent. This high-loom establishment was transferred in 1607 to the grand gallery of the Louvre. In 1613 Girard was succeeded by his son Henri, who carried on with du Bourg. Closure came about 1650. Notable tapestries include the *History of Jeptha* after Voüet and *Pharaoh's daughter saving the infant Moses from the Waters*; both had yellow grotesque borders on a blue ground and the King's armorials supported by angels, in grisaille;

3. workshops established in 1601 at Hôtel des Tournelles and directed by the Sieur de Fourcy, superintendent of the royal buildings. Weavers were of Flemish origin.

Not content with the speed of output of the three existing Parisian workshops, which all used high-warp looms, Henri IV of France courageously decided on a bold innovation. He contracted with two of the best tapissiers in the Low Countries, Marc de Comans and François de la Planche (known in his native Oudenarde as Frans van den Planken), to transfer their low-warp establishments, with some considerable number of Flemish low-warp weavers, to Paris in 1607, to set up a manufactory with 60 looms and 20 in Amiens or elsewhere. The Paris workshops were to be in the Maison des Canaye in the Faubourg St Marcel, close by the river Bièvre. The district was known as the Gobelins from the fifteenth century dyeworks established there by Jean Gobelins. In short time the Faubourg St Marcel manufactory became the most successful in France; the unique conditions under which de Comans and de la

Planche had contracted to make a transfer to Paris, coupled with the rapidity of weaving and high standards, crushed effective competition. There has been speculation as to the precise abilities—as businessmen or craftsmen—of the two founders; parallel with their tapestry production they were concerned with swamp drainage, brewing, grain imports from Malta and making soap. In about 1633 the founders were succeeded by their sons, Charles de Comans (died in the same year and succeeded by his brother Alexandre), and Raphael de la Planche. Following disagreement between Alexandre and Raphael, the latter was appointed to establish a new manufactory in the Faubourg St Germain and took many of the weavers with him. Alexandre de Comans died in 1651 and was succeeded by his brother, Hippolyte, who remained in control until the formation of the Gobelins shop by Colbert in 1662. Raphael's son, Sébastien-François, assumed the directorship of the St Germain workshop in 1661 but lacked business ability, and the premises closed in 1667. The provincial workshops of Amiens, Tours and Calais (1604–20) were linked with the St Marcel workshop and so it is impossible to determine in many instances exactly where tapestries were woven. The St Marcel works was split up into ten small boutiques, each in charge of a master weaver whose monogram was woven into every tapestry produced; a characteristic of this workshop. An inventory of 1627 suggests that over 1000 tapestries had been woven since 1601. Among the most important were a set of the *History of Constantine the Great* from designs by Rubens, for the Barberini family before their Rome atelier was established, *Abraham's Sacrifice* and *Metamorphoses of Arethusa*. Designers included Voüet, Fouquières, Corneille, Guyon, Champagne and Lerambert. Master weavers included Philip de Maecht, Hans Tayer, Lucan van den Dalle and P. Bernard.

By royal command the French tapissier Pierre Lefèvre (formerly director of the Florentine manufactory) returned to France in 1647 to direct a high-loom workshop in the garden of the Tuileries. He returned to Florence several times, leaving his son, Jean, as director, and died in Florence in 1669, by which time Jean was at the Gobelins. *The Toilette of a Princess* is a well known Lefèvre piece.

Where Henri IV had failed, Louis XIV was successful. In 1662 the Parisian workshops were amalgamated in *La manufacture royale des meubles de la Couronne* and Louis placed his minister Colbert in charge, with Charles le Brun as the professional director of the artistic élite of France. The Hôtel of the Gobelins and adjacent buildings were purchased and made ready to receive artists and craftsmen of the highest reputation, including tapissiers, sculptors, goldsmiths, cabinet-makers and others, to make the Gobelins a multi-discipline works for the production of almost every type of art and craft required for the use of the king and his court. Tapestry production was split among five individually contracting workshops, each under a 'contractor' with the power to hire or fire. The three high-loom contractors were Jean Jans, Jean Lefèvre and Henri Laurent; the low-loom ones were Jean Delacroix and Mosin. The contractors competed for contracts and weavers were paid according to their output. Every finished piece bore the signature of the contractor or master weaver. The five workshops employed 250 workmen, excluding apprentices, and in 28 years produced 19 complete sets of high-warp and 34 sets of low-warp tapestries. The finest set was *The History of the King* (*see* 49). Other notable hangings were the *History of Alexander, Elements, Seasons, Acts of the Apostles,*

Pictures at the Vatican (both after Raphael), *Triumphs of the Gods* after Noël Coypel, *The Grotesque Months* and *The Indian Hangings* (*see* 56).

In 1690 the veteran director, Charles le Brun, resigned after guiding the Gobelins Manufactory through many years of unequalled success; it had eclipsed Brussels, and Mortlake in England was dying. Pierre Mignard replaced le Brun, and the sons of Jans and Delacroix were made contractors for the high- and low-warp loom workshops respectively, with two additional low-warp contractors, Souette and de la Fraye. The wars towards the end of the seventeenth century imposed strict economy in France, so the Gobelins was closed from 1694 to 1697 and the weavers sought work elsewhere. In 1699 Jules Harduin Mansart was appointed superintendent and the new director was Robert de la Cotte, who held that position until 1735. The golden age of the Gobelins had passed and a state of comparative lassitude continued well into the eighteenth century.

Italy

The decline of the Florentine manufactory started during the reign of Cosimo II (1609–21). The chief workman, Papini, was succeeded by Jacques Elbert van Hassell, or van Asselt, who, in turn, was replaced by Pierre Lefèvre in 1630 (later the 'tapissier to the King of France'). Under Ferdinand II (1621–70) production increased but never achieved sixteenth century excellence; portraits, portières, religious subjects, furnishings and hangings made to cartoons of Raphael and Romano were the main products. After the death of Lefèvre in 1669, Giovanni Pollastri established the workshop of St Mark, and Giovanni Battista Termini of Florence set up a Rome manufactory which lasted for 17 years. On returning to Florence he was appointed to direct its manufactory, but died in 1717; the manufactory closed in 1744. Florentine masters signed their tapestries which, between 1604 and 1693, comprised some 37 items including 12 histories, sets or series.

Founded by Cardinal Francesco in 1672, the Barberini family's manufactory in Rome was by far the most important seventeenth century development in Italy. It was a private enterprise charged with the responsibility to weave tapestries for the Barberini palace, but also accepted commissions for the Duke of Ferrara and others. The Cardinal had gained a knowledge of manufactory management by placing orders at the Parisian workshops of St Marcel and Fontainebleau, as well as by visits and correspondence. Pietro de Cortona was appointed artistic director, and Jakob van den Vliete of Oudenarde was the master weaver under the name of Jacomo della Riviera; his son-in-law, Gasparo Rocci, was appointed master weaver on Jakob's death in 1639. Products included many sets executed in the most lavish manner such as the *History of Constantine the Great* (now in the Philadelphia Museum of Art), the *Life of Urban VIII*, and the *Life of Christ*. The manufactory closed soon after the Cardinal's death in 1679.

Flanders

During the first half of the seventeenth century the competitive effects of the new manufactories in France, England and Italy, coupled with wars and general unrest, resulted in almost mass-emigration by weavers, despite government attempts to encourage weaving by offering special privileges, taxation concessions and so on. With the introduction of special display facilities in Brussels for tapestries, the marketing activities of Antwerp were transferred gradually from 1655, with great benefit to Brussels workshops. The most famous Brussels tapissier during the first part of the seventeenth century was the Widow Geubels, the wife of the former Jacques Geubels whose mark appears on many tapestries of his time. She carried on her husband's business to become the most successful woman tapissier in history with her sets and series of *Histories of Joshua, of Troy, of Cleopatra* and *of Noah*, and *Diana Hunting*. After her death in 1629 the manufactory was carried on by her partner Jan Raes, who associated with Franz van den Hecke (died 1665). Their output was prodigious and included a *History of Cyrus*, the *Acts of the Apostles* and *Consecration of Charlemagne*. The *History of Decius* tapestries, from cartoons drawn by Rubens in 1618 and woven under his supervision, were possibly intended for Baron Zouche's new house at Bramshill, near Basingstoke, England, which is now the Police College; on its walls is a set of four *Decius Mus* hangings without the original borders. Other Brussels workshops of prominence included those conducted by François van Cotthem (c1641–59), Bernard van Brustom (c1626–40), Martin Reymbouts (c1609). The second half of the century brought to prominence the workshops of Everard II Leyniers (1644–80), the son of Gaspar (died 1649); Jacques van der Borght, or Borcht, who, with le Clerc, de Vos, and Cobus, wove for William III of England (1688–1702), the *Battle of Bresgate, Battle of the Boyne* and *Landing at Torbay,* the whereabouts of which are unknown. Albert Auwercz (1657) was prominent also with his allegorical signed pieces of *Sapientia, Monarchia* and *Magnificentia*, and myths series including *Diana* and *Flora*. The list of lesser names is too long to reproduce here.

Antwerp came to be more of a weaving centre during the late seventeenth century than previously, with the workshop of Gerard van der Necken and Jean van Leefdeal, Nicolas Nauwelaerts and Pierre and Michael Wauters. The existence of the 'headquarters' studio of the artist Peter Paul Rubens (1577–1640) and the fact that his father-in-law, Daniel Fourment, conducted a tapestry marketing, cartoons and materials business in the town, must have contributed greatly to the late seventeenth century popularity of Antwerp tapestries. The industry in Oudenarde followed the pattern of Brussels with a weaving population depleted to 1000 or fewer early in the century, and growing again towards the 1690s. The pattern in Ghent, Alost, Tournai, Valenciennes, Enghien and Arras was the same, with Tournai displaying the best resistance to the trade recession of the first half of the century and picking up rapidly soon after, perhaps as a result of Philip Béhagle of Oudenarde transferring his energies there in 1678 to set up a manufactory to weave tapestry 'more fine and exquisite than that made in the Low Countries'. He employed 50 workmen and his name with the Tournai mark appears on a number of famous pieces including the *Conquests of Louis XIV,* although some authorities claim the set was made at Beauvais after Béhagle was appointed Director of the Royal Manufactory there in 1684.

Spain and Peru

A small Flemish colony under François Tons was established at Pastraña, New Castile and in 1623 some of its products were exhibited and highly commended in Madrid. By 1625, the four looms in the Gutierrez workshop, near St Isabel, in Madrid, were under the management of Antonio Ceron and it is possible that Velazquez's picture of *The Spinners* was painted in this workshop in about 1651 (*see* 46).

The influence of the Spaniards upon tapestry woven in Peru is most marked in the seventeenth century. There are two styles: one peculiar to the mountainous regions and distinguished by the quantity of old Inca symbols, patterns and the interlocking of different coloured threads when they meet on neighbouring warps; the other, that of the coastal region, in which there are European and Chinese elements of design, with the slit technique.

Denmark, Norway and Sweden

To celebrate his triumph over the Swedes in the War of Kalmar (1611–13), King Christian IV of Denmark had a great set of tapestries, depicting the various episodes, made for him at the Delft manufactory. No doubt this gave Christian V of Denmark the idea that he should do the same to commemorate the Scanian War (1675–9) against Sweden. These hangings were woven in brilliant colours between 1684 and 1692 to the designs of Peder Andersen and Wilcken Ribolt in a royal tapestry manufactory at Copenhagen, directed by the brothers van der Ecken and manned by Flemish high-loom weavers (*see* 51).

In seventeenth century Norway home-weaving possibly was encouraged by the church as a congenial and inspiring occupation for the long, dark and cold winter nights. A number of medium-sized panels from this period survive, like that depicted in 45. Similar activities were pursued in Sweden as a continuation of the popularization of weaving described in the last chapter.

Germany

In 1604, Duke Maximilian of Bavaria established a manufactory in Munich which was manned principally by French refugee weavers from Aubusson. Although the enterprise closed within 12 years it put the city on the map as a centre for excellent tapestries, and may be regarded as the forerunner of the present manufactory. Another manufactory to employ former Aubusson, weavers was in Berlin; founded in 1686 by the Great Elector Frederick William of Brandenburg (1640–88), the Berlin workshop's main production was tapestries for the palaces of King Frederick I of Prussia (1688–1713) whose death signalled closure of the manufactory.

Bibliography
The Bible
Cowie, L. W. *Seventeenth-Century Europe.* Bell, London (1965)
Official Guide. *Bramshill House Police College.* HMSO, London (1971)
Thomson, F. P. & E. S. 'Tapestries in Westminster Abbey', *Westminster Abbey Occasional Paper,* pp. 6–10, December 1973, London

Plate 36 (*opposite*) Designed by Micheline Beauchemin and woven by her entirely in silk specially dyed in Japan, this very beautiful panel entitled *Wings no. 2* hangs in the Canadian Embassy in Tokyo (*Micheline Beauchemin, Quebec*)

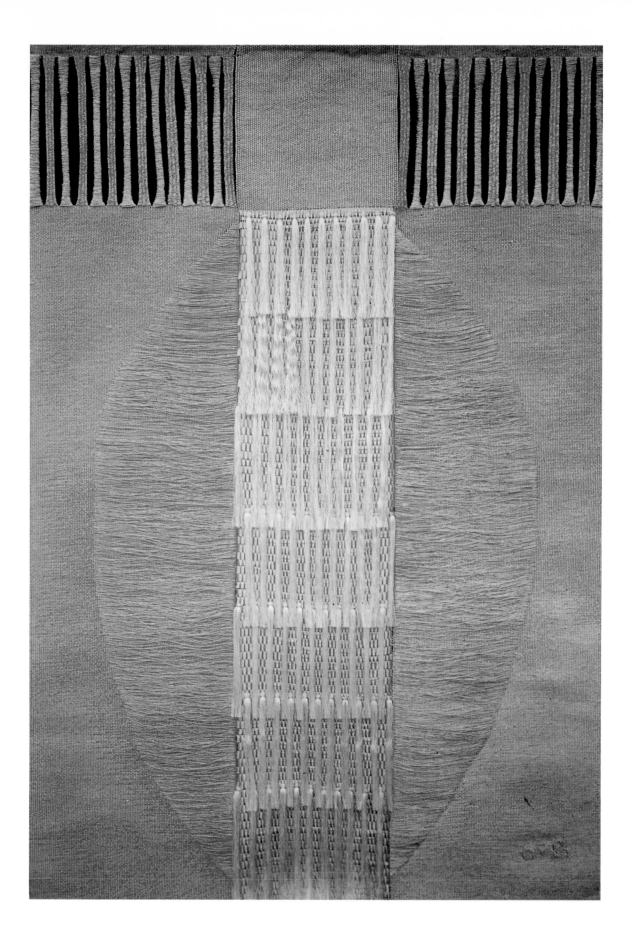

Plate 37 *Lifescape* was designed and woven by Helen Frances Gregor as a memorial to Dr John Deutsch, who contributed much to Canada's academic and industrial life. The tapestry hangs in Queen's University Centre at Kingston, Ontario and incorporates Dr Deutsch's academic hoods (*H.F. Gregor, RCA, Toronto, Canada*)

Plate 38 *Lundu* was designed and woven in the São Paulo atelier of Norberto Nicola, one of Brazil's most outstanding pioneers of contemporary tapestry. He has endeavoured to create a distinctive national style, with considerable success (*Norberto Nicola, São Paulo, Brazil*)

Plate 39 (*opposite*) *Trillium Hills* was designed and woven by Lithuanian-born, Canadian Anastasia Tamošaitis. The design typifies the harsh but challenging environment of nature's many shapes in the tundra and forestlands, lakes and rivers, of the Province of Ontario, Canada (*Mrs Anastasia Tamošaitis, Kingston, Ontario, Canada*)

Plate 40 *La Joie de Vivre* was based on a painting by the French artist Max Ernst, and woven on a low-warp loom in one of France's newest and most outstandingly successful ateliers (*Atelier Yvette Cauquil-Prince, Paris and Corsica*)

5 From the Eighteenth to the Mid-Nineteenth Century

Tapestry industries were in a bad way at the start of the eighteenth century. The Gobelins manufactory in Paris was only just recovering after being closed from 1694 to 1697 as part of the plan for French national economy. Although boasting the name of a royal manufactory, the industry at Aubusson, Felletin and Bellegarde in provincial France was in a very feeble state following the king's failure to give the aid he promised in 1664: the appointment of a competent painter to make new designs and an expert dyer. In Brussels the industry was reduced to nine master weavers, 150 workmen and about 50 looms. The Mortlake workshops in England had suffered successive bouts of neglect and maladministration since the accession of Charles II; Mortlake was finally closed by royal warrant on 9 April 1703. In Italy, the death of Cardinal Francesco in 1679 was followed soon after by closure of the Barberini workshops in Rome. Thereafter the main activity again was centred on Florence, where the workshops closed before the mid-century. The Rome workshop of Pope Clement XI did not open until 1710.

The main uses for tapestry were what they had always been; broadly for decoration, comfort, furniture coverings, occasionally for personal wear, and for animal coverings such as a saddle cloth. According to whether the piece was designed for personal use or as a gift or bribe calculated to move events in the direction the head of state or other person desired, the artist was ordered to make the tapestry a visual recitation of biblical episodes, classical history, deeds of courage or daring by a monarch or lord, or a cheerful wall-covering for a boudoir. Hangings were commissioned for their intrinsic grandeur or beauty. The day was still some two centuries away when tapestries would be commissioned or traded fundamentally as investments, and assessed more for their capital appreciation potential than for elegance or beauty! If the latter value had been put on tapestries in earlier times there might not have been such a patchy production programme for royal workshops, although the whim of the moment would have tended to dominate and pull down standards.

The productivity of the Gobelins and other workshops has been expressed in terms of the average number of square metres of tapestry made by a weaver in, say, a month. These averages, and any conclusions based on them, are likely to be unreliable. Workshop conditions varied enormously and measurement parameters were not standardized. For example, some weavers were required to visit the wool store each time they had to recharge their bobbins with weft; other workshops required an apprentice to take the rosary to the store, match the colour the weaver needed and then wind the wool on to the bobbins. The weaver's productivity would be influenced by the number of good daylight hours he could work, the warps per unit length, whether work was at a high- or a low-loom, whether slits were to be avoided by interlocking the weft, the variety of colours and tints to be used in weaving detail, and so on. Tapestry manufactories of old had no ergonomic specialists to maximize human

EDMUNDUS DUMMER de
Swathlin g: in Com.Southton
GEN: Anno Domini 1701 ÆTAT:LXXIX

55 English tapestry portraits are comparatively rare and so, in view of the historical significance of this one, it is very fortunate it has been preserved so well. This *Portrait in Tapestry
of Edmundus de Dummer* was almost certainly woven by John Vanderbank, the chief arras-
worker at the Great Wardrobe in Great Queen Street, London in 1701 – the year Dummer
died, aged 79. His son, Edmund Dummer of Swaythling, was by 1711 the Clerk of the Great
Wardrobe; in that year he and his brother Thomas – then Deputy Keeper of the Great
Wardrobe – and other members of the family petitioned the Earl Marshal of England to
confirm their right to use the armorials which had been used by their ancestors. The Petition
shows that the Dummers had a long history of distinction in England. The semi-lion of the
armorial shown in the portrait is black, although the Petition described it as blue. When the
arms were re-granted in 1721 the semi-lion was described as being black. If the armorial of
the portrait is correctly coloured, the black shows that the tapestry must have been woven
before 1711 or after April 1721. One of the responsibilities of the Deputy Keeper of the
Great Wardrobe was to see to the lining of the many tapestries made by Vanderbank, who
produced *Chinoiseries*, *Grotesques*, a few series of *Venus and Cupid*, sets of the *Elements* after the
Gobelins designs of Charles le Brun, and many more. The function of the Great Wardrobe
was the production and maintenance of textiles, furnishings and so on for the monarch
(*Victoria and Albert Museum; Crown Copyright*)

56 *The Indian Hunter* is one of ten *Tapestries of the Indies* woven in the years 1708–10 by the Gobelins in Paris, to the order of Grandmaster Ramon Perellos y Rocafull of Malta. The designs were taken from paintings given in 1679 by Prince Maurice of Nassau to Louis the Fourteenth of France, and were the work of two artists, Franz Post and Eckout, who had accompanied the Prince during his expeditions to South America and Africa between 1636 and 1644. From the time Louis received the paintings, the Gobelins was engaged on weaving *Indian Hangings* for more than a century, for the popularity of these visions of exotic landscapes, fearsome animals and strange natives was great. The tapestries woven for Perellos were for decoration of the Grandmasters' Palace in Malta. In the archives of the Order of St John of Malta, kept at the Royal Malta Library, there is the original contract made in Paris with the Gobelins manufactory in the persons of de Mesmes and Etienne Leblond 'Ordinary Weaver of Gobelins Tapestries to the King' (*Fr. Marius J. Zerafa* OP, *Curator of Fine Arts, and the Speaker of the Malta House of Representatives*)

57 *May Dance*, woven in Brussels between 1700 and 1720, and measuring 335 × 406cm (11ft × 13ft 4in), is made of wool and silk. It is typical of the rural scenes that were a feature of many so-called Teniers (or Tenières) tapestries, such as the *Marriage Feast at Cana, The Seaports* and *Peasants Dancing in Front of an Inn. Time Enchanted by Love* from David Teniers' picture painted in 1683 is one of the better known, less rural tapestries (*Fine Arts Museum of San Francisco*)

efficiency, nor were there specialist layout planners, or time and motion study engineers to root out superfluous physical activity by the weaver. The health and safety conditions of nearly all workshops would have been condemned under the provisions of western countries' twentieth century factory acts. A few master weavers of the Middle Ages—when tapestry-weaving was Europe's most widespread and highly subsidized industry—were, admittedly, practical and enlightened in their production planning; but when tapestry manufacture was in recession at the start of the eighteenth century, scientifically evolved production was still some 200 years in the future. The technical development destined to have greatest effect was the abolition, from the third quarter of the eighteenth century, of hand-spinning of the various threads, with the invention by Hargreaves, Arkwright and Crompton, of practical spinning machines.

France

Recovering from its enforced closures in 1694–7, the Gobelins based its early eighteenth century design repertoire initially on old cartoons and a set depicting the *History of King Louis XIV*. Earliest of the new designs were by Claude

Audran the younger, with figures by Corneille and Louis de Boulloigne, and animals by Desportes, for eight panels depicting *The Triumphs of the Gods,* started in 1700, and proved very popular, repeats being woven as late as 1770.

Appointed in 1662 to rationalize tapestry-weaving in Paris, the king's minister, Colbert, whose firm guidance was so responsible for bringing into being the Manufacture Royal des Meubles Couronne (the Royal Manufactory of Furnishings for the Crown), was replaced in 1699 by the new superintendent of royal buildings, arts and manufactures, Jules Harduin Mansart. He died in 1708 and was replaced by the Duc d'Antim. The professional director of painting and design appointed in 1662, Charles le Brun, resigned in 1690 and was succeeded by the ineffective Pierre Mignard, in turn replaced by Robert de la Cotte in 1699, who remained in office until 1735.

During the first decade of the eighteenth century a start was made on weaving a set of *Indian Hangings,* ordered for decoration of the Grandmaster's Palace in Malta (*see* 56). This set proved so popular that designs based on it were made by Alexandre François Desportes and framed—according to the fashion of the time—in simulated wood. From 1738, *The New Indian Hangings* were copied many times; a series woven by Neilson in 1774-6 is in the Austrian State collection. In 1711 a series of eight tapestries representing the *Old Testament,* after Antoine and Charles Coypel, was put on the looms, to be followed soon after by a corresponding series depicting the *New Testament,* and a 12-piece set of *Ovid's Metamorphoses* begun in 1717. Four *Old Testament* panels were woven between 1715 and 1731 by Jans and Lefèvre, and the *New Testament* ones by Restout and Jouvenet. Five panels of *Scenes from the Iliad,* after A. and C. Coypel and Charles Herault, woven by Jans and Audran, followed between 1722 and 1732. Then came *The New Portière of Diana* and *The Arms of France,* both after P. J. Perrot, and the *Arrival and Departure of Mehemet Effendi,* after Charles Parocel. The designs, dating from the *Iliad,* display a design shift compared with those used by the Gobelins until the end of the

58 *The Camp* is a tapestry from *The Arts of War* series, which numbers many hangings woven by many manufactories, but is generally regarded as being centred on tapestries depicting the *Victories of the Duke of Marlborough,* also appearing under the title of *Marlborough's Victories.* Hangings record in detail the heroism and horror, the daily events and routine boredoms, the dress, panoply and customs of battles fought at Blenheim, Ramilles, Oudenarde and Malplaquet. *The Camp* was one of several of the series woven by Judos de Vos in Brussels between 1720 and 1725 (*Victoria and Albert Museum; Crown Copyright*)

seventeenth century. A new and grander style is apparent as the fashion turns to the art of the boudoir. This movement was accelerated by the series of tapestries designed by Charles Coypel representing the *History of Don Quixote* (*see* Plate 26). In contrast to the grand historical compositions of the past, Coypel arranged his motifs in small pictures framed in simulated carved and gilded mouldings placed on a wide and richly decorated ground, the whole enclosed in a frame of similar character. The first of these settings—there were seven in all—was by Belin de Fontenay; the most popular was by Tessier. These hangings have found a place on the most exalted palace walls.

The artist-director of the royal tapestry manufactory of Beauvais, Jean Baptiste Oudry, was appointed inspector of the Gobelins in 1733. In 1735 Robert de la Cotte was succeeded by his son, Robert. The Duc d'Antim was succeeded in 1736 by Orrey, who fell into disfavour and was succeeded by Lenorman de Tournehem, Madame de Pompadour's uncle. He survived long enough to be replaced by 'La Pompadour's' brother, M. de Vandières, the Marquis de Marigny, who held office from 1751 to 1773. Among the new artists to supply designs was Jean François de Troy, director of the French academy at Rome. Between 1737 and 1740 he supplied seven cartoons for the *History of Esther* with borders by Perrot to simulate carved and gilded wood; the set was woven 13 times by Cozette and Audran. De Troy also designed cartoons for the *History of Jason,* which was woven with alternate borders. One set with borders by Cheillon was woven by Audran, the other by Gravelot was woven by Cozette (*see* Plate 27). There is nobility of conception in these splendid compositions that recalls, and perhaps surpasses, that of le Brun, while, in addition, there is a certain Italianate ease and absence of restraint. These designs by the leading artists of the time had a marked influence upon the technique of weaving. Hitherto the craftsmen had used a colour-scheme of their own, partly traditional and formal. The new models were full of subtle colour and delicate grey tones, and the application of the fine bold decorative colour-schemes of le Brun and his school resulted in utter failure when applied to the new designs. The painters and the manager were indignant. Oudry bitterly complained in 1748 of this '. . . work of pure routine, which represented neither the tone nor correctness of the pictures supplied for execution', and scolded the craftsmen for using merely 'tapestry colours'. The struggle between the weavers and the painters grew acute, but ended some years later in submission by the weavers.

Then it was that Gobelins' tapestries became merely woven pictures; exact and lifeless copies of the painted original. The number of dyes multiplied and not all were colour fast. But that was not all. After the death of Oudry his instructions continued to prevail and were even supplemented, until an impossible standard for weaver qualification was set. In 1756 the corporation of the trade in Paris recommended that a skilful weaver of high- or low-loom tapestries, repairer or restorer of tapestry, or weaver of Savonnerie carpets, should be master of all the rules of proportion, especially those of architecture and perspective, and have some knowledge of anatomy, of taste and accuracy in drawing, in colouring and in shading, of grace in arrangement and grandeur of expression of all styles and classes, figures, animals, landscapes, palaces, rustic buildings, statues, vases, woods, flowers and plants of all kinds. He should have a knowledge of sacred and secular history, and should be able to apply properly the rules of good manufacture, and to discern that which produces beauty of texture and colouring—that is, the different qualities of silks, wools and hangings, which frequently require to be turned over, or raised, or altered to the eye, for which reason weavers themselves have always been permitted to dye the materials they employ. With the great improvements incorporated in 'Vaucanson's low loom'—the work of the low-loom at this period was declared to be superior to that of the high-loom—with the 1000 dyes each graded in 12 tints, and tapestry-weavers who possessed the foregoing qualifications, what more was to be desired? Despite such competent weavers all was not well at the Gobelins, which was engaged mostly in weaving furniture coverings rather than grand hangings. The competitive influence of François Boucher at the Beauvais manufactory was taking the wind out of the Gobelins' sails so much that the Marquis de Marigny was compelled on the death of Oudry in 1755 to offer Boucher the position of inspector at the Gobelins. Boucher accepted, but subsequently did not design half the quantity of hangings he had done for Beauvais. By 1772 the Gobelins authorities owed their contractors—Audran, Neilson and Cozette—a considerable amount of money; in lieu of payment they were empowered to sell tapestries and seek private commissions.

With the accession of Louis XVI (1774–93), design emphasis shifted from romanticism to restraint; considerable changes in executive and artistic personnel accelerated as the fateful and lean years of the French Revolution approached, a period the Gobelins survived with its belt drawn tight and thanks to the diplomacy of the administrative director Guillaumot. In 1770 Boucher was succeeded as inspector by Noël Hallé and du Rameau, who, in turn, were succeeded between 1783 and 1790 by Taravel and Belle. The administrative director was the architect Soufflot 1755–80, the Court painter Pierre 1781–9, the architect Guillaumot 1789–92, the former weaver-contractor Audran 1792–3, Augustin Belle 1793–5, Audran again 1795, Guillaumot 1795–1807, M. M. Canal 1807–10, the painter, Lemonier, 1810–16, the retired artillery officer, Baron des Retours, 1816–33, Lavocat 1833–60, Badin again 1860–71, the chemist, M. E. Chevreul, 1871, the engineer, Alfred Darcel, 1871–85, Gerspach 1885, Jules Guiffrey 1885–1908. High-loom contractors included Jean Jan's son, Jean 1691–1731, Jean Lefèvre's (or Lefèbure's) son 1697–1736, Monmerque 1730–49, Cozette 1749–88, Cozette's son 1788–92, de la Tour 1703–34 and Audran (father and son) 1733–92. Low-loom contractors included Jean de la Croix's son 1693–1737, Souette 1693–1724, de la Fraye 1693–1729, Cozette 1736–49, E. le Blond 1701–27, E. Claud le Blond 1727–51 and the Scotsman, James Neilson, 1749–88, who so much improved the low-loom that it was regarded as more capable than the high-loom; he also experimented and improved dyeing, and was principal of the school of instruction. The contracting system was abolished in 1790 in favour of payment by salary. Oudry's elegance and demands as a painter on the weavers up to his death in 1755, coupled with Charles-Antoine Coypel's (1694–1752) rococoesque designs and François Boucher's similar demands, placed ever greater pressure on the dyer, with eventual development by Chevreul of the immense range of colours and tints described in Appendix 3. Napoleon used the resources of the Gobelins to record his exploits; a set of tapestries is now in the Mobilier National, Paris. Nineteenth century painters included Carle Vernet (1758–1836) and Jacques Louis David (1748–1825); subjects were contemporary or models of the past. A further crisis in about 1850 nearly closed the Gobelins and it was

59 The first tapestry depicting *The Battle of the Boyne* was woven in 1703–7 by Josse de Vos in Brussels, for William the Third (1689–1702) of England. The second tapestry shown here, of *The Battle of the Boyne,* was woven in Robert Baillie's workshop in Dublin, Ireland. The designer is said to have been Johann van der Hagen, a landscape, marine and scenic painter working in that city. The weaver was a Huguenot refugee, John van Beaver (died 1750), formerly of Flanders. Baillie was commissioned to supply six hangings for decoration of the Irish House of Lords, and the tapestry depicted here was hung there on 11 September 1733. It was signed JOHN VAN BEAVER and initialled RB for Robert Baillie. Measurements are 518·5 ×640cm (17×21ft) and materials are wool with silk highlights; the warp is probably linen. The scene depicted is of William III at the crossing, and the death of Schomberg. Since 1802, the House of Lords building has housed the Bank of Ireland, where this tapestry still hangs (*Bank of Ireland, College Green, Dublin*)

Plate 41 (*opposite*) The Nürnberger Gobelin Manufactur during the second half of the twentieth century has carried out a research and mathematical analysis investigation into the visual impact of colour in tapestry design, in association with Dr Herbert Bayer of New York. This is one of the designs produced during research (*Nürnberger Gobelin Manufactur, Federal Republic of Germany*)

Plate 42 (*overleaf*) *Nightsun* was woven by Münchener-Gobelin Manufactur to the design of Dirk Holger, a former student at Atelier Tours de St Laurent, under Jean Lurçat, in 1964–5. Holger established his own atelier and has used it as a base for a vigorous campaign to promote the teachings of Lurçat (*Atelier Jean Lurçat, Munich*)

not until a century later, under the influence of Jean Lurçat's design renaissance, that its economic future appeared more assured.

The early eighteenth century position of Bellegarde, Felletin and Aubusson has been described, except for the hostility created by Felletin's weavers in 1698 when they 'pirated' Aubusson's blue selvedge instead of using their own brown colour. They wove landscapes, the *Hunts of Louis XV,* a reduced series of Oudry's designs, the *Battle of the Granicus* after le Brun and signed M.R.D. FELLETIN. P. VERGNE (about 1780), *Hunts of the Bear, Boar* and *Stag* (illegally woven with a blue selvedge), the *Seasons,* the *History of Joseph, Constantine,* and landscapes with châteaux, woods and birds. Designated a royal manufactory from 1727, Felletin was aided by Aubusson artists Roby and Finet. Aubusson, a low-loom establishment, incorporated its name and the weaver's initials in its blue selvedge from 1732; painters included Jean Joseph du Mons 1731–55, Jacques Juliard 1755–80, and Ransom from 1780. Subjects included decorative landscapes and verdure-like pieces comparable with those of Oudenarde. In the second half of the eighteenth century modified versions of Beauvais cartoons by Oudry, Boucher and Huet were woven; warps were always wool. Typical was Huet's *Pastorals with Blue Draperies,* also Chinese subjects and furniture coverings.

Lille was prosperous at the end of the seventeenth century and continued so under Guillaume Werniers, son-in-law of de Melter who had steered the manufactory to success with the help of weavers taken on from Brussels. On the death of Werniers in 1738, Pierre Pannemaker and the widow Werniers failed in their attempted business partnership and direction came under François Bouché from 1749 to 1773. The industry seems to have deteriorated between 1773 and 1781, when Etienne Peyrolle worked but two looms. Under Werniers was woven the *Story of Don Quixote,* some *Teniers,* the *Marriage Feast at Cana, Portraits of Baldwin, Count of Flanders* and his wife *Marie* with

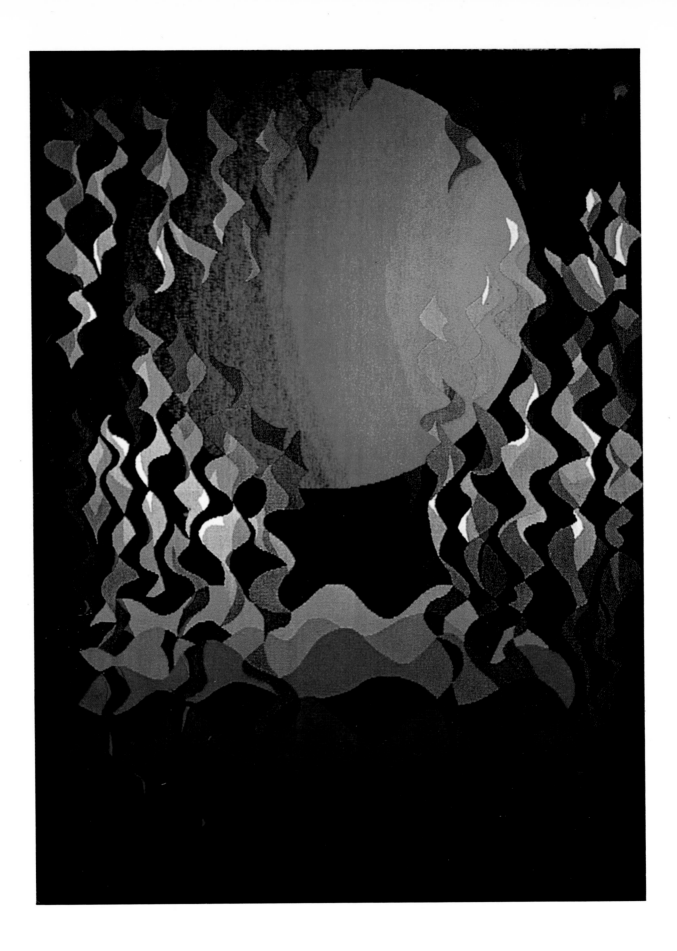

family, after Arnold Wuez, *Christ Calling Little Children* and *Peasant Scenes*. Later hangings included the *History of Psyche* and a *Portrait of Charles Rohan*, Governor of Flanders.

The seventeenth century manufactory established by Duke Leopold at La Malgrange, Nancy, produced a set of the *Victories of Duke Charles V* designed by Charles Herbel (died 1702), and woven by Charles Mitté in about 1705; it bears the double cross of Lorraine; all hangings are now in the Austrian State collection. Other hangings included ten pieces representing the *Months* after Coclet. Others associated with the manufactory were Pierre Durand (died 1755) and his son Nicholas, and Jean Bellat of Aubusson from 1717, who may have had an independent high- and low-loom workshop.

60 *The Audience of the Emperor* is typical of the *Chinese Hangings* woven by the Beauvais manufactory from early in the eighteenth century. The cult of Chinoiserie was first promoted by Marco Polo's accounts of his journeys between 1271 and 1295, and then revived by the dramatic landscapes of the seventeenth century painter Robert Robinson, who may have produced cartoons for the 'Chinese' tapestries woven by the Soho workshop, London, about the second quarter of the eighteenth century. *The Audience of the Emperor* represents a slight break with earlier types of 'tentures chinoises' in that an even more extravagant mixture is portrayed. The seated potentate, possibly intended to be the Grand Mogul, is holding a reception. He is seated on cushions beneath an extravagantly ornate cupola with a high roof overhead, which is a mixture of Moorish and Gothic constructional and decorative features, and suggests that the artist had gained some of his ideas for it from the upper part of a hot-house for tropical plants. Surrounding the canopy is a cloth through which an elephant pushes his trunk and one large ear, to the left. On the carpeted steps, three visitors make deep obeisance. At the far left a noble lady sits in a wheeled chair harnessed to two black slaves crouching with their heads bowed and almost invisible against the edge of the carpet; behind her are two attendants. The tapestry measures 317.7 × 488cm (10ft 5in × 16ft 6in); materials are wool and silk. The date of weaving is earlier than 1732 (*Fine Arts Museum of San Francisco*)

Adrién de Meusse of Oudenarde and Beauvais had a high-loom at Gisors from 1703 and wove a portrait of *Louis XIV* last seen in Gisors Museum. Jean Baert of Oudenarde was subsidized by the magistrates of Cambrai in about 1703 to establish a manufactory there. He was succeeded by his son Jean Jacques in 1741, and his son, Jean Baptiste Baert, died there in poverty in 1812. Products of the Baerts included three hangings of *Peasants Dancing and Carousing*. Many small workshops existed in France almost on a cottage industry basis; if not actually weaving original pieces there was always work for the competent and trustworthy in the tapestry repair and cleaning, or alteration business.

The Beauvais manufactory suffered a great loss with the death in 1704 of Philippe Béhagle and, although his widow and eldest son, Philippe, continued the works until 1711, when the brothers Filleul were appointed, and the artist le Pape continued in office until 1721 to be replaced by Duplessis, there was a steady decline. The Filleuls had introduced *Chinese Hangings* with cartoons by Vermansal, Belin de Fontenay and others (*see* 60). Noël Antoine de Mérou managed the works from *c*1721 to 1734, to be replaced by the brilliant but strict artist-director Jean-Baptiste Oudry; he speedily raised manufacture to a pitch of excellence and popularity essential to the survival of a privately owned but state-subsidized enterprise catering for noble and wealthy patrons. The drawing school was re-established and new designs produced by Oudry himself including lively sets of *Fables of La Fontaine, Rural Pastimes, Hunts of the Wolf, Stag* and *Fox, Comedies of Molière* and *Amours of the Gods*. Oudry appointed Nicholas Besnier his partner and business boomed, to be followed by even greater prosperity in 1736 with the first of François Boucher's great series of tapestries, *Les Fêtes Italiennes*, in 14 pieces; looms were busy from 1736 to 1762. The *Chinese Hangings* made from sketches by Boucher, started in 1743, proved equally popular and were copied many times. Other Boucher designed sets or hangings include the *History of Psyche, Amours of the Gods, Fragments of Opera* and *The Noble Pastoral*. Besnier died in 1753 and was replaced by André Charlemagne Charron; in 1755 Boucher replaced Oudry as inspector to the Gobelins. Charron kept pace with fashion by ordering new designs; Deshayes cartoons included the *Iliad of Homer,* and *History of Astrea*; he died in 1780 and was replaced by de Menou who continued to 1793. The latter's term of office was distinguished by a high output of tapestries including *Les Convois Militaires, Sciences and the Arts* and *Continents,* and the weaving of carpets like those of the Savonnerie. Closed in 1793, the establishment was reduced to six weavers when it opened again in 1794 with Camousse as director. He was replaced by the artist Jean Baptiste Huet who died in 1814 and was succeeded by his sons until 1819, when Guillaumot became director and transferred all the high-loom weavers to the Gobelins; he resigned in 1828 and was succeeded by the Marquis d'Ourchies until 1831, when Guillaumot's son, Jules, took over but died within a year. Successive directors were Grau Saint Vincent 1832–48, Pierre Adolphe Badin 1848–76, Jules Dietérle 1876–82, Jules Badin 1882–1918.

Italy

Reference was made in the preceding chapter to closure of the Florence manufactory in 1744. Many of the weavers went to Naples where both low- and high-loom work was done until the manufactory closed in 1799. Hangings included the *Elements* after le Brun, the *Consecration of the Virgin, Rape of Proserpine, Birth of the Virgin, Royal Munificence* and *Apotheosis of Charles III*; one of the last pieces is signed DESIDERIO DI ANGELIS 1796. Pope

Philippus Cettomai F. MDCCXC.

Clement XI established a manufactory in the Hospital San Michele, Rome, in 1710 and appointed the Parisian weaver Jean Simonet and painter Andrea Procaccini with a staff of three workmen to inaugurate it. The enterprise flourished, and from 1717 to 1770 was directed by Pietro Ferloni with Victor Demignot as principal weaver. Among its products were portraits of Popes (*see* Plate 25), the *Purification of the Virgin, Descent of the Holy Spirit* and *Christ on the Cross,* after Raphael. In 1770 Giuseppi Folli succeeded Pietro Ferloni, and Felice Cettomai was appointed papal tapissier; presumably the subject of 61 was a relative. Shortly after Philippo Percoli was appointed director the works closed for a period, but were producing tapestries in 1831 to be closed on the entry of the Italian troops into Rome. Pope Benedict XV re-established the workshop, which wove a panel after the *Madonna* of Pinturicci. Up to the end of the eighteenth century some 50 pieces and sets from original cartoons, or after Rubens or Raphael, had been woven to the highest standards.

In about 1734, some Rome weavers founded a workshop in the Place de

Santa Maria di Trastevere under the direction of Antonio Gargaglio. Products included *Pope Paul confirming the statutes of the Jesuits*. In 1737, Charles Emmanuel III of the House of Savoy appointed the former Florentine manufactory low-loom craftsman, Victor Demignot, to establish a workshop in Turin, wherein the high-looms were to be under the direction of Antonio Dini of Rome. The latter went to Venice in 1754 and high-loom work was discontinued. The Chevalier de Beaumont produced the cartoons until 1766, when Laurent Pécheux of Lyons replaced him. Demignot died in 1743 and was replaced by his son, Francis, who continued until 1784. Antonio was the next and last director. By 1755 the workshop had produced some 34 pieces, mostly of classical subjects. Dini's workshop was continued by his daughters Luisa and Giuseppa until about 1789.

Flanders

Judocus (or Jos) de Vos employed 12 looms in Brussels from 1703 to 1707 and with Jerome le Clerck and Jan Cobus may, in hindsight, be regarded as one of the principal tapissiers who restored the reputation of that city after the depressing period at the start of the eighteenth century. He produced the *Descent from Torbay, Battle of Bresgate* and the *Battle of the Boyne* for William III (1688–1702) of England. Between 1712 and 1721 a set of reproductions of the *Conquest of Tunis by Charles V* was woven to the 1535 cartoons of Jan Vermayen, and used to replace tattered remnants of the set woven originally by Wilhelm Pannemaker, by order of Emperor Charles VI of Austria. Jos de Vos's many hangings included *Victories of Prince Eugene, Amours of Venus and Adonis, Pastoral Scenes,* the *Triumph of Commerce, Peace, Justice* and so on. *Scenes of Shepherd Life*, a fine series after Teniers including *Rural Scenes (see* 57) and the *History of Alexander* series, after le Brun, are in England's Hampton Court Palace. Jos de Vos left a son, Jean François, who had eight looms in 1736. The father was such a brilliant tapissier that he has often been thought of as a Gobelins weaver, an

62 From the time that the Great Wardrobe was moved from Great Queen Street, London, to Poland Street in the Soho district, the name of John Vanderbank as chief arras-worker fades from the records. In his place, Paul Saunders appears, more often described as 'tapestry maker' seemingly with the object of persuading his lordly masters that he was capable of better things than the almost continuous and humdrum work of cleaning, repairing and restoring the colours of court and stately tapestries. It appears that he was allowed to weave hangings for private clients, for some of these fabrics are outstanding. The finest is a set entitled *The Pilgrimage to Mecca*. Several copies were made of this popular set, which is distinguished by its landscapes, softly defined trees, classical buildings, ruins and watercourses enlivened with small figures dressed in Oriental attire. Saunders was a man of many parts. He was a cabinet maker, upholsterer and State undertaker, as well as tapissier. Most of his tapestries were signed, including these (*Collection Ulster Museum, Belfast*)

idea enhanced by the somewhat similar style of Paris and Brussels at that period. Similarly, an artist who worked almost entirely for the French and died in 1690, Adam van der Meulen, has sometimes been regarded as the designer of Brussels tapestries almost certainly designed by Lambert or Philip de Hondt.

The van den Hecke family of Brussels were also prominent eighteenth century weavers. Jean-François van den Hecke's sons, François and Pierre, came to notice in 1730; little is known of the former, but the latter was a low-loom weaver whose chief works were the *History of Psyche* after Jan van Orley, the *Four Seasons, Elements, Peasant Festivals, Pleasures of the World,* and a set after Teniers. He died in 1752.

The Leyniers came to prominence in the seventeenth century after Urban (1674–1747) was apprenticed in his father's workshop at 11 years of age; his father, Gaspard Leyniers, was a dyer. Urban was accorded the privileges of a master in 1700 and soon entered into partnership with Henri Reydams, a master weaver of Brussels with five looms. The latter died in 1719 and was succeeded by Urban's brother Daniel; business developed rapidly until 1728, when Daniel died and was succeeded by Urban's son, also called Daniel, a

dyer like his father and grandfather. He associated with Pierre van der Borght in the production of some tapestries, for example a series depicting a *Landscape* and *Scenes of Peasant Life*. Daniel Leyniers gave up business in 1767–8 and was succeeded by a son, François or Daniel François Leyniers, mentioned in connection with a *History of Moses* in 1768. Tapestries produced by the Leyniers up to 1717 included the *History of the Duchy of Brabant* (Hôtel de Ville, Brussels), *History of Don Quixote*; up to 1728: the *History of Telemachus,* after Jan van Orley (copied many times); up to 1745: *Peasant Life,* after Teniers, *Friezes of Arabesques, War and Peace* and *Military Life,* woven in about 1740 by Daniel Leyniers and Pierre van der Borght (or Borcht) from cartoons by Hyacinthe de la Peigne (Austrian State Collection); up to 1767: *Landscapes with Foliage, Triumph of Mars* (Bowhill House, Selkirk, Scotland) and *Acts of the Apostles*. Tapestries were all clearly signed.

The workshops of Jacques van der Borght (or Borcht) with eight looms, and that of son Gaspard with five looms, were active in 1700. Another son, Jacques François, signed many tapestries including the *Sacrament, Subjects after Teniers, Story of Achilles*, after Jan van Orley. Tapestries are initialled F.V.D.B., P.V.D.B., I.V.D.B., IAC.V.D.B. for François, Pierre (son of Gaspard), Jacues, or Jacques (son of Jean François) van der Borght, respectively with the name shown sometimes as BORGHT. François disappears from the records after 1761, and Gaspard (or Jaspar) died *c*1742. Pierre received privileges *c*1742 and died in 1763. His brother, Jean François lived until 1772 and left a son, Jacques van der Borght, who carried on the family tradition with three high-looms; with his death in 1794, the great Brussels industry died too. Notably van der Borght tapestries include also *Hunting Scenes* (Austrian State collection), the *Continents, Founding of Rome, Odyssey, Wars of Troy, Jerusalem Delivered,* a *Fishmarket* (Bowes Museum, Barnard Castle, Durham) and *Dutch Figures outside an Inn.* Gaspard (Gaspar or Jaspar) worked in association with Jerome le Clerc from 1676 to 1742: they signed tapestries 'A. Castro' and 'Le Clerc', respectively.

Oudenarde's eighteenth century history is similar to Brussels's with the family of Jean, Ferdinand, Jacques, David, Pierre and Jean Baptiste Brandt

64 This painting by Copley of the scene in the old House of Lords, in London, when the Earl of Chatham collapsed on 7 April 1778, shows one of the tapestries depicting *The Defeat of the Spanish Armada.* This sixteenth century tapestry was lost when the building was destroyed by fire, but an engraving of it appears in 48. Chatham was taken ill whilst speaking about the position of British colonists in America. He died a month later at his country home (*Tate Gallery, London*)

145

the most prominent in weaving from 1691 to 1787, and the van Verren's from 1699 to later than 1723. There were small manufactories at Ghent and Bruges from 1750, Douai from 1726, Valenciennes from 1739 and Arras from 1740.

Flemish eighteenth century tapestries are characterized, like those of France, by borders woven in imitation of gilded frames; nineteenth century pieces often have no borders but closely resemble painted pictures.

Germany

The Munich manufactory, re-established in about 1718 by Maximilian II Emmanuel, Elector of Bavaria, employed French weavers. Subjects were similar to those of the seventeenth century when, to the orders of Maximilian I Emmanuel, Hans van der Biest wove between 1604 and 1615 a set of battle scenes, such as the *Storming of the Castle of Verona,* to Peter de Witte's cartoons. The eighteenth century manufactory survived until 1802. Productions included 'art of war' hangings such as *A small body of Cavalry crossing a Plain,* now in Schleissheim New Palace in Munich, and *The History of the House of Bavaria,* the *Triumph of Bacchus* and *Flora,* a *Banquet of the Gods.*

After his resignation, the workshops of P. Mercier in Berlin were directed by his brother-in-law, Pierre Barrabon, and Mercier appears to have moved to weave in Dresden; the *Parting of Prince Frederick-Augustus with his Father* is signed P. MERCIER Dresden, and dated 1716. In 1708, Frederick I of Prussia presented to General James of England—later the Earl of Stanhope—a set of *Chinese Grotesques* designed and woven in the Beauvais style but at Berlin, and with one tapestry signed J. BARRABAND (Jean Barrabon succeeded his father). During the last half of the eighteenth century, Charles Vigne directed the Berlin high-loom workshops and may also have had an interest in those of Dresden. Hangings included pieces in the style of Teniers. French weavers worked in small workshops established to supply the patron's needs at Würzburg, Erlangen, Schwabach and Heidelberg.

Spain

The royal interest in tapestries continued, despite the closure of the workshop near St Isabel in Madrid towards the end of the seventeenth century. Eventually Philip V of Spain (1713–46) found a Flemish master of weaving, Jacques van der Goten of Antwerp who, with his four sons, seemed better equipped to establish a successful manufactory; they were installed in the Casa del Abreviador, near the gate of St Barbara, in Madrid. The first piece off the low-looms was the *Poultry-seller,* scarcely a royal piece to inaugurate what soon was called the Real Fábrica de Tapices y Alfombras de Santa Barbara (Royal Factory of Tapestries and Rugs of St Barbara); *Peasant Scenes and Hawking* followed. Jacques van der Goten died in 1725 and was succeeded by his sons, François, Jacques, Cornelius and Adrian. The establishment was strengthened in 1729 by the addition of a French high-loom weaver, Antoine Lenger, whose survival was shorter than that of van der Goten senior. Jacques van der Goten took over high-loom weaving and produced the *Virgin with the Pearl,* after Raphael. The high-loom workshop was transferred to Seville under the management of Andrea Procaccini, formerly of the San Michele papal manufactory in Rome; Jacques van der Goten remained director, and a *History of Telemachus* after Michael Angelo Houasse was woven. The move to Seville was unsatisfactory and in 1733 the looms and weavers returned to Madrid, eventually settling in the old workshop of Gutierrez, in the street of St Isabel, but returned to the St Barbara building in 1756. Productions included a *History of*

65 This late eighteenth or early nineteenth century tapestry depicting *The Annunciation* was woven in Sweden's southern province of Skåne, and is intended to be a seat or table cover. Tapestry-weaving was a home industry in southern Sweden before King Gustav Vasa (1523–60) commissioned Flemish weavers to establish a workshop under his patronage and make hangings for the royal palace. Apprentices were indentured and after working the minimum stipulated number of years as trained craftsmen, some were enticed to work in the castles of provincial noblemen who wished to equip their castle similarly. By this means, a knowledge of tapestry techniques gradually spread. The economic returns for provincial professional weavers not enjoying the patronage of a nobleman were not great, so the craft gradually developed for many into a part-time occupation, or a pastime for middle- and upper-class women; sometimes they joined together and hired the services of a professional artist to make designs. Some of the weavers from the royal workshop travelled from one group of provincial weavers to another, offering them advice, materials and cartoons, or undertook to market designs no longer required. By the mid-eighteenth century tapestried upholstery in the better-class homes started to give way to other fabrics, and weaving was more the occupation of lower-class homes, although it remained of high quality with intriguing designs (*Victoria and Albert Museum; Crown Copyright*)

Don Quixote after Procaccini, the *History of Cyrus* and the *Conquest of Tunis* woven in 1740 using the ten surviving panels of Pannemaker's smaller series in place of cartoons; both sets are now in the Royal Collection of Spain. Towards the end of the eighteenth century, the artist Francisco Bayeu produced cartoons of Spanish everyday subjects such as the *Repast at the Inn* and *The Vendor of Barley-water,* which stirred national pride. Then came Goya with no fewer than 45 popular subjects, such as the *Fair at Madrid, The Ball, Women at the Fountain,* and *Children Climbing a Tree.*

Cornelius van der Goten, the last son of the founder, died in 1786. He was succeeded by a weaver from Antwerp, Lievin Stuyck, and work continued as before until 1799 when Stuyck petitioned the King to allow Juan Bautista Stuyck to weave carpets in the Persian style. Lievin Stuyck was informed that his nephew might work thus, and both the tapestry and carpet-weaving industries continued until 1808 when the French entered Madrid, and the industry ended. When the establishment opened again in 1819, pile carpet-weaving was the primary industry and tapestry eventually was hived off in 1889 to No. 2 Calle Fuenterrabia, and dropped completely.

66 This *Tapestry Portrait of Catherine the Great of Russia* was woven about 1783 by Cozette at the Gobelins manufactory in Paris. It is a magnificent but delicate portait of fine texture, measuring (with its frame) 42 × 35·5cm (1ft 4½in × 1ft 2in). Tapestries were little known in Russia before Peter the Great established, in present day Leningrad, in the years 1716 and 1717, the first Russian Tapestry Manufactory. To launch it he was obliged to appoint foreign artists and craftsmen who could initiate production and train native apprentices. Among the foreigners was Philip Béhagle II, the son of the late Director of the Royal Manufactory of Tapestry at Beauvais, France; he was put in charge of dyeing and manufacture. Supplies of materials and communication difficulties hampered progress for several years but the Imperial Tapestry Factory – as it came to be called – survived for over 140 years (*Messrs Christie's, Fine Art Auctioneers, London*)

Russia

Tsar Peter the Great of Russia (1682–1725) established a tapestry manufactory at St Petersburg (Leningrad) in 1716 as part of his programme of reform, which included broadening the arts and crafts of his realm. Foreign specialists were recruited on five-year contracts which bound them to organize the workshops, produce tapestries, and train Russian craftsmen and apprentices. The director was an architect, le Blond, of Paris. Philippe Béhagle II had charge of the weavers and dyeworks. Weavers were recruited from Flanders and Paris, and included Bourdin, P. Camousse, Gauchere, Grignon, Houet, Magney and Vavoque. An attempt to weave a copy of the *New Indies* after Desportes proved abortive because there were no local supplies of suitable materials, and orders placed abroad were not serviced rapidly or adequately. During the first decade of existence the workshops produced only minor pieces such as *Dogs and a Cat, Still Life,* woven by Vavoque (Leningrad Museum) and *The Battle of Poltava,* woven by Béhagle and Kobyliakov (Hermitage Museum, Leningrad), made to the design of Louis Caravaque. This tapestry is still regarded as Russia's first great masterpiece of the tapissier's art. By the end of the first quarter of the eighteenth century, as many Russians as foreigners were working the looms, and in about 1732 the manufactory was placed under the Ministry of the Household and changes were made to improve conditions and status. The portrait of *Empress Anna Ionnovna* of 1732 was probably the last tapestry woven by Béhagle. Later attempts to weave the *New Indies* series were highly successful; by 1746, 18 of a series had been woven and were installed at Peterhof. Other hangings included *Grotesques,* verdures and classical compositions. In the 1740s production all but stopped, but was revitalized again in 1755 with a new set of directives and control by the Senate. By 1764 some 150 persons were employed and before the end of the century the workshops reached their highest achievement with the production of tapestries after Russian and European artists. Subjects included biblical, mythological, classical and historical motifs in the form of hangings, chambers and furnishings. Some of the better known include *Views of Pavlovsk,* the *Seizure of Kazan, Vladimir and Rogneda* and a series of portraits. The manufactory closed in 1859. Few tapestries from the manufactory exist outside Russia; most are in the Hermitage Museum in Leningrad, and the Armoury in Moscow. There is one, however, in the English National Trust's Blickling Hall, at Aylsham, Norfolk.

Norway and Sweden

The position of tapestry-weaving was much the same in both countries in the eighteenth century. Until about 1725 a few itinerant weavers continued to journey from place to place to carry out commissions. They were increasingly ousted by the growing use by the wealthy and middle-class families, of manufactured textiles such as silks, satins, brocades and padded coverings for furniture. Even walls no longer sported tapestries; if not painted with complex designs, biblical or allegorical scenes, there was a covering of paper, sometimes hand-painted or block-printed. The demand for tapestry coverings for benches and chairs had all but ceased as a professional art.

Instead, tapestry-weaving changed into a folk-art and a cottage- or home-based industry which used materials at hand: the vegetable dyes and the pelt wool of native sheep, with linen thread from local flax. Although the district of Gudbrandsdalen in Norway is usually credited with having been the centre for tapestry-weaving, there is reason to believe that a home-based industry was more extensive. In Sweden, the main eighteenth and early nineteenth century activity was based on Dalarna in the north-west central part of the country, and Skåne in the far south. The Anderson family of Everlöv were famous weavers from the early eighteenth century and produced countless smallish pieces such as cushion and table covers in brilliant colours. Hälsingland is a province some 200 miles north of Stockholm, which has as its county symbol the blue flax flower; tapestried chair-coverings from that county, dated 1763, are very finely woven (*see* 65).

China and Japan

K'o-ssu tapestry production continued and reached high artistic perfection in China during the eighteenth and early nineteenth centuries (*see* 67). Some attempt was made to copy European styles while 'overlaying' them with a Chinese attitude to colour rendering and composition balance, perhaps as a tribute to western missionary influence, or with the object of attracting overseas customers.

Japanese 'tsuzure-nishiki' or polychrome tapestries, with weft threads made of thick cotton covered with silk, silver or gold, were woven throughout the eighteenth and nineteenth centuries, and produced a rather coarse-looking and robust fabric. Use included clothing, hangings, curtains and furniture coverings. Factories produced both Japanese and European style hangings.

England

The history of the Great Wardrobe in Great Queen Street, London, has been outlined in Chapter 4 up to the year 1727, when John Vanderbank retired and was succeeded by Moses Vanderbank and John Ellis. In about 1742 the Wardrobe was moved to Poland Street, Soho, to a building still standing in 1979. Paul Saunders took over the position of chief arras-worker or, as he called it, 'tapestry maker', although much of his work consisted of cleaning, repairing and renovating colours. He was a man of many parts, being a cabinet-maker, upholsterer and State undertaker (he laid out the remains of the Duke of Cumberland) as well as tapissier. The tapestries he wove for private clients prove his competence, although there appears to have been a partnership with another weaver, George Smith Bradshaw, judging from the way some tapestries are signed. He wove the *Pilgrimage to Mecca* (*see* 62), *Vases of Flowers* and chair-seat covers illustrating *Aesop's Fables*. Bradshaw's tapestries are still at Ham House, near London, and once were described as 'among the most beautiful tapestries ever produced'. These represent the *Fountain,* the *Dance,* the *Swing* and the *Fruit-gatherers* and are based on paintings by Watteau and Pater. Saunders died in about 1771.

The Lambeth manufactory probably remained active into the eighteenth century. Stephen Demay (or De May) was a descendant of the Stephen and Philip de May (or de Meij) who worked at Mortlake in about 1645 and the Matthew de May who worked in the Great Wardrobe in 1673. Stephen Demay was established as a tapissier who altered tapestries in 1700, and signed his work with the shield of St George and S.D.M. He worked much for Lord Nottingham. A naturalized Frenchman, Peter Parisot established a tapestry workshop at Paddington, London, where in 1750 he was joined by two carpet-weavers from the French town of Chaillot, and shortly after moved to new premises in Fulham, where he secured the patronage of the Duke of Cumberland. Parisot produced tapestries in the style of the Gobelins and carpets like those of Chaillot. He had a dyeworks and also a school of instruction at Fulham in south-west London. Although patronage was powerful and production was considerable, the enterprise ran into difficulties and failed in 1755. James Christopher le Blon, a painter, established a manufactory near the Mulberry Ground in Chelsea, London, in about 1723 with the object of weaving tapestries in the same manner as brocades. One of his productions, a *Head of Christ*, is in London's Victoria and Albert Museum; the manufactory was short-lived.

Ireland

When the Irish Houses of Parliament were being rebuilt in 1728–9, Robert Baillie, 'Upholder' of the City of Dublin, was invited to furnish tapestries. This was in response to a petition he presented in 1727, in which he stated:

> . . . That the Petitioner, understanding a new Parliament House is to be built, is emboldened, from the Encouragement this most Honourable House has always given to the Manufacturers of this Kingdom, to offer his Service for perpetuating the Particulars of the late glorious Revolution, and the remarkable Incidents in the Wars of Ireland, by preparing suits of Tapestry for such Parts of the House of Lords as shall be thought proper, containing their History. . . .

Baillie proposed six tapestries but only two were woven: *The Defence of London-derry* and *The Battle of the Boyne* (*see* 59). The artist was a Fleming working in Dublin, Johann van den Hagen, and the weaver was a former employee of the Gobelins in Paris, John van Beaver. He was admitted to the Corporation of Weavers of Dublin, in the Guild of the Blessed Virgin Mary, on 25 October 1738, and died at his house in World's End Lane, Dublin, on 28 August 1750. The two tapestries were hung in September 1733. King William is depicted in 59 with sword in hand, mounted on a charger and directing the issue. Baillie had conducted a tapestry manufactory for some years before the two

67 This early nineteenth century k'o-ssu panel – depicting Immortals and scholars welcoming a princess riding through the skies on a ho-ho bird – is characteristic of the highest quality tapestries of the time. In the foreground girls play with a tame deer on a mountain path. Taoist emblems appear in several places. The size of the hanging is 128 × 65 cm (4ft 2¼in × 2ft 1½in). Chinese k'so-ssu (cut-silk) tapestry-weaving continued until well into the first quarter of the twentieth century, but many examples exhibited a decline in standards compared with those woven up to about the first quarter of the nineteenth century. Later examples sometimes have designs embellished with paint (*Phillips and Company, London*)

tapestries were woven, and had manned his workshop with Flemish and French weavers. The Dublin Society tried to encourage weavers by awarding premiums or prizes. In 1743, van Beaver won £10 for his *Feast of Bacchus*, and in 1745 Richard Pawlet won £10 for his *Settee Bottom*. Van Beaver won again for his *Meleager and the killing of the Boar*, but will be remembered best for his magnificent tapestry portrait of *King George II* woven in 1738. The industry came to an end before the nineteenth century.

Bibliography
Thomson, W. G. *Tapestry Weaving in England*, Batsford, London (1915)
Wace, A. *The Marlborough Tapestries at Blenheim Palace*. Phaidon, London (1968)

Acknowledgements
Acknowledgement is made to the following, with thanks for information sent, or advice given: G. W. A. Dummer, MBE, CEng, FIEE, FIEEE, FIERE; A. H. Zouche-Gordon; Miss Wendy Hefford, Victoria and Albert Museum; G. Hughes-Hartman, Sotheby & Co., London; N. H. MacMichael, FSA, Archivist, Westminster Abbey, London; C. P. Claxton Stevens, and Paul Whitfield, Christie, Manson & Woods, London; William Wells, formerly of the Burrell Collection, Glasgow, Scotland; Revel Oddy, Royal Scottish Museum, Edinburgh.

6 A Century of British Tapestry Renaissance

During the last quarter of the nineteenth century a noble effort was made to revive tapestry-weaving in England. The Royal Windsor Tapestry Manufactory opened in 1876 and, although it closed within 15 years, its influence was out of all proportion; it triggered off a chain reaction that is still apparent in the five continents. Although it perpetuated a style of design and attitudes to the function of tapestry as a form of magnificent wall-paper, the Manufactory was influential enough to make the intelligentsia consider tapestry afresh.

The Royal Windsor Tapestry Manufactory

Established in still-existing premises off Albert Road in Old Windsor, and close to the Castle, the Manufactory was manned by weavers whom the Franco-Prussian war had driven from their homes in Aubusson and Beauvais. An influential committee of management was formed in 1877 to direct the Manufactory and also to give it the same degree of royal recognition as that enjoyed by tapestry workshops in other countries: *President* : His Royal Highness The Prince Leopold, KG. *Vice-Presidents* : HRH The Princess Louise, Marchioness of Lorne and HRH The Princess Christian of Schleswig Holstein. *Members* : The Duke of Westminster, KG; The Marquess of Bute; Sir Richard Wallace, Bart.; F. Cunliffe-Owen, CB; Louisa, Marchioness of Waterford; The Countess of Breadalbane. *Hon. Secretary* : The Lord Ronald Gower. *Director and Secretary to the Committee* : H. Henry. *Offices* : 17 Orchard Street, Portman Square, London. The looms were under the direction of Mr Henry. The artist 'in residence' was T. W. Hay.

Prince Leopold was the youngest son of Queen Victoria; both Vice-Presidents were her daughters. The Duke of Westminster—Hugh Lupus Grosvenor (1825–99)—was deeply interested in tapestry and a well-known connoisseur. The third Marquess of Bute—John Patrick Crichton-Stuart (1847–1900)—appears to have been keenly interested in 'the elegant art'; an interest his descendants continued to exhibit energetically until well into the mid-twentieth century (*see* 68). Sir Richard Wallace (1818–90) was instigator of the great treasure house of art bearing his name, the Wallace Collection, off London's Manchester Square. He was well versed in the magnificence of tapestry through his French-born wife, and his own residence in Paris. The Director of London's South Kensington Museum, Francis Cunliffe-Owen (1828–94), knighted in 1878, was a fount of wisdom on the influence of tapestry on the history of art. (The Museum was renamed the Victoria and Albert Museum in 1899, and in 1909 restricted to art collections only.) Louisa, Marchioness of Waterford (died 1891), was, like the third Marquess of Bute, descended from the third Earl of Bute; she was a fine artist in her own right. The Countess of Breadalbane was a daughter of the fourth Duke of Montrose and would have been very familiar with the best of the tapissier's art; the family seat at Taymouth Castle had Audran tapestries after Tessier that had belonged to Madame de Pompadour's brother, the Marquis de Marigny.

68 The third Marquess of Bute, John Patrick Crichton-Stuart (1847–1900) (*National Museum of Wales, Cardiff*)

Right from its foundation the Royal Windsor Tapestry Manufactory produced hangings of a very high standard of design and workmanship and, at the Paris Exhibition of 1878, was awarded a Gold Medal for eight pieces depicting *The Merry Wives of Windsor*; the cartoons were by T. W. Hay. Sir Albert Sasson purchased the set for installation at 25 Kensington Gore, London. E. M. Ward, the Royal Academician, designed the cartoons for *The Battle of Aylesford* tapestry, woven in 1878, and for the *English Country Pastimes* set made for Vanderbilt. Four hangings each measuring 335·5 × 732cm (11 × 24ft) were made for the Member of Parliament, H. A. Brassey. These were the *Aylesford* piece and two designed by J. E. Hodgson RA: *The Siege of Rochester Castle and the Burning of Rochester Bridge* and *The Men of Kent Marching in Front of Harold*; there is no record of the fourth piece. A set of four tapestries made for Lord Aldenham depicted *Morte d'Arthur,* sometimes referred to as *Subjects from Tennyson's 'Idylls of the King'*. The Corporation of the City of London commissioned four tapestries still hanging in the Mansion House, the official residence of the Lord Mayor of London: *A Joust on London Bridge, Queen Elizabeth Opening the Royal Exchange, The City Champion Receiving the Banner of the City on the Steps of Old St. Paul's* and *Queen Victoria Visiting the Mansion House on the Occasion of Her Jubilee in 1887* (see 69). Other tapestries are in Windsor Castle, the Victoria and Albert and other museums, and public and private collections.

Royal Windsor tapestries have been likened to those of the Gobelins of the period. Research has confirmed the great care taken by the designers to ensure historical accuracy of the scenes and details portrayed. The line is clear and decisive, the colour rich and vigorous and, of course, the techniques of weaving excellent. Some three years after the Manufactory closed in 1890 several of its hangings were exhibited at the Chicago World Fair. These pieces kindled much interest throughout the Americas and no doubt materially helped William Baumgarten to establish, in 1893, the first tapestry workshop of recent times in the Americas. Mr Baumgarten's atelier initially was on New York City's Fifth Avenue, where he employed Mr Foussadier—formerly of the Royal Windsor Manufactory—as his Chief Weaver.

The Merton Abbey Tapestry Works

In 1861 a young man named William Morris (1834–96) recently down from Oxford University's Exeter College, where he had studied medieval art and literature, formed a rather strange commercial venture with his friends Philip Webb (architect), Ford Madox Brown (designer), Dante Gabriel Rossetti and (later, Sir) Edward Burne-Jones (both artists). Morris enlisted his friends as un-named partners in the firm of Morris, Marshall, Faulkner and Company. P. P. Marshall (surveyor and engineer), a friend of Brown's, and C. J. Faulkner (mathematician) initially kept the books. Premises were in London's Red Lion Square. A publicity brochure proclaimed the Company's experience as 'Fine Art Workmen in Painting, Carving, Furniture and the Metals'. Among its employees were several who made their mark individually in later life such as (Sir) Frank Branwyn, painter of murals and designer of tapestries, whose home in Queen Caroline Street, Hammersmith, was close by Morris's home at Kelmscott. The Company prospered rapidly and expanded to take on the manufacture of stained glass, wallpaper and chintzes. In 1865 a move was made to nearby Queen Square. Dissension developed among the un-named partners and so the firm was reconstituted in 1875 as Morris and Company. In 1877 showrooms were opened in London's West End, at 449 Oxford Street.

Plate 43 (*above*) *A Vivaldi* is typical of the hangings produced in the Barcelona atelier of one of Spain's most outstanding twentieth century tapissiers, Maria Asunción Raventós. Harmonious but brilliant colours are emphasized by a wide choice of weaving techniques, which combine to create a sense of romance, adventure, warmth and yet visual harmony. This gifted designer-weaver has combined tapestry techniques to create a wealth of invigorating forms (*Maria Asunción Raventós, Barcelona*)

Plate 44 (*overleaf*) Weavers at work on a loom of the Portalegre Tapestry manufactory are following an ancient craft in the most modern conditions that technology can provide. The British Company, Imperial Chemical Industries, established a terylene polyester fibre plant in association with the manufactory, to produce beautifully coloured materials for the tapestries (*Manufactura de tapeçarias de Portalegre, Portugal*)

69 This tapestry of *A Joust on London Bridge* in 1390, between David de Lyndsaye, Earl of Crawford, and Lord John de Welles, Ambassador to Scotland of Richard the Second was designed by Richard Beavis (1824–96) and woven at the Royal Windsor Tapestry Manufactory (*City of London Corporation*)

And in 1881 the entire manufacturing complex was moved out of London to Merton Abbey on the banks of the river Wandle, near the present-day 'tennis mecca' of Wimbledon. The old Mortlake Tapestry Manufactory that had closed during 1703–4 was to the north-west, 17km (10 miles) away, but sufficiently close for many people to confuse Merton Abbey with Mortlake.

Morris visited the Royal Windsor Tapestry Manufactory in 1878 when *The Battle of Aylesford* tapestry was being woven and caustically remarked that only the royal patronage of the Manufactory made their tapestries saleable. He visited the Gobelins workshops in Paris to see how they made tapestries and expressed the view that both the Windsor and Paris establishments were prostituting the potentials of the art. He was convinced that a new school

70 (Above) *The Forest,* a tapestry designed by Morris, Webb and Dearle and woven in 1887, like that below, at the Merton Abbey Tapestry Works. (Below) *The Achievement,* a tapestry designed by Sir Edward Burne-Jones and woven in 1894. Only the left and centre parts are shown (*Victoria and Albert Museum; Crown Copyright*)

based on Gothic concepts of excellence was the only remedy that could save tapestry-weaving from oblivion, and so, in 1879, he designed and had made a high-warp loom like those he had sketched at the Gobelins. In the seclusion of his bedroom at 'Kelmscott' in Hammersmith Mall, on the north bank of the river Thames in west London, he rose early each morning to teach himself the arts of designing and weaving tapestries. He was aided only by his observations in Windsor and Paris and by a small eighteenth century book in the French language, *Arts et Métiers.* Jokingly, he called his first tapestry *The Cabbage and the Vine,* listed in books since as *The Vine and Acanthus.* Although he was to claim later that a child could be taught the techniques of weaving but to master the art requires years of training and artistic experience, he immediately started to instruct others including a young assistant, Mr Harry Dearle, who rose to be manager and chief designer of tapestry at Merton Abbey.

Tapestry-weaving started at Queen Square in 1880, with trial verdures and furniture pieces. Morris developed strong views on how weaving should be arranged. He insisted that only the high-warp loom offered the gamut of facilities required and it must be positioned in the workshop to ensure that maximum light fell on the face of the tapestry. The weaver was to work from the back and to view the front by mirror-image through the warps. Great care was to be taken to ensure that the mirror was never tilted, otherwise a distorted image would result. Morris had the cartoon placed behind the weaver, who was obliged to turn to consult it. The insistence on the weaver receiving the maximum amount of available light emphasizes the inadequacy of artificial light in those days; there was nothing to equal good, white daylight. Despite risk of fire, many weavers of old were forced to work by candlelight or rush-taper. Oil and gaslights survived until the 1930s in some inner town districts. Edison and Swan did not invent their electric lamp bulbs until 1879, and it took another three-quarters of a century for many industrial and home premises to have access to an electricity supply. Ancient tapestries displayed now under controlled lighting conditions are often better seen than by the weavers who made them, or by the clients who commissioned hangings for the walls of their castle or manor house.

Morris and Burne-Jones initially worked together on designs, with the latter concentrating on figure-work and Dearle contributing verdures, borders and accessories. Colours were strong; garishness was taboo. Single colour weft strands appear in early tapestries; blended strands producing a greater range of tints appear in later Merton Abbey tapestries. Slits were prevented by interlocking colour boundaries. Textures varied from 3·9 w/cm (10 w/in) to 6·3 w/cm (16 w/in) with a very occasional 16·5 w/cm (42 w/in). Lesser known Morris tapestries may be difficult to identify because he did not use a workshop, designer's or weaver's mark, apparently relying on his distinctive style and occasional woven lines of verse, to identify his products. Sixteen years after Morris's death the likeness of a bishop's mitre and the words MERTON ABBEY or M.A., sometimes with the weaver's name, or initials, were woven into the blue selvedge.

Morris's scathing criticism of tapestries produced by the Gobelins and the Royal Windsor Manufactory was ventilated in his lectures and, in one entitled 'The Lesser Arts of Life', he claimed the Gobelins workshop had changed tapestry-weaving from being a fine art to a mere 'upholsterer's toy':

> It would be a mild word to say that what they make is worthless; it is more than that. It has a corrupting and a deadening influence upon all the lesser arts of France ... a more idiotic waste of human labour and skill it is impossible to conceive. There is another branch of the same stupidity, differing slightly in technique, at Beauvais; and the little town of Aubusson in mid-France has a decaying commercial industry of like rubbish.

In his *History of the Merton Abbey Tapestry Works*, the late H. C. Marillier wrote of Morris:

> He wished to revive the art on its pristine Gothic lines, when tapestries were designed and woven as hangings, with simple colours and little more perspective than would be permissible in a stained glass window.

In some respects, Morris was in advance of his times. If he had lived to be a 100 years old or more, he would have found a strong ally in Jean Lurçat of France. Morris and Sir Edward Burne-Jones established a design style that was so different from that of their contemporaries that, with the great influence they had, they had the power to make a wide public take note. Perhaps Morris's main contributions to tapestry were the many debates his outspoken criticism and assertions provoked, and the way in which he managed to involve people, who, in the normal course of their lives, probably would not have been drawn into the art forum. His breadth of interests and activities in politics, literature

71 The fourth Marquess of Bute, John Crichton-Stuart (1881–1947), the founder of the Dovecot Tapestry Studios at Corstorphine, near Edinburgh, Scotland (*The Most Hon. the Marquess of Bute*)

72 William George Thomson (1865–1942), the Organizer and first Director of Weaving at the Dovecot Tapestry Studios (*Author's copyright*)

73 (1) A view in 1912 of the ancient Dovecot of the demolished Forrester castle built in the late fourteenth century by Sir Adam Forrester; (2) The Dovecot Tapestry Workshop about 1930; and (3) Weavers working at a high-warp loom dating from about 1690, which came from the manufactory in London's Soho; Richard Gordon, the head weaver, is at the far right (*Author's copyright*)

and several categories of art touched on the life of a large public in Britain and abroad. Through his campaigning zeal countless people were forced into making their own assessment of tapestry in relation to the arts, and also to consider the place of the arts in relation to civilization.

The second great renaissance of tapestry that started in 1876 is interlocked by a thread of weavers who were employed by the Royal Windsor Tapestry Manufactory, the Merton Abbey Workshops and the Dovecot Tapestry Studios near Edinburgh. The names of some may be found on selvedges: Gordon Berry, H. Carnegie, Richard Carter, John Henry Dearle, William Elliman, Robert Ellis, George Fitzhenry, John Glassbrook, William Haines, John Keich, William Knight, John Martin, George Merritt, Mrs Jean Orage, Harry Plant, George Priestley, Frederic Reed, Edward Russell, Percy Sheldrick, William Sleath and Walter Taylor. Dearle eventually was appointed the Works Director of Merton Abbey. Ellison and Haines were recruited by Merton Abbey from the Royal Windsor workshops. Glassbrook and Berry were recruited by the Dovecot Studios in 1912 from Merton Abbey. Reed and Sheldrick were disabled ex-soldiers from the First World War, recruited by Merton Abbey. Mrs Jean Orage was employed on weaving at the Oxford Street showrooms of the Merton Abbey works. Others not specially mentioned were all Merton Abbey weavers. As a small boy the author knew John Glassbrook and Gordon Berry who were both killed, ironically enough, in the ancient tapestry weaving countryside of Flanders, during the First World War. Their names are entered on the War Memorial standing by the Parish Church in Corstorphine. The author also remembers Mrs Jean Orage, who retired to live at Askerswell in Dorset and died there in the 1960s.

The Merton Abbey looms' first work of importance was the *Goose Girl* woven in 1881 to the design of Walter Crane, and measured 239 × 183cm (7ft 10in × 6ft); it was purchased by Mr Pope of Cleveland, Ohio, the first of several American patrons of the Merton works. The Victoria and Albert Museum of London has the cartoon. *The Forest* (*see* 70 above) was designed by Morris, Webb and Dearle and woven in 1887; it measures 122 × 335·5cm (4ft × 11ft) and was sold to Mr A. A. Ionides; it is now in the Victoria and Albert Museum, as is *The Achievement* panel, which is one of six hangings of various sizes designed by Sir Edward Burne-Jones, and woven in 1894 by Martin, Taylor, Sleath, Ellis, Knight and Keich, for W. K. D'Arcy of Stanmore Hall, west of London (*see* 70 below). The theme of the set was the quest for the Holy Grail. The set was sold by Sotheby's in 1920 to the Duke of Westminster and, in the same salerooms, the Earl Grosvenor, the Duke's heir, sold three tapestries of the set on 20 April 1978, for £104000. Between 1881 and 1927 over 60 sets of hangings or panels were woven at Merton Abbey; several were so popular that copies were ordered. Notable among copies (in addition to the *Holy Grail* set) were: *St George* (designer: Sir Edward Burne-Jones; woven 1887; repeated 1895); *The Adoration* (Burne-Jones; 1890; 1895, 1900, 1901, 1902, 1904, 1907); *Angeli Laudantes* (Burne-Jones and Dearle: 1894; 1898, 1902, modified version 1904, 1905); and *Flora* (Burne-Jones; 1896; 1898, 1900, 1904, 1915, 1920).

The Dovecot Studio at Corstorphine and the Edinburgh Tapestry Company

A legend has been published often that the third Marquess of Bute consulted William Morris as to how a new tapestry workshop should be set up. A

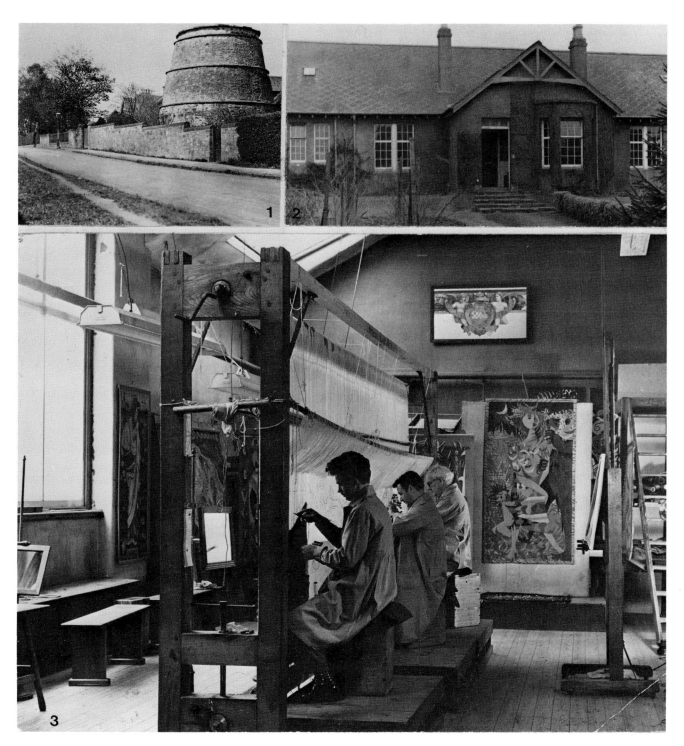

booklet published by the Scottish Committee of the Arts Council of Great Britain, *The Jubilee of the Dovecot Tapestries 1912-62*, states: 'On the death of the Marquess it fell to his son to carry out the plan.' Research has failed to unearth any evidence to support the legend, which has been queried by several historians who were dubious about the likelihood of the third Marquess seeking advice from a man who had so loudly criticized the Royal Windsor Tapestry Manufactory. But referring to unpublished family records, the author is convinced the meeting did take place, probably at the South Kensington

Museum in the presence of its director, and with William George Thomson (1865–1942) as an additional consultant.

Morris died in October 1896 and Henry Dearle took over artistic direction of the Merton Abbey workshops. Except for difficulties caused by the First World War, the increased urbanization of the immediate surroundings and the adoption of a few improvements in technique, production of tapestries continued much as in Morris's time until 1940, when the Second World War caused closure. No attempt was made to open the works again, or to continue Morris's distinctive style as a particular form of art.

Here it is necessary to give a brief account of how William Thomson came to be involved with tapestry. He was born at Roman Camp Cottage, a gatehouse on the Gordon Castle estates at Fochabers, by the Spey river, in Scotland's northern province of Morayshire, and at three years of age was lamed by poliomyelitis. Consequently, after matriculating from Milne's High School (founded and endowed by Alexander Milne, an emigrant Fochaberian who had made a fortune in cotton in New Orleans) he chose to study at Gray's School of Art in Aberdeen to be an artist. From Aberdeen he won scholarships successively to London's Royal School of Art, and to Paris and Madrid. His first encounter with tapestry was when, as a small boy who had just discovered how much his paralysed legs would impede his mobility, his father's employer —the first Duke of Richmond and Gordon—gave him a Gordon Castle tapestry-covered chair to console him, and his maternal grandmother drew his attention to the tapestry by telling him of her memories of the magnificent and romantic wall-hangings she had seen during her student days in Leyden, from whence she had returned to her native Aberdeenshire to be one of Scotland's first qualified midwives. (The former Gordon Castle chair was auctioned in the early 1970s by Parke Bernet in New York, from the home of Professor J. C. Thomson of Pennsylvania.) While studying art in Paris and Madrid William Thomson had been captivated by the colourful design and beauty of Gothic tapestries. Finding there was no comprehensive book in the English language on the subject of tapestry, he determined to write one. In pursuit of this aim he taught himself the Flemish and Basque languages to facilitate translation of archaic documents and, acting as a commission agent in the purchase of tapestries and ancient Hispano-Moresque carpets for clients, he travelled widely in Europe to research information for his manuscript. He returned to London in 1893 to seek work that would support him while he wrote the book.

Before the advent of colour photography the South Kensington Museum employed artists to make precise coloured reproductions of items that the Museum wished to record. Thomson was appointed to make coloured drawings of tapestries, and concurrently was appointed an Examiner in Art by the Board of Education (now the Ministry of Education and Science). He found lodgings in Bute Street, close to the South Kensington Museum and District Railway station, thinking it was more homelike to live in a street named after a Scottish noble family. He could not have dreamed the name would have greater significance for him in the years to come. A meeting with William Morris was inevitable. They were both examiners in Art and one of Morris's first commissions had been work for the Museum, to which he had given a model high-warp loom (*see* 2). Thomson set about making renewed contacts with all who might be in a position to progress his manuscript. He knew several Merton Abbey weavers, including John Martin and Mrs Jean Orage, an acquaintanceship which later resulted in him being accused of having tried to entice some Merton weavers to join the Dovecot Tapestry Workshop near Edinburgh. A letter written by the Merton Abbey Workshop's manager, H. C. Marillier, and published in *The Times* proved Thomson to be innocent; the enticer was the new workshop's designer, Skeoch Cumming.

From the start of his work at South Kensington, Thomson received repeated offers of employment from tapestry workshops in the United States. His reply was always the same: he would remain in London to complete the manuscript of his book. *A History of Tapestry* was published in 1906, and was accorded high commendation. The first comprehensive book in the English language on the subject, it enabled English-speaking people to study tapestry in depth for the first time. Thomson moved to 'Holly Cottage' (now number 62) High Street, Hampton, to be nearer Hampton Court Palace, where he was working on tapestries. Largely as a result of friendship with the Palace's superintendent, Mr Chart, Thomson was instrumental in helping to establish— with Miss Louise Chart and Miss Elizabeth H. Tann—one of the first commercial tapestry repair workshops. The premises at first were in Mr Chart's house in the Palace Yard, and then in the nearby town of Surbiton.

From about 1909, the fourth Marquess of Bute had employed an Edinburgh artist, Skeoch Cumming, to make designs for tapestries. By 1910 sufficient progress had been made for the Marquess to order the building of a workshop on a plot of land near the centre of the ancient village of Corstorphine, 8km (5 miles) west of Edinburgh, on the modern A8 trunk road. The old dovecot at one side of the plot had provided eggs and meat for the inhabitants of the once mighty castle of the Forresters, but the last vestiges of the Castle had disappeared in 1878. A French descendant of the Forresters wrote of the castle:

J'ai visité Corstorphin en 1875; il ne reste de l'ancien Corstorphin House que la base d'une vieille tour massive qui s'élève encore d'une vingtaine de pieds . . . non loin de l'Eglise de Corstorphin.

Thomson was appointed by the Marquess of Bute to the position of Organizer and first Director of Weaving of the Dovecot Tapestry Workshop at Corstorphine, and moved there in 1911 to supervise the new building and its equipping. From the sketches he had made at the Gobelins and elsewhere, he made drawings of the high-warp looms for the workshop and arranged with a local carpenter to make them. He set about the task of finding weavers, local suppliers of materials, and attracting apprentices. It was a daunting challenge to build up from nothing, in that small village with no tradition of handwoven tapestry, an enterprise that demanded the selfless devotion of very specialized and highly skilled craftsmen. Britain had very few suitably expert weavers.

From the tower of Corstorphine Parish Church, built in the fifteenth century on the site of a twelfth century religious foundation, a flame had burned from sundown to sunset for more than 300 years until 1769, to guide travellers across the treacherous marshes thereabouts. One might well ask: what better place could there have been to rekindle the romance and warmth of Scottish tapestry crafts than by a former swamp, symbolic of those in warmer climes some 400000 years before, by the side of which prehistoric man had mastered the art of making the first crude tapestry, by intertwining rushes about a framework of reeds or saplings?

The head weaver designate, John Glassbrook, arrived from Merton Abbey on 16 January 1912, and set about the task of dressing the looms. Gordon Berry, also from the Merton Workshop, arrived a little later and was appointed Master Weaver. Contrary to what has been published elsewhere, it must now be said that neither Glassbrook nor Berry were trained by William Morris. They would have been only 13 or 14 years old at the time of his death in 1896 and were not named as weavers at Merton Abbey until 1906. Apprentices Wood and Anderson signed on in July 1912, and apprentices Richard Gordon and Ronald Cruickshank in January 1913. Skeoch Cumming continued as the designer. The Marquess of Bute exercised overall control as the Managing Director. Initially the enterprise was called the Dovecot Tapestry Workshop, or Studios, with an occasional lapse into the Scottish 'Doo'cot', of Corstorphine. The earliest surviving document is a receipt, which fixes the date business started; not in 1912, as has been widely publicized previously:

Received from the Most Noble the Marquess of Bute, the sum of £500 (Five Hundred Pounds), to establish a banking account to meet cost of Loom, Materials, and other expenses in connection with the tapestry to be woven at Corstorphine.

W. G. Thomson 9th Oct. 1911.

As the outline of the first tapestry was transferred from the cartoon to the warp threads, Thomson reflected on the chain of circumstances that had brought him—a Thomson kinsman descendant of the Sir Adam Forrester who had built Corstorphine Castle and had died there on 13 October 1405—to Corstorphine to re-establish tapestry-weaving in Scotland. If a Lord Chamberlain of Scotland and Keeper of the Great Seal had regarded Corstorphine as a good place to found a dynasty which survived for ten generations, then surely this was a good omen for the Dovecot Tapestry Studios?

A tapestry measuring 404 × 986cm (13ft 3in × 32ft 4in) made of wool and with a texture of 7 w/cm (18 w/in) was to be the first project. The title was *The Lord of the Hunt,* and the scene was a Highland stag hunt of old, rich in detail of dress, arms, hounds, horses and the wild life of Scottish moor and forest. Surely a most ambitious piece to inaugurate weaving by a group who had not worked as a team before! Great care was taken to ensure accuracy of detail of every feature depicted. Preparation of the design and cartoon involved countless revisions; a considerable library of reference works was compiled to check and cross-check the historical accuracy of all features. The main loom, and the smaller apprentice-training loom, were warped up by mid-March 1912, and weaving started. Almost immediately there were difficulties in translating the design in terms of tapestry. The weavers were obliged to unpick what they had woven the day before, or they had to wait until the designer decided how a detail should be represented, or until he caught up with their progress. Although Skeoch Cumming is widely credited with having designed *The Lord of the Hunt* tapestry, there is reason to think he learned the arts of tapestry designer —and rather belatedly found that an artist is not automatically a tapestry designer—as a result of his association with weaving the Dovecot's first tapestry. There is evidence that William Thomson, who was both a qualified and experienced artist and tapissier, was obliged to undertake considerable redesign in order to translate Cumming's ideas into a weavable form. There is some evidence that he did far more than interpret Cumming for, in truth,

Plate 45 (*opposite above*) *Peter and the Wolf* is a lovely tapestry designed and woven by Gabriella Hajdal in her Budapest studio. The theme is based on an old story (*Gabriella Hajdal, Budapest; photograph Karoly Szelenyi*)

Plate 46 (*opposite below*) The tapestries of Jan Hladik surely demonstrate finally that the secret of good tapestry is a combination of imaginative design brilliantly executed and then woven by a master of the craft. *The Message* (left) dates from 1974–5 and measures 270 × 230cm (8ft 10½in × 7ft 6½in). *Marie* (right was woven in 1975 and measures 275 × 195cm (9ft × 6ft 6¾in) (*Jan Hladik, Prague*)

Plate 47 Contemporary Swiss tapestry design and workmanship is illustrated in this panel from the loom of Moik Schiele. The numerous colour changes and the geometrical accuracy necessary to produce the design must have made *All IV* exceptionally difficult to weave. Exhibited at the Jacques Baruch Gallery in Chicago, this 200 × 200cm (6ft 6¾in × 6ft 6¾in) hanging of cotton, wool, silk, linen and synthetic fibres has a texture of 2 w/cm (5 w/in) (*Moik Schiele* SWB W.C.C, *Textilements, Zurich*)

Plate 48 This 'documentary' tapestry by the Polish designer and weaver Stefan Poplawski was inspired by the international statesmen's meeting in Helsinki in 1975 and is characteristic of the style this tapissier has evolved, with considerable distinction. Measurements are 178 × 309cm (5ft 10in × 10ft 1½ in); warp is linen and weft is sisal (*Stefan Poplawski, Poznan, Poland*)

Plate 49 Japanese contemporary handwoven textiles emphasize fibre manipulation more than pictorial representations. *R-2* tapestry wall-covering in the Obayashi Building Office was designed and woven in 1974 by Mihoko Matsumoto. Materials are cotton and wool. Measurements are 190 × 700cm (6ft 3in × 23ft). The thick vertical warps are bound concentrically with wool thread to give the design in white, and contrast to the coloured parts. Lower and upper parts of the hanging are plain weave with knotting. Simple in plan, the total effect is arresting and elegant (*Mihoko Matsumoto Atelier, Nara, Japan*)

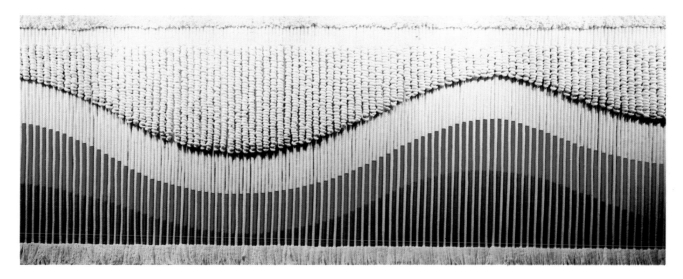

Plate 50 *Trees and Flowers,* one of the Wassef products. When Ramses Wissa inaugurated tapestry-weaving instruction among the boys and girls of Harrania, near Cairo, he could scarcely have dreamt that their inspired designs and fabrics would receive world acclaim (*Werner Forman Archive and Studio Ramses Wissa Wassef, Egypt*)

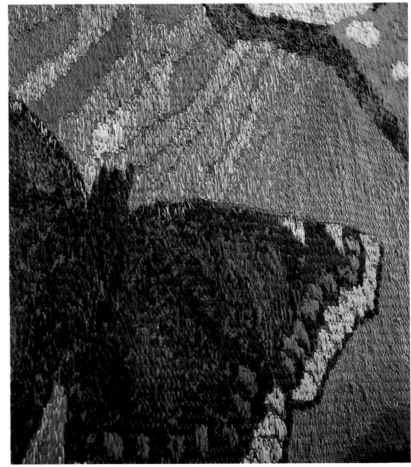

Plate 51 Swedish tapestry designer, weaver and lecturer, Hans Krondahl, spends his holidays at his cottage deep in the forest and countryside of southern Sweden, where he draws inspiration for design motifs. Shown here is a detail of one of his recent hangings, commissioned for the restful décor of a military research establishment. (*Hans Krondahl, Brösarp, Sweden*)

Thomson was better qualified to design a tapestry and especially one depicting a Scottish hunt. His boyhood had been spent on the Gordon Castle estates where his father was the chief gamekeeper to the first Duke of Richmond and Gordon; there was little Thomson did not know about the customs of lords of the hunt, and of the habits of animals and birds of Scottish forests and moors! A succession of letters written to him by the Marquess of Bute emphasize the continuing problem of design, and also hint at some of Cumming's personal problems (*see* 74). Another letter written by the Marquess to Thomson, dated 19 September 1913, from Dumfries House, Old Cummock, Ayrshire, states: 'The matter of getting new designs executed seems to me an important difficulty.' The Marquess wrote on 4 October 1914 from Edinburgh:

> I am bound to say I am much disappointed by the design being in such an unfinished state all through. What is best to be done one scarcely knows. It is obvious that the weavers must be losing heart under the obvious fact that the new designs cannot be forthcoming after the completion of the present one, and when that time is reached they will be left to seek another apprenticeship. I cannot help thinking it would be best to put off the weavers until more of the design was done—but of course they would have to be put off on full pay.

As stated previously, the reason given for making a start in 1910 on the building of the tapestry workshop was that Cumming's designs were sufficiently advanced to warrant it. So why were the weavers repeatedly being held up for want of designs as late as October 1914? *The Lord of the Hunt* was not completed and cut from the loom until 1924, so the Marquess's comment could scarcely refer to anything else than *The Lord of the Hunt* tapestry. The author has always understood that his father was obliged to produce a workable design— possibly based partly on Cumming's sketches—which could be interpreted in terms of the tapestry-weaver's palette and skills. The painting reproduced as Plate 28 depicts the right side of *The Lord of the Hunt* tapestry of 75. The painting was made by the author's father in Corstorphine and is very likely part of the original for the tapestry.

The Dovecot workshop closed in 1916 following mobilization of the weavers to fight in the First World War. John Glassbrook and Gordon Berry were killed in battle and are commemorated on the War Memorial by Corstorphine's old Parish Church. But they are remembered in another place, too. There are three Merton Abbey tapestries in the north aisle of the Henry VII Chapel in Westminster Abbey; the panel depicting *Edward the Confessor* was partly woven by Glassbrook. The panel depicting *Henry II* was woven in 1911 by Berry, Glassbrook and Martin.

Richard Gordon and David Anderson replaced Berry and Glassbrook as Head Weavers when the workshops re-opened in 1919. Scottish wool supplies were short and eventually the Gobelins in Paris provided supplies. In 1923, Dovecot weavers visited the Gobelins manufactory. The following is quoted from a letter written by David Anderson, on about 23 June 1923, to the Marquess of Bute's secretary, Captain Alexander Rawlinson:

> At the Gobelins, where we received a courteous welcome from the director and a fine reception from the tapissiers, we learned a great deal.
> The head tapissier proved to be a very artistic fellow, and as our visit was as interesting to them as the Gobelins was to us, we practically spent all the daytime for a week with them. Their interest in the Scottish tapestry, especially on

learning of its size, was very acute. It is bigger than any of the numerous pieces on which they are at present engaged.

They, of course, have hundreds of years of tradition behind them, and the process now is just the same as it was in the seventeenth century, but the designs are comparatively poor and in most cases not suited to tapestry.

Their dyeing establishment which is of course on the premises and is necessarily the finest possible, dyes fourteen thousand different shades of colour. The dyer himself, with whom I became friendly, has offered concessions both in the supply of wool and dyes, and silk and dyes, which I think could entirely alter our system of buying dyes from London which are not up to the Gobelins standard, and at a cheaper cost.

There are one or two things which I should like to show to Lord Bute, on our tapestry, which in the future can make our work even better still.

Our visit to Paris was simply invaluable, as we noted practically everything without let or hindrance, and I think our future dyes, which is a vital question, are sure to be, at any rate superior to the ones which we are at present using. As far as designs go, I am glad to say that neither historically or in grandeur, can any of the Gobelins designs approach our 'Lord of the Hunt', and with a continuance of those fine historical cartoons we should soon be on the way to becoming foremost in the tapestry world.

William Thomson broke his connexion with the Dovecot Studios in 1919, and moved to live in Hampstead, London, following the proposal that he should head a tapestry-weaving and training workshops complex to instruct and give congenial employment to hundreds of war-disabled ex-members of the fighting services. This magnificent plan had widespread support but was wrecked on the rocks of parliamentary politics. Then came an approach from America through his brother, James C. Thomson (of the Continental Illinois National Bank and Trust Corporation, of Chicago), inviting him to head a tapestry manufactory and concurrently to advise a consortium of antique collectors in the United States. But by the early 1920s his second book, *Tapestry Weaving in England from the earliest times until the end of the eighteenth century* (published in 1915), was making calls on his time in the capacity of a consultant. One of his principal clients was the Viscount Curzon of Kedleston who, despite his responsibilities as Secretary for Foreign Affairs in the ultrasensitive climate of the post-war world, kept up a continuous correspondence regarding the Curzon family's tapestries at Montacute and elsewhere.

Until the Second World War forced the closure of the Dovecot Studios in 1940, weaving of monumental tapestries continued and included *The Duchess of Gordon*, *The Prayer for Victory*, *The Time of the Meeting* and *The Prince of the Gael*, the designs for which are all attributed to Skeoch Cumming; *The Admiral Crichton* and *Verdure Piece* designs are attributed to Alfred Priest. *The Prince of the Gael* hanging was not completed. With *The Lord of the Hunt*, all these tapestries remain the property of the Marquess of Bute. A rather astonishing comment on them was published in the brochure commemorating the Jubilee of the Dovecot Studios in 1962, and published by the Scottish Committee of the Arts Council of Great Britain:

Fashions change and these tapestries appear closer to the eighteenth and nineteenth centuries when there was often a danger of the weaver imitating the qualities of oil painting and producing a textile that was neither good painting nor good tapestry. They remain, nevertheless, fine examples of weaving craftsmanship.

7 April. 1914.

Dear Mr Thomson

We got back again about 10 days ago. I found a letter from Lady Cowdray asking about the tapistry and saying she would like some made for her house — I think in Scotland. I wrote to her that at present we were unable to take on other work, but that I hoped to be able to do so in time. How is the work getting on? and is my

portrait finished? I fear I cannot get North before th 3 of May when I intend going to Edinburgh to see the Tapistry. Mr Cumming is I hope well to the fore. Any thoughts of excuse or feelings of compassion that I may ever have had towards him in his times of trouble have now entirely ceased to exist. I have myself abstained

for many weeks from both smoking and drinking! Yours sincerely

Bute

---

6 May. 1915.

Dear Mr Thomson

About the gold weaving — You say you could not with the green alone get sufficient difference between the flowers and the leaves, but this does not matter as we would never in a real border be doing flowers. You have taken some flowers as subject for this trial but my suggestion

was a partridge. It does not matter what is now woven — but what we want to ascertain is the amount of any particular colour necessary when it is being used alone with gold. I suppose gold and blue go best but we were trying gold and green because they

seemed the most difficult to deal with. A border of red and gold but having more red than gold in it would I think be good round a dark panel.

Yours sincerely

Bute

I enclose a specimen of coloured velum I have got. Please let me

know what you think of them. I am much taken by the last orange coloured one. Velum seems at all events to take colour well.

74 Two letters written by the fourth Marquess of Bute to W.G. Thomson (*Author's copyright*)

The writer of these criticisms remained anonymous, and presumably did not know of the immense difficulties which attended the establishment of the Studios, nor was he in a position to make any allowances for the continuing design difficulties which marred at least the early years.

These seven tapestries remain important because they mark the end of a period when a devoted patron of the arts could afford to commission great hangings which, until then, reflected all that was best and most noble in 'the elegant art'. They are on one side of the watershed dividing tapestries conforming to certain widely accepted standards of professional excellence, materials and texture from those on the other side, composed of various constructions, materials and textures which in some degree may qualify as 'tapestry'. It would be a barren exercise to compare physically dissimilar objects unless allowances are made for the differences. So one might just as well compare a painting by Rembrandt with a *Punch* cartoon as try to compare these seven tapestries with many in the modern idiom. A gifted weaver, provided he is permitted to exercise his abilities and make his own interpretations, can do more than produce an imitation of an oil painting. Loose use of the term 'tapestry' to describe many things makes re-definition of 'tapestry' most urgent.

When weaving started again at the Dovecot in 1946 the Marquess of Bute was compelled to relinquish control through ill-health. A management board was appointed composed of his brother, Lord Colum Crichton-Stuart; two of

172

75 *The Lord of the Hunt* tapestry. Weaving this magnificent hanging was the first task when the Dovecot Studios started work in 1912; it was not completed until 1924 (*The Most Hon. the Marquess of Bute*)

his sons, Lord Robert Crichton-Stuart and Lord David Crichton-Stuart; and his younger daughter, Lady Jean Bertie. The name of the enterprise was changed to the Edinburgh Tapestry Company Limited. Ronald Cruickshank was appointed Manager and Head Weaver, Richard Gordon and John Louttit were appointed Master Weavers, and young apprentices were engaged. And so, almost concurrently, the post-war fervour for reform and improvement which had so much motivated Jean Lurçat and his friends in France had an equally energetic counterpart in Scotland. Prominent artists were commissioned to make designs, and they were given help in converting their skills to the best advantage in terms of the tapissier's 'palette'. Tapestries were woven to the design of Edward Bawden CBE, RA, Sir Cecil Beaton CBE, Sir Frank Brangwyn RA, Louis le Brocquy, Sir Stephen Gooden CBE, RA, John Maxwell RSA, Henry Moore OM, Michael Rothenstain, Sax Shaw (who grew so enthusiastic that he wove his own designs), Sir Stanley Spencer CBE, RA, Graham Sutherland OM, Sir Francis Rose (Artistic Advisor (1948–50)), Julian Trevelyan, and many more. Clients included members of the British royal family and the nobility, American and British state and national bodies, commercial and industrial enterprises, churches, foundations and individuals. By the end of 1953 some 84 pieces had been woven, including a few rugs. Texture varied from 3·9 to 6 w/cm (10 to 15 w/in) except for rugs with about 1·79 to 2 w/cm (4 to 5 w/in). Sizes ranged from about 269 × 223·5cm (8ft 10in ×

7ft 4in) to chairbacks and other small pieces of about 56 × 53cm (1ft 10in × 1ft 9in). Tapestries included *The Wine Press* (*see* Plate 29), the *Arms of Queen Elizabeth the Queen Mother, The Tinkers, The Lion and the Oak Tree, The Fighting Cocks, Farming, The Garden of Fools, Stein Carpet* and *Watered Rug.*

Ronald Cruickshank resigned from the Edinburgh Tapestry Company in 1952 to start his Golden Targe tapestry workshop in Edinburgh. Subsequently he received so many inquiries from the United States that he emigrated there to help the America Crafts Movement to stabilize its programmes of instruction and weaver workshops. Richard Gordon was appointed Manager and Head Weaver at the Dovecot in Cruickshank's place, and continued in this responsible position until his retirement in 1963. He had by then worked at the Dovecot Studios for 50 years (barring the two periods of closure between 1916–19 and 1940–6). In 1979, Richard Gordon was Britain's oldest and most experienced tapissier, living out a happy retirement in his native city of Edinburgh, linking the old with the new in his continuing interest in tapestry.

The Bute family's connexion with the Edinburgh Tapestry Company ceased in 1954, when it passed under the control of Messrs. John Noble and Harry Jefferson-Barnes. The position of designer, which had been held by Sax Shaw, was combined with Archie Brennan's continuing position of Master Weaver, and it fell to him to broaden the range of designs and weaving techniques that would reflect more fully the modern idiom in tapestry development.

Never a large organization, nor sited in pretentious buildings, the Dovecot Studios have nonetheless exerted a profound influence on twentieth century art, architecture, textile industries and the social scene. It is necessary to emphasize most strongly that the Studios' success is the result of the sum total of faith, energy, devotion, inspiration and loyalty contributed by a relatively small group of extremely gifted and imaginative people, all of whom were determined that Scotland should nurture one of the most intellectually rewarding of all the arts. But without the vision and initiative of the fourth Marquess of Bute, it is certain that Britain today would not be counted among the founding pioneers or producers of magnificent handwoven tapestries. There can be no praise too high for the sacrifice and courage of the Bute family, which kept the Dovecot Studios alive during the difficult 1912–54 period.

The Poland Street Workshop

It is most important that several tapestries with a Scottish motif, designed by Mr Sacheverall-Coke and made between 1897 and the early twentieth century in London's Soho, in Poland Street, should not be mistaken for Dovecot tapestries. Established by former Royal Windsor Tapestry Manufactory weavers from Aubusson under the direction of one of their number, Michel Brignolas, the Soho atelier made tapestries for a Scottish clan chief, including a *History of the Clan MacIntosh, Tragedy of the Bog-na-Gicht, Lady MacIntosh raising the Clan for Prince Charles Edward, Combat on the North Inch, Perth* and *Treachery of the Cummings.*

The Kensington Weavers

During the first half of the twentieth century the Kensington Weavers were active above a handicrafts shop in Kensington Church Street, in west London, but closed about 1960. The weaver-directors were K. Grasset and Maggie Thomas. Two tapestries are in the Museum of London.

Contemporary Tapestry

During the second half of the twentieth century tapestry-weaving in Britain

174

has been encouraged by the British Crafts Council and various educational bodies. Only time will tell how many products from these looms will be accorded lasting appreciation. Among the few really brilliant professional designer-weavers may be included: Dorothy Ablett, Mary A. Auty, Hilda Breed, Peter Collingwood, Elizabeth P. Hamilton, David Holbourne, Pat Holtom, G. Burnett, Eta Ingham-Mohrhardt, Gerald Laing, James J. More, Tom Phillips, Maggie Riegler, Miriam Sacks. Eleanor Scarfe, Dorothy E. Urquhart and Crissie W. H. White.

There is need for stability in the definition of 'tapestry'. Otherwise genuine tapissiers sometimes are obliged by popular demand to design and weave things that often are more eye-catching than truly artistic, more examples of lazy or careless construction than planned new forms of expression, more a failure to learn and employ all the techniques of design and weaving than to produce a fabric worthy of 'the elegant art'. The day may not be far distant when the British Advertising Standards Authority, or its counterpart in other countries, is required to arbitrate on the veracity of an advertisement for 'tapestry'. In recent years the public has been induced to pay to visit exhibitions of 'tapestry' composed of draped, suspended, coiled, folded, piled or layered rope, cord, twine or yarn, chair-seat or hessian webbing and strips of plastic or seaweed; also, folded, pleated, or shaped and sewn pieces of paper, plastic, tree-bark, cardboard, wood-shavings, papier mâché and machine-made fabrics; or pastiches of weavers' bobbins, match-sticks, cigarette-ends, balls of wool heaped or scattered against a wood, fabric, metal, plastic or frozen-fluid and continually refrigerated backing; also, what appears to be bags made of ordinary commercial sackcloth sewn into huge or weird shapes and then stuffed, or inflated with balloons, and piled up randomly in heaps or suspended. There has also been an exhibition called 'tapestry' of commercial sackcloth cut into the outline of human forms, and then puckered by drawing some of the threads, to resemble the appearance of a decaying corpse.

And what has been the public's reaction to this interpretation of 'tapestry'? To answer, one should recall Hans Christian Anderson's story of the emperor who was persuaded by the court tailors to order an excellent suit of very modern clothes; the best his empire had seen! When the clothes arrived, the emperor dressed himself in them and set forth in procession through his country. And as the procession passed by the people who had gathered to see him in his finery were, at first, struck dumb with amazement, and then applauded madly. They had never seen such exquisite clothes! And so the procession continued, with the crowds remarking on the magnificence of their emperor's new clothes until a small boy, who was in the front line of the spectators, turned to his mother, and with a puzzled look on his face asked, 'Why is the Emperor naked, Mummy?'

The truth is that the public is easily misled, particularly with respect to contemporary art. A book which could include all 'off-beat' interpretations of 'tapestry' would have to be many times the size of this book, so let us study tapestry woven in the traditional way but designed in the modern idiom, and show charity towards those whose work proves that embellishment with other art-forms enhances effect or beauty.

In conclusion, it is worth recording that one of several reasons for the closure of the Royal Windsor Tapestry Manufactory in December 1890 was that orders started to fall off when the Victorian campaign for cleanliness got under way, and it was found that tapestries were very difficult both to keep clean and to clean when dirty. Not a few contemporary hangings may have a short life unless owners discover a miraculous way to clean them, or are prepared to tolerate them as they gather dust!

Bibliography
Cullingham, G. *The Royal Windsor Tapestry Manufactory*. Historical Records Series published by the Royal Borough of Windsor and Maidenhead, Windsor (1979)
Marillier, H. C. *History of the Merton Abbey Tapestry Works*. Constable, London (1927)
Morris & Co. *The Merton Abbey Arras Tapestries*. A catalogue (1906)
Thomson, W. G. *A History of Tapestry*. E. P. Publishing Co. (1973)

Acknowledgements
It is appropriate to make acknowledgement at the end of this chapter to the following persons who kindly provided special information for consideration and without whose help it would have been impossible to give so much historical detail: Murray Adams-Acton, Miss C. Armet, Mrs L. Bardner, Archie Brennan, Mrs J. Chaplin, Miss L. Chart, Gordon Cullingham, Richard Gordon, Fiona Mathison, the Baron Nelson of Stafford, Mrs Jean Orage, John H. C. Piper, Sax Shaw, Dr J. C. Thomson, Hans Tisdall, and Miss F. and Miss H. Webster.

7 A Century of World Tapestry Renaissance

The late nineteenth century revival of interest in tapestry weaving that stimulated the establishment of the Royal Windsor Tapestry Manufactory, and the design revisionist activities of William Morris of the Merton Abbey Workshops, had a counterpart in several countries, particularly following widespread publication of the weaving philosophies propounded by Morris. The Frenchmen from Aubusson who had helped the Windsor Manufactory to come into existence had many friends at home who were eager to find work in more promising places, and who looked further afield than to the British Isles. They knew from relatives and friends who had gone before to set up looms in Italy Germany, the Scandinavian countries and so on that any true master of the art of dyeing and of weaving, who could grow or find the plants that give the primary dyes of blue, red and yellow, and also the metallic salts required for mordants, and who could take wool from animals or plants and spin it into thread, was certain of a welcome in many lands. They knew that, given lodgings and the basic materials, a good design and a trustworthy loom, they could create lovely furnishings for a lordly castle or a stately home, and continue to delight their patron.

The Development of Tapestry in North America

The hard life imposed on early settlers and shortages of wool and other raw materials shut out both the opportunity to weave or to purchase fringe luxuries such as tapestry. By the latter part of the nineteenth century there were individuals with the means to purchase pieces from abroad, such as Mr Pope of Cleveland, Ohio, who purchased the *Goose Girl* from the looms of William Morris in England. His outspoken criticism of contemporary décor strongly influenced the eventual back-to-the-crafts movement in America, and encouraged people like Louis Comfort Tiffany of New York to specialize in high quality components for domestic furniture and décor. Towards the end of the century some ethnic groups were starting to revive native homeland crafts including Swedish rya and other tapestry weaves.

The United States of America

The display of Royal Windsor Tapestry Manufactory hangings at the Chicago World Fair in 1893 boosted the American Crafts Movement and, at the same time, persuaded William Baumgarten of New York to capitalize on the new national interest by importing looms from France, appointing as his master weaver the French-born former Windsor employee J. Foussadier, inducing Aubusson weavers to cross the Atlantic, and establishing a manufactory at 321 Fifth Avenue, New York City in 1893. Baumgarten's first trial tapestry, a chair-seat cover, is in the Art Institute of Chicago collection. A year later he moved to former hotel premises at Williamsbridge by the Bronx river, which then had clear water suitable for his dyeworks, and almost immediately received his first major order. Mr P. A. Widenner of Philadelphia required a suite of 13 hangings, portières and chair-coverings in the style of François Boucher, the

inspector of the Gobelins (1755–70). This order established Baumgarten as a master tapissier who made magnificent copies of the best European tapestries of the eighteenth and early nineteenth centuries. Orders were showered on him by America's leading families and state institutions, such as the Rhode Island State House, where tapestries from his looms are still. But from soon after 1904, when he was awarded the highest honour of the St Louis Exposition, his business declined, and it closed in 1912. A tapestry woven by Baumgarten's first American apprentice is in the Metropolitan Museum of Art. Members of the Foussadier family continued weaving until about 1925.

Competition for Baumgarten came in the person of Albert Herter (1871–1950) who had studied and worked at the Gobelins Manufactory and was trained by Jean-Paul Laurens. Herter idolized the Gothic style and admired William Morris. As well as being a first-rate tapestry designer, he was a good businessman who exploited his idea that Americans' innate nationalism would make them acutely interested in Gothic-style tapestries depicting important events in American history; he knew that Morris's back-to-Gothic-simplicity campaign had made a favourable impression on the American arts intelligentsia.

The Herter looms, called initially the 'Aubusson Looms', were established in 1908 on New York City's East 33rd Street. Weavers were brought from France, and Herter designed and wove a number of Gothic-style samples to demonstrate the contrast with the heavy and pompous classical style favoured by Baumgarten. The Aubusson Looms flourished and one of the first large orders was for a set of hangings depicting the *History of New York* in 26 panels to be hung in New York's Hotel MacAlpin. The surviving 21 panels are now in the collection of the Metropolitan Museum of Art. Materials were wool, cotton, artificial and natural silk woven with a texture of 6·3 w/cm (16 w/in). Scenes include Henry Hudson's discovery of the Hudson River and the purchase of Manhattan in 1626. The Fine Arts Museums of San Francisco have a Herter hanging of a pirate ship, woven in 1913 and signed H.L. The Art Museum of Cranbrook Academy of Art has the *Great Crusade* (*see* 76). This hanging was commissioned by Mr G. C. Booth in 1918 and depicts people prominent in the fight for justice throughout history. Herter broke his connection with the Aubusson Looms in 1923, which moved to 841 Madison Avenue, New York and adopted the name of Herter Looms. The depression of the 1930s killed the demand for semi-luxury fabrics and the manufactory closed in 1933–4.

The third notable early twentieth century tapestry workshop was founded by Lorentz Kleisar at Edgewater, New Jersey, in 1913. Called the Edgewater Looms, it produced several impressive hangings but it also succumbed to the 1930s depression. Notable Edgewater hangings include one of the City of Newark in the nineteenth century, woven with vegetable-dyed wool and silk in 1925, and now displayed in Newark Museum. The Institute of Texan Culture, San Antonio, has an Edgewater hanging depicting Santa Anna's surrender to Houston, supported by a border depicting people prominent in the history of Texas.

The 1945–50 post-war back-to-the-crafts movement was as strong in the United States as in Europe. But it was soon found that the time had passed

77 Jean Lurçat's *Spirit of France* was woven at Aubusson during the darkest days of the Second World War. It suggests an attitude of defiance which could have brought him into conflict with the Nazi occupying forces (*California Palace of the Legion of Honour; gift of Mrs Marie Stauffer Sigall*)

when any medium-sized tapestry workshop could exist on a purely commercial basis; labour costs were too high. Survival of the tapissiers' art was, in future, to exist and be nurtured in many small workshops and guilds scattered throughout the United States, except for a few closely-knit ethnic and religious communities which regarded tapestry-weaving as part of their way of life. On the other hand, state and national authorities, often prodded by inspired architects, came to recognize tapestry as an important medium for the decoration of renovated or new buildings. At high level the idea increasingly took hold that tapestry was no longer just a picture on the wall, a way to fill an unsightly corner, a break in the architectural montony of a building, or a convenient but unobtrusive method of modifying the acoustics of an echoing building or room. Tapestry could be used for all of these purposes, admittedly. But it also had a definite place of its own in twentieth century art and architecture. It was to be an essential ingredient in the ergonomics of spatial relationship between man and his environment on the one hand and, on the other, an intellectual stimulant. Tapestry was not to be treated as a luxury for a few, but as the aesthetic composition of a hospital, school, public library, city hall, newspaper office, boardroom, bank, clubhouse and even crematorium (*see* Plate 30). Distinguished designer-weavers demonstrated that a purpose-designed hanging could be just as stimulating and visually satisfying as any of the archaic and magnificent 'Triumphs' series hanging in the New Tapestry Court of London's Victoria and Albert Museum. Moreover, it was shown that modern production methods placed purpose-designed tapestry within the bounds of economic price.

Among America's new tapissiers was Ronald Cruickshank (1898–1969), late of Edinburgh's Golden Targe Studios and, before that, Manager and Head Weaver of the Edinburgh Tapestry Company's Dovecot Studios at Corstorphine. His background included a stint as weaver at the Gobelins in Paris, involvement with the Scottish Century Guild that had promoted William Morris's design philosophy (founded in 1882 by Arthur H. MacMurdo (1851–1942)), and with the Aubusson-centred Association of Tapestry Painter-Designers. In Cruickshank's view the American Society of Tapestry Designers had exposed weaknesses of the nation's hand-weaving industry and its designers' position. He felt strongly that American designs should be woven by native weavers rather than sent abroad for execution, and he put his finger on weaknesses in the training of American weavers as much as on the failure by designers to orient their ideas towards what was practical in the workshop.

Cruickshank set up his high-warp loom in his new home in Louisiana in the early 1960s. His services were so much sought that he had difficulty in finding enough time to carry out commissions. He was an Associate Professor at the University of Southwestern Louisiana, a counsellor at workshops, and teacher at courses nation-wide. His great popularity and the demands made on him probably contributed to his untimely death within the decade. He was working at his home on the hanging illustrated in Plate 33 at the time of his death; the weaving was completed by his widow, Mrs Beatrice Cruickshank. One of his main teachings was that the combined physical properties of a tapestry coupled with its aesthetic appeal made it superior to sculpture and stained glass in architecture. He warned tapissiers to guard against American preoccupation with size, pop-art of the moment, and extravagance in weave, materials and texture. He believed that a tapestry should average about 152 ×

183cm (5 × 6ft), or not be larger than a competent weaver could complete within some 15 working weeks; anything much larger is likely to try the patience of the weaver, who should be spared risks of boredom, or exhaustion of his initial enthusiasm. The Cruickshank Tapestry Weavers of California and many other guilds carry on his teachings. Examples of his hangings are in several collections.

One hesitates a little before including the work of Swedish-born Helena Hernmarck in a section devoted to American tapestry. But this extraordinarily gifted artist-innovator-designer-weaver seems to have found her final home in New York City. Whilst still a student at Stockholm's School of Arts, Crafts and Design, Miss Hernmarck developed a design technique which gave her widespread recognition; one of her early pieces—*Beta*—is in Stockholm's Nationalmuseum. Before settling in New York she had studios in England and Canada. On arriving in America she concentrated her approaches on architects and interior decorators. She developed several techniques to reduce tapestry production costs, such as the photographic enlargement— however large the tapestry—of the cartoon in the form of a photocopy which shows the individual dots composing the original. She weaves on a Swedish low-warp loom 335cm (11ft) wide. Tapestries greater in height than this are woven as strips. Any slight variation in length between strips is taken up by pulling gently on the warps of one strip until both lengths are equal. The palette is restricted, with tint gradations obtained more by using weft strands of different thickness than by the use of different colours. Weft is usually wool but may include a shimmering acetate, acrylic, metallic or synthetic yarn. Warps are always linen. The dot-prints of the photostat cartoon laid under the warp are a guide—depending on their size and density—to the choice of weft thickness and weave technique to produce the required visual effect. The colour photograph of the design is always kept by the loom for reference.

The weaving technique is an ingenious combination of endless variations of

78 Honorata Blicharska, like Stefan Poplawski (*see* Plate 48) is a Polish tapissier who has experimented with portraits in tapestry. Her London exhibition in 1978 attracted much attention. *Patti Hansen* is a double impression in different tints (*Honorata Blicharska, Warsaw*)

tabby, basket, double or over-weave. Weft strands of different thickness but the same colour produce contrasts suggestive of deep and light colour. The tapestry surface undulates in thickness, and different weave types give emphasis. Miss Hernmarck says her techniques may be copied by others, but success depends almost entirely on their ability as designers and visual interpreters. Her very individual style has produced many commissions and include: *Bay Street in Toronto*, 1969 (in Los Angeles County Museum), *Steel 1*, 1973 (Bethlehem Steel Corporation), *Poppy Field* (Security Pacific National Bank), *Surfing* (Australian Mutual Provident Society, Melbourne), *The Rain Forest* (Messrs. Weyerhaeuser, Seattle) and *Sailing* (*see* Plate 34).

A large number of small workshops manned by one or two weavers are affiliated with national organizations which encourage tapestry, and there are also sponsoring organizations such as the National Endowment for the Arts which support individual artists. Vacation courses and workshops are numerous and several universities encourage outside ideas by appointing visiting foreigners to temporary posts. Prestigious artists are helped to design tapestries through the agency of an editor, who translates their cartoons in terms of a weaver's needs and commissions a workshop.

The Museum of International Folk Art at Santa Fé, New Mexico, has worked to revive traditional Spanish colonial textiles (*see* Plate 35). The author is indebted to Nora Fisher of this Museum for permission to quote the following from their Catalogue, which quotes from *The Primary Structure of Fabrics*, by Irene Emery:

The simplest possible interlacing of warp and weft elements produces plain weave. If the warp and weft elements are equally spaced and either identical or approximately equal in size and flexibility, the plain weave can be described as balanced. A number of the simple Rio Grande yardage fabrics are, or are thought to have been, balanced plain weave. If the wefts are sufficiently numerous and sufficiently compacted to completely cover the warps, the fabric is weft-faced. Differing from the yardage fabrics, the Rio Grande blankets are all weft-faced plain weave. The vast majority are woven with bands of weft stripes. Amongst this group of fabrics, a large percentage were woven double-width. Irene Emery has clearly explained this method which is used for weaving a wide fabric on a narrow loom:

'If the weft is continuous but always interweaves twice (over and back) with the warps of one layer before shifting to the other layer, the two layers of the fabric will be joined by the common weft only along one edge and, when removed from the loom, will spread flat and form a single simple-weave fabric double the width that was set up in the loom. Thus, it is only the construction method that is double, not the finished fabric. If the method of construction is known it is entirely reasonable to describe and classify such a fabric as double-woven, or as double-width.'

The double-woven weft-faced plain weave Rio Grande blankets can easily be identified for they are characterized by a group of heavier, paired warps at the exact center of the textile. The Rio Grande blankets which contain motifs are tapestry-woven. Irene Emery has this description of the technique:

'Weft-faced plain weave identifies the weave when it lacks the special characteristic of discontinuous-weft patterning. It is when that characteristic is added that weft-faced plain weave becomes tapestry weave. Tapestry weaving generally involves two fundamental principles: hiding the warp with closely packed wefts to secure solid colour, and weaving independent wefts back and forth each in its own pattern area.'

The latter quotation is a most valuable additional definition of tapestry. The following is quoted from the Catalogue's *Brief Introduction* by Dorothy Boyd Bowen:

> What we have come to term the Rio Grande blanket was the most commonly produced and widely distributed of the 19th-century New Mexican Spanish goods. It was woven in the settlements and ranches along the Rio Grande and its tributaries for three centuries, and was a staple of the economy as well as a necessity for survival . . . It was traded far south into Mexico, east into the United States, west to California, and in all directions to the Indians. . . . Blankets were intended for wearing during the day and for bedding at night. More complex designs based on the Saltillo Sarape do not have evidence of neck slits or wear at the center seam, which indicates they were wrapped around the shoulders, unlike many Mexican sarapes which were woven with neck slits to be pulled on over the head. . . . The typical Rio Grande blanket has the following physical characteristics: designs include wide bands and zones of narrow stripes, later with Saltillo sarape motifs introduced. Colors are the natural-undyed white and brown churro wool, combined with natural-dyed yarns including a great deal of indigo, yellow, madder, tiny areas of cochineal, and much reddish to golden tan. These textiles were woven on the narrow treadle loom either in two widths or in one width with multiple center warps, in either weft-faced plain weave or tapestry weave. Later weaves have wefts of short-staple Merino wool brilliantly colored with synthetic dyes.

It must be emphasized that these are Spanish Colonial textiles which, with the introduction from Spain of churro sheep, by Francisco Vasquez Coronado in 1540, upgraded Pueblo Indians' weaving compared with their pre-Conquest use of cotton and other vegetable fibres, which they wove on a vertical loom.

Canada

Despite the historical link between one of the Vice-Presidents of the Royal Windsor Tapestry Manufactory's Committee of 1877 and the Royal Canadian Academy of Arts, scant encouragement was given to tapestry until the second half of the twentieth century. From then the Royal Canadian Academy of Arts, founded in 1880 by HRH Princess Louise and Marquess of Lorne, more than made up for past omissions by establishing a small but select and powerful Society of Tapestry Designers and Weavers. This body has done much to impress governmental authorities at national and local level with the peculiar properties of tapestry and its place in architecture, the social environment and art. In fact, public appreciation is reaching a par with that displayed throughout the Scandinavian countries. But then, it might be argued, the warmth and colour of tapestry displayed in public buildings, commercial premises, industrial offices and the home, are a natural development which greatly help to counter the rigours and depressive effects of living in northern latitudes, where winters are long, bitterly cold with many hours of darkness and life on the outside bleak and rather colourless!

The tapestries chosen for illustration as typical of modern Canadian hangings are, by coincidence, all the work of women, which is another parallel with twentieth century tapestry production trends in Scandinavian countries. *Wings no. 2* designed and woven by Micheline Beauchemin is depicted in Plate 36. Woven in natural silk with a palette of 20 colours with five tints each of gold and silver, this beautiful panel has a texture of 3·9 w/cm (10 w/in). It hangs in the Canadian Embassy in Tokyo. Miss Beauchemin pioneered fire-resistant tapestry curtains for the stage of Ottawa's National Art Centre's

Opera House. Having seen how light is retained within the boundaries of round glass fibres—the sort used for multi-channel telephonic communication using fibre-optic technology—she had fibres of nylon made with a cross-section half-round and half-flat. Using fibres of this shape, spun into weft threads of several colours, she wove her 2 ton fire-resistant stage curtains, which scintillate like cut-glass. Her loom is represented by hangings in the following places: London's Kensington Town Hall, Montreal Airport, the School of Architecture in Winnipeg and Kansas City's Hallmark Center. Pieces are signed M.B. at the bottom, right corner, or on the reverse.

When Queen's University, Ontario, wished to commemorate the life and work of Dr John Deutsch, they commissioned Helen Frances Gregor to design and weave the hanging depicted by Plate 37. Called *Lifescape*, it measures 305 × 915cm (10 × 30ft) and symbolizes Dr Deutsch's academic eminence by incorporating his 17 academic hoods in geographical order across panels of woollen weave coloured to suggest Canada's arctic snows, the earth mosaic of the prairies, the colours of the Laurentian Shield and marine blues of the seas surrounding the land; metal bars symbolize Deutsch's industrial interests.

Lithuanian-born Canadian Mrs Anastasi Tamošaitis rather specializes in hangings that recall ancestral roots in the northern countries. Her *Trillium Hills*, depicted in Plate 39, was woven in 1970 on a high-warp loom and measures 183 × 244cm (6 × 8ft) with a texture of 5 w/cm (12·7 w/in), and an average of 18 wool weft yarns per cm (45·7 wy/in). Tapestries designed by her artist husband and woven by Mrs Tamošaitis often echo folklore or nature and include *Spring*, *Gardening*, *Rocks* and *Sunset*. A Tamošaitis tapestry hangs in Montreal City Hall.

South America

Various international agencies have attempted to revive tapestry weaving in the Andean mountain region, but with little success. South America's main source of tapestry is centred on the workshops of Brazil, where Genaro de Carvalho in Bahia, and Jacques Douchez with Norberto Nicola of São Paulo, are prominent. The latter has worked to create a Brazilian national style and has achieved considerable international recognition. *Lundu* or *Dance*, in Plate 38, is a typical Nicola workshop hanging, which reflects the multifarious moods, gestures, sounds, colours and scenes of South American folk dance. It measures 260 × 290cm (8ft 6in × 9ft 6in).

A few workshops have grown up round university-inspired schools of applied art, such as that of the University of Chile, or have been originated by European immigrants, as in Colombia and Argentina. Mexico City houses the Taller Nacional del Tapiz.

France

During the latter part of the nineteenth century French tapestry stagnated as a result of unimaginative administration of state manufactories. During the short life of England's Royal Windsor Tapestry Manufactory, the Gobelins in Paris was administered by Baudin (1860–71), provisionally by the chemist, Chevreul (1871), by the engineer, Alfred Darcel (1871–85), by Gerspach (1885), and by Jules Guiffrey (1885–1908). Gustave Geffroy (1908–26) was administrator when French artist-designers were so stirred by the teachings and weaving of William Morris in England that they were in a mood for revolution. The late nineteenth century production of the Gobelins included hangings for the high court of the palace at Rennes. Guiffrey commissioned Jean Paul

79 African plaited hair styles inspired this tapestry technique, originated by Swedish-German tapissiers working in Swaziland on a developing countries project (*R. and E. Brenner-Remberg, Mbabane, Swaziland*)

Laurens to make cartoons for the *Apotheosis of Colbert*, which was to be the widest tapestry then existing, 793 × 1283cm (26 × 42ft); it took six weavers six years to complete. Other subjects were *Duke Jean de Berri at Bourges* after Cormon, the *Godchild of the Fairies* by Mazerelle, *Ovid's Metamorphoses, Sujets de la Fable* by Albert Maignan and *Poet and Syren* by Gustave Moreau.

The Beauvais manufactory was directed by Pierre Adolphe Badin (1848–76), by Jules Diéterle (1876–82), by Jules Badin (1882–1918) and by Jean Ajalbert, who belatedly tried to improve the workers' conditions and work prospects. The first of a series of four hangings commemorating the *Victory of the Great War* after Anquetin was hung in the Musée des Invalides, Paris, in 1926.

During the first third of the twentieth century, Aubusson prospects deteriorated and manufactories closed. The Gobelins and Beauvais enterprises amalgamated under the name, 'Manufacture Nationale de Beauvais aux Gobelins', of Paris. And in 1933, Madam Marie Cuttoli attempted to halt the French tapestry industry's slow death by commissioning the greatest artists of the day to design tapestries. Despite the support of Picasso, Rouault, Braque, Derain, Dufy, Miró, Léger and Lurçat among others, all that emerged were picture-like tapestries more costly than the original painting! But influential attention had been drawn to the plight of tapestry. Miró and Lurçat continued their collaboration in search of a solution, and the latter collaborated with François Tabard, the master weaver of the long-established workshops at Aubusson of Tabard Frères et Soeurs. In 1939 the Ministry of National Education appointed the painter, Marcel Gromaire (1892–1971), and Jean Lurçat (1891–1966) officially to study, in association with Aubusson weavers, every possible means of re-establishing French tapestry production on a profitable and vigorous foundation. Despite the German occupation of France soon after, and the near-impossible living conditions at their working base in the village of La Creuse, Lurçat and his associates worked out a practical rationale for more economic design and weaving, as their first objective. Lurçat started by examining, classifying and coding the characteristics of materials used. He then reduced the number of colours and tones or shades to the basic variety essential for the palette of a competent weaver, and gave each one an identifying code that would be a standard for recognition purposes. He then formulated a set of standard instructions to facilitate communication between designer and weaver.

Like Morris, Lurçat admired the Gothic style of tapestry, and his next task was to set design guidelines that would break away from production of picture-like tapestries. He sought to create an art-form combining the vision of the designer with the inspirational interpretation of the weaver—to make tapestry a joint creation. With the eventual liberation of France, followed by peace in 1945, Lurçat and his associates astonished the world of art by producing their vital new form of tapestry. The looms of Aubusson, Beauvais and the Gobelins were soon partners in the creation of hangings inspired by great artists including Henri-Georges Adam (1904–67), Jean Arp (1887–1966), André Beaudin (born 1895), Alexander Calder (born 1898), Charles-Edouard J. Le Courbusier (1887–1965), Fernand Léger (1881–1955), Alberto Magnelli (1888–1971), André Masson (born 1896), René Perrot (born 1912), Jean Picart-le-Doux (born 1902), Marie E. Vieira da Silva (born 1908) and Marc Saint-Saëns (born 1903). The great impact made by Lurçat from 1945 was all the stronger and impressive because Europe and much of the rest of the world had been starved, through many long years of war, of creative and colourful art.

The major tapestry workshops of Paris are: Manufacture Nationale des Gobelins; Manufacture Nationale de Beauvais aux Gobelins; Atelier du Marais (Yvette Cauquil-Prince); Atelier de Saint-Cyr (Pierre Daquin); Atelier de Suresnes (Claire Radol); and Marie Moulinier, Plasse-Lecaisne. Outside Paris: Anne de Quatrebarbes and Jacqueline de la Baume-Durrbach. All but the first and seventh use low-looms, as does the Aubusson-Felletin workshops. Other ateliers include Berthaut, Braquenié, Brivet, Coupé, Goubely-Gatien, Hamot, C. & P. Legoueix, Pérathon Soeurs, Raymond Picaud, Pinton Frères, Tabard Frères. The National School of Tapestry is at Aubusson. The State manufactories train their own staff. Other workshops in and around Paris are private ventures. The Felletin looms of Pinton Frères wove the Chichester Cathedral reredos tapestry designed by John C. H. Piper (see Plate 32).

L'Association des Peintre-Cartonniers de Tapisserie was formed by Lurçat and others in 1945 to act as a 'pep-group' in the dissemination and acceptance of the principles he and his associates had formulated for the renovation of France's tapestry industry. Madame Denise Majorel founded La Demeure Tapisseries Contemporaines d'Aubusson Sculptures Estampes in Paris in 1950. The function of this organization was to achieve world-wide publicity for the new tapestry. The Parisian and Corsican atelier of Madame Cauquil-Prince weaves magnificent hangings (see Plate 40), and also continues research guided by Lurçat principles. *La Joie de Vivre* measures 240 × 290cm (7ft 10½in × 9ft 8in) and is typical of the hangings produced by this relatively new workshop. In 1976 the French Government invested Madame Cauquil-Prince with the much coveted Ordre du Mérite National in recognition of her contributions to the art of tapestry.

It is still too soon to place the contributions of Jean Lurçat and his associates against the background of tapestry's historical development, despite the euphoria created by the display of tapestries woven by him and his 'school'. In the past there have been great movements with sudden changes in design philosophy and fashions. Perhaps his main contribution will be seen as the breaking of the rigid attitudes created by the masters of tapestry that had engulfed them, but from which they could not escape. There now appears to be a tendency to go too far in the opposite direction; to be too free in the interpretation of what is tapestry, and this can easily change into a force just as self-destructive.

Lurçat demonstrated his 'new tapestry' by designing and weaving more than a thousand pieces. He was engaged on *Chant du Monde* at the time of his death in 1966. In June of 1962 he helped to ensure that tapestry would continue to be discussed and appreciated globally by inaugurating the first of the biennial exhibitions of tapestries of all countries, which continue to be held by the International Centre for Ancient and Modern Tapestry in Lausanne, Switzerland. The tapestry in 77 was one of Lurçat's earliest 'new tapestries'.

Germany

In the last quarter of the nineteenth century attempts to re-establish tapestry looms met with varying success, the best being the Scherrebek, Schleswig-Holstein manufactory which operated from 1896 to 1903. The Bauhaus School of Design produced heavy-fibred tapestries from abstract designs, under the direction of Frau Anni Albers, the wife of Professor Josef Albers. From about the end of the 1940s manufactories were established in Munich and

Nuremberg. The Nürnberger Gobelin Manufaktur has carried out important research on colour technology in association with the Austrian-born American painter and graphic artist, Dr Herbert Bayer (born 1900), a former student of the Bauhaus School of Design. A Nürnberger tapestry measuring 190 × 150cm (6ft 2¾in × 4ft 11in), designed by Professor Ernst Weil, is illustrated in Plate 41.

Dirk Holger (born 1939), a former student of Jean Lurçat's, is one of the Federal Republic's most outspoken critics of the so-called three-dimensional tapestry, which its designer-weavers claim should be accepted as legitimate tapestry. Himself both a designer and a weaver, Holger produces imaginative and clear-cut images in brilliant colours (*see* Plate 42); this is a hanging measuring 180 × 132cm (5ft 11in × 4ft 4in) woven for him by the Münchener Gobelin Manufaktur. He has established his own workshops equipped with low-warp looms, under the name of Atelier Jean Lurçat, in Munich, and uses these premises as a base to campaign nationally for greater appreciation of tapestries in architectural planning and interior décor. Holger has exhibited much internationally, particularly in the United States of America, where he has won a considerable following for his philosophies and his fabrics.

There are quite a number of home-industry tapestry-weavers scattered throughout the Federal Republic of Germany, some self-taught and some trained at the Professional High School of Textile Arts or at the Fine Arts Academy in Nuremberg where Hanns Herpich, the designer of hangings, is director of the textile workshops.

Spain

The Spanish Royal Tapestry manufactory in Madrid turned increasingly to the production of pile carpets towards the end of the nineteenth century and, in 1889, moved premises to 2 Calle Fuenterrabia, to the east of the old basilica of Atocha in Madrid. During the twentieth century manufactories, such as that of Alfombras y Tapices Aymat SA of San Cugat del Vallès in Catalonia, have continued to produce carpets, tapestries and other fabrics; its tapestry designers have been Josef Guinovart, Josep M. Subirachs and others. The Taller de Artesantia Textile workshop in Madrid, manned by five enthusiastic designer-weavers who spin and dye their own materials, has in recent years made the Colonia del Retiro a centre for the devotees of natural materials. The workshop produces traditional tapestry using vegetable dyes and weaving materials such as wool, cotton and linen. Aurelia Muñoz of Barcelona is a distinguished designer-weaver whose rather coarse-woven traditional weaves are planned as three-dimensional sculptures. Her creations have been exhibited internationally and appear in several places on a semi-permanent basis, for example in New York's Spanish Tourist Office, the Royal Scottish Museum in Edinburgh, and the Stedelijk Museum in Amsterdam. By far the most exciting of Spain's twentieth century tapestries are designed and woven by M. Asunción Raventós at the studio Taller Jesús 14, in Barcelona. This gifted and imaginative artist, designer and weaver experimented and produced several distinctive fabrics but has successfully combined an impression of Spanish colourful brilliance, romance and adventure, positiveness and vivacity in a series of multi-hued hangings of which a part of one is shown in Plate 43.

Portugal

Since the sixteenth century the town of Portalegre has been a centre for wool industries and in the year 1771 a weaving mill was established in the former

Colégio de São Sebastião, built by the Jesuits in the seventeenth century but abandoned when they were banished. The woollen mill was called Fábrica Real (Royal Manufactory) and recruited foreign technicians to ensure that products were of the highest quality and wide in variety. One of these technicians was a Joseph Larcher, who, within two years of arriving to work at the Royal Manufactory, left to found a dyeing workshop on his own account. This workshop developed rapidly and became the Fábrica de Lanifícios de Portalegre, which was taken over by the firm of Francisco Fino Lda, with each administration in turn taking a pride in keeping their methods and products up-to-date and seeking a worldwide market. In 1965, Francisco Fino Lda collaborated with Imperial Chemical Industries of Britain to establish Finicisa-Fibras Sintéticas, SARL, for the production of terylene polyester fibres. Since about 1946 Francisco Fino has used the old Royal Manufactory workshops to stage a revival in both hand-woven rugs and tapestries, using some of the most modern looms and techniques; Plate 44 shows weavers at work at one of the modern high-warp looms. This Manufactory celebrated its two-hundredth anniversary in 1973 and has a museum exhibiting some of its tapestries, designed by, among others, Jose de Ameda Negreiros, Fred Kradolfer, Jean Lurçat, Carlos Botelho, Guilherme Camarinha, Renato Torres, Vieira da Silva, Thomaz de Melho, Eduardo Nery, Louis Le Brocquy, Mark Adams, R. Burle Marx, Sidney Nolan and Sture Nilsson; over 160 designers' work has been woven, and slightly less than half the designers were foreign. Innumerable awards have been won for the many magnificent tapestries this Manufactory has produced since the early 1950s. About 80 per cent of hangings are exported.

Hungary

Hungary's geographical position, coupled with 150 years of occupation by the Turks and the many forms of political influence on its national culture, has had the effect of exerting a wealth of different types of artistic impression. Folk crafts were strong but tapestry does not appear to have been much in evidence until about the start of the twentieth century, when William Morris's pre-Raphaelite movement in England stimulated efforts to establish a workshop similar to that of Merton Abbey. Noémi Ferenczy (1890–1957) was the first of the new movement in Hungary to make a mark. Since childhood she had been surrounded by the artistic atmosphere of her family—her father, Károly Ferenczy, was the leading master of the painters' colony of nineteenth century Nagybánya—and she was reared upon the art treasures of the museums of Europe; in Paris she learned the traditional high-warp technique of weaving from one of the staff at the Gobelins. In 1913 she set up a loom at Nagybánya, and designed and wove her own tapestries with (according to an article in the *New Hungarian Quarterly* of January–March 1963, by Éva Kovács):

> . . . a zeal reminiscent of religious devotion and the same profound concentration as the unknown masters of the Middle Ages. . . . Her early works show her full understanding of the noblest traditions of the medium. In them she was chiefly inspired by medieval tapestries, with their lavish ornamentation of foliage, fruits and flowers and strictly two-dimensional composition. The colouring of her pieces, with their cold blues and greens, also recalled these medieval tapestries. The experience that inspired her first major work, 'The Creation' (1913), was the series of stained glass windows of Chartres Cathedral. This tapestry, divided into nine squares and edged with a luxuriant border, imbued the Biblical story with pictorial qualities showing complete indifference to traditional represent-

ation. She did not depict the story of the Bible, but her lavish decorative imagination filled up the surfaces with curving and sweeping branches bearing heavy fruits and fantastic flowers and with immobile animals. The purple-robed figure of God the Father, engrossed in meditation in the centre, and beneath him, the first human couple helplessly holding each other's hands are scarcely more than decorative motifs.

Tapestries woven by this pioneer include *Flight into Egypt* (1916), *The Bricklayer* (1933), *The Woman Weaving* (1932), *The Muse* (1937) and *The Town* (1938–9 and 1956–7). Again, quoting from the above-named source:

> She dedicated her works to the embellishment of homes, and this fact determined the scale of her tapestries which, apart from a few large compositions, are generally one or two square metres in size. Every minute part of the surface is wrought with the same care, permitting all details to stand out perfectly, without ever leaving the large surfaces empty.

Lenke Széchenyi is another tapissier who has helped to pioneer modern tapestries in Hungary and has an interesting philosophy based on a background as a painter:

> The yarn has never excited me. I never work according to the rules of weaving, but I weave in compliance with the independent laws of painting and drawing. Gobelin-weaving is a branch of painting. From the various coloured yarns one can blend colours and shades with exactly the same sureness as one mixes oil paint on the palette. Why does the gobelin excite me more, for all that? When I paint I get carried away by my own enthusiasm, while the mechanics of the loom act as a control inclining one to steadier conceptualization.

Her tapestries include several based on myths, including *Astral Realms*, *Earth*, *Apple* and *The Legend of the Metamorphosis*.

The tapestry shown in Plate 45 is from a photograph by Kàroly Szelènyi of Gabriella Hajdal's magnificently designed and woven interpretation of *Peter and the Wolf*, inspired by Prokofiev's musical suite. This tapissier normally uses no more than ten colours and works on a low-warp loom. The following is quoted from *New Hungarian Quarterly*, no. 51, of 1973, and was written by Lajos Németh:

> Gabriella Hajdal . . . designs—or rather paints—gobelins and tapestries. Despite this her gobelins are not woven pictures but rather painting-like tapestries. Noémi Ferenczy was her Hungarian forerunner. She had remained within the limits determined by woven materials, but at the same time put a richer meaning into her work than is customary in merely ornamental and decorative work. Noémi Ferenczy has created her own individual homogeneous style—the themes and style of Gabriella Hajdal's works are extremely varied. She experiments from abstract, geometrical work to Surrealist compositions with mythological themes. Unity in her work is achieved by mastery over her material, the love for her art, the richness of her colour schemes and variety of form rather than by a consistent notion of style and form. Her colours are very different from those of her predecessor, Noémi Ferenczy, whose gobelins had a peculiar colour harmony of pastel shades. Gabriella Hajdal's colours are glowing and saturated, but never gaudy. She experimented with a revival of long-forgotten techniques of embroidery as well.

Peter and the Wolf was designed and woven in 1959 and was Gabriella Hajdal's first tapestry. It measures 200 × 350cm (6ft 7in × 11ft 6in), and recounts the old Russian story of Peter, who goes into the forest and plays with birds. He notices a cat and warns the bird to beware, lest the cat catches and eats it. Then a wolf comes, and Peter realizes he may be eaten himself, so he climbs a tree and waits for hunters to come and dispatch the wolf.

Czechoslovakia

During the last 100 years the Slovak arts and crafts movement has changed from being largely a rural occupation, carried on in the home of farmers, shepherds and forest workers as a folk art source of extra income, to being the professional activity or profitable hobby of city-dwellers. The changes of attitude to hand-woven textiles were stimulated principally by Antonin Kybal and Alois Fišárek, of the Prague College of Industrial Arts. The former established his own studio in 1928 and created designs for the textile department of the Co-operative concern. His main interests were carpets and tapestries, and under his leadership the College of Industrial Arts worked intensively with industry. A woman, Marie Teinitzerová, should be credited with having revived the art of tapestry on traditional lines; the tapestry design philosophy of William Morris did not go unnoticed by Slovaks of the latter part of the nineteenth and the early years of the twentieth century, and created controversy among tapestry design revisionists which, in turn, stimulated greater interest and activity. During the last half of the twentieth century workshops have multiplied to provide competition to the two manufactories, at Jindrichuv Hradec and at Valasské Mezerici: the former appears to favour mostly low-warp, and the latter, high-warp looms. Notable designer weavers include Rudolf Schlattauer, Vera Drnkova-Zarecka and Luba Krejci. But perhaps the most outstanding are Jan Hladik (born 1927) and Jenny Hladiková (born 1930), whose studio workshop is in Prague. Both work on high-warp looms and have produced some remarkable tapestries, strong in imaginative and sensitive design, and woven with all the skill that a true master of weaving can command. Two of Jan Hladik's wonderful hangings are shown in Plate 46.

Switzerland

With Lausanne as the centre for CITAM, the International Centre for Ancient and Modern Tapestry, founded by Jean Lurçat in 1962 with the object of encouraging tapestry techniques and appreciation, and a history of flax spinning and weaving going back to Swiss lake-dwellers of the Stone Age, it is scarcely surprising that Switzerland has an exceptional number of tapissiers producing excellent hangings. Plate 47 depicts a tapestry from the Zurich loom of Moik Schiele.

Poland

Until the early twentieth century tapestry-weaving was part of the folk culture of rural Poland but, from about 1926, a new impetus was given by the activities of a Warsaw co-operative factory and educational bodies such as the Poznan Academy of Art, the Warsaw School of Fine Arts and similar institutes in Sopot and Lodz, coupled with the Union of Polish Artists. Designer weavers experiment widely in outline and interpretation and there have been exhibitions outside Poland of tapestries which should be described only as macabre or hideous or, at the other extreme, extremely beautiful. Plate 48 shows a tapestry woven by Stefan Poplawski (born 1945), a graduate of Poznan Academy of Art, who has exhibited extensively abroad and won high commendation for his use of tapestry as a means of topical recording of notable events; his other similar hangings include *Valencia 1937* and *Conversation*,

191

which records a meeting between the President of the United States of America —Jimmy Carter—and Edward Gierek. Honorata Blicharska of Warsaw has been fascinated by the use of tapestry as a recording medium, too, but has adopted a different technique (*see* 78). The following is quoted from the Camden Arts Centre's brochure of her 1979 exhibition there, and was written by Warren Hadler of New York's Hadler Galleries:

> ... Blicharska's work has been developed on a series of levels. There are links to the traditions of early textile portraiture, with references to both Coptic and European works. She has also pursued contemporary problems of colour and space on the woven surface through the telescopic manipulation of her loomed grid structure ... Blicharska seems to relish the implied contradiction of her use of photography as a 'cartoon' for her portraits. 'Taking pictures as a model, a mechanical process of portrayal, allows for limitless duplication. I approach this process in a new way using a very old technique—weaving. I attempt to duplicate the duplicate. I magnify this face from a photo, and by reconstructing it from miniscule woollen threads, every grid on the loom becomes for me a profoundly explored space. The individual spaces are abstract, but they grow with physical distance into a reality. I create a new face which is now impossible to duplicate, unless of course it is photographed.' If there is one individual aspect of Blicharska's images that transfixes the viewer, it is the eyes. They reveal the coldness, the façade, of these humans who themselves are used as a façade upon which we hang our cultural fantasies.

Japan

Since 1945 hand-woven textile production has grown at an astonishing rate and latterly has been encouraged and co-ordinated by the Japan Craft Design Association. Considerable effort has been devoted to creating what may be called a Japanese style as distinctive as the k'o-ssu hangings of old. Many so-called tapestries are distinctive but involve stretching almost to breaking-point the definition of tapestry to include them as such. Many of these textiles are immensely ingenious but are better described as draped, or moulded and stiffened thread sculptures, some comprising piles of thick thread arranged like mouldings. Exponents of these techniques include Masakazu and Naomi Kobayashi, and Sachiko Morino, all of Kyoto, Akiko Shimanuki of Kamakura City, Hiroko and Masafumi Y. Watanabe of Tokyo; Toshiko Tsutsumi of Kamakura City has evolved intricately woven, knotted and bound, golden and bright reddish-brown wall hangings that recall the decoration of some Japanese warriors of old, or seen in early twentieth century shrines. Plate 49 is a hanging woven by Mihoko Matsumoto, a Member of the Japan Craft Design Association and teacher at the Kawashima Textile School. Her education included graduateship at Musashino Art University and fabric design studies at America's Cranbrook Academy of Art.

Africa

In most parts of Africa there is a long heritage of basket, rush and grass-weaving for a variety of purposes, ranging from hut construction to the making of clothes. In recent years various international agencies have attempted to exploit native skills by introducing new techniques, equipment and European teachers, with the object of improving living standards of the community. In some respects, improvements based on weaving industries stemmed from the work of missionaries during the nineteenth century.

The introduction of the spinning wheel has been attributed to Swedish missionaries, but the author is convinced that the Banchory (Scottish) born pre-ordination master carpenter and builder, the Reverend William Dower, who went to southern Africa on behalf of the London Missionary Society in the 1860s, was much more likely to have been responsible for making and distributing spinning and weaving equipment among African tribes. Some short time after arriving in Africa he was appointed missionary to the great chieftain Adam Kok and was the founder of the modern town of Kokstad, near the twentieth century African homeland of the Transkei.

The Fund for Research and Investment for the Development of Africa (FRIDA), the Swedish International Agency for Development (SIDA), the United Nations Development Programme (UNDP) and the Geneva-based International Labour Office (ILO) have all been involved in establishing training and production workshops in African and other developing countries (e.g., Abu Dhabi, United Arabic Emirate), in which hand-woven tapestry has been a major craft. In Africa, notable activities have centred on Ethiopia, Botswana, Swaziland, Lesotho and South Africa generally. During the first quarter of the twentieth century Anglican church missionaries established weaving workshops in Lesotho as a means of increasing employment for women. In 1967 the Thabana-li-'Mele Handicrafts Centre (TLM) was founded by the Swedish-born Peter and Ulla Gowenius in Lesotho, after they left the Rhorkes Drift Workshop in Natal, South Africa. Experiments were started in spinning local mohair and weaving it into tapestries and other fabrics. The working staff has increased from 50 people in 1974 to over 120 now employed at the Centre and in surrounding village workshops. In recent years the work has been directed by an International Labour Office and SIDA expert, the Norwegian-born Bjørg Kristiansen White who, from 1973 to 1974, directed, under immense physical difficulties, a similar tapestry workshop at Gambella, established without adequate feasability studies or support by the Ethiopian Ministry of Community Development and Social Affairs. TLM uses high-warp looms of rather simple construction and, on account of the high price of mohair, is making increasing use of karakul wool. Weavers are encouraged to produce their own designs, which frequently portray local animals and people. Viewed through European eyes, the visual impact could be improved by greater attention to weaving; i.e., outlines which should be clear-cut go in a stepped pattern because the weaver has not changed his weft colour sequentially so as to produce a straight line of colour change. A local trader who set up tapestry workshops at Teyateyvaneng under the name of Tullycraft has succeeded in producing a definite style and a weaving technique that is more refined, with the result that this small workshop is reportedly having difficulty in meeting demand in the United States and Europe for its products. If materials cheaper than mohair could be used and the price of tapestries reduced, there might be a better market, provided improvements in design do not advertise too blatantly 'developing country art'. The Copts of the first millennium often did better. When Rolf and Elizabeth Brenner Remberg of the Federal Republic of Germany and Sweden went to Swaziland on a two-year contract to advise on textile production at the Mbabane Crafts Centre, they were intrigued by Africans' hair-plaiting customs. Using a low-warp loom and linen thread, they experimented with a texture of 4 w/cm (10 w/in) and produced model tapestries like that shown in 79. These techniques were copied and embellished by native designer-weavers to produce simple but striking hangings which have aroused much attention and commendation in Africa and abroad. The largest hanging so far measures 200 × 300cm (6ft 7in × 9ft 10in). The tapestry is woven in two steps; first the weaving and knotting is done on the loom; then the plaited format is added. There are innumerable variations of this simple but arresting theme which has a most professional and yet typically African appearance, and can be varied by harmonious blending of tinted threads.

In 1947 an Egyptian teacher established a tapestry-weaving school as a means of giving basic training to the youth of Harrania, near Cairo. The School prospered and turned into one of the most outstandingly successful mid-twentieth century centres for training in tapestry design, and the production of brilliant and exciting hangings. The Harrania Tapestry Workshops founded by Ramses Wissa Wassef produce tapestries that have found a global market and are so often copied that one is advised to check authenticity before purchasing a piece reputed to have come from a Harrania loom. The English and Arabic weavers' mark is depicted in Appendix I (*see* 91 MG 3 and 5). A tapestry is depicted in Plate 50.

Sweden

The Handarbetets Vänner (Friends of Textile Art Association) founded in 1874 by the Swedish feminist Sophie Leijonhufvud-Adlerparre in association with the liberal oriented Rosalie Roos had the prime object of creating work which would help to give women independence; it came to serve as a model for establishment of similar national societies elsewhere. The Association now has the largest private studio in Scandinavia with resources for the production of complex textiles. In 1950 the Association came under the influence of Edna Martin and outside artists were given increasing opportunity to create cartoons for textiles scheduled for public buildings such as hospitals, the Swedish National Records Office, Lund City Hall, Stockholm's Cultural Centre and the National Bank of Sweden. Cartoon artists included Max W. Svanberg, Lennart Rodhe, Olle O. Hagalund and Eva Scheffer. Textile folk art declined towards the end of the nineteenth century but was channelled into new and more resilient self-expression from 1899 with the establishment of Föreningen för Svensk Hemslöjd (the Association for Swedish Handicrafts), followed in 1912 by the National Association (Svenska Hemslöjdsföreningars Riksförbund).

The most active textile artist of the first half of the twentieth century was a woman, Märta Måås-Fjetterström, who founded a weaving workshop at Båstad, southern Sweden, in 1919. She mostly engaged in weaving rugs with designs inspired by Persian and archaic Swedish peasant art but, like William Morris in late nineteenth century England, she was a campaigner who made society think about the relevance of art to civilization and she influenced many people. She died in 1941 and her position on the board of her Båstad company was filled by Barbro Nilsson, who was already known nationally as a brilliant tapissier and a creator of monumental hangings woven in association with some of the most outstanding artists of the century. She engaged Marianne Richter and Ann-Mari Forsberg who would, in due time, take over the traditions and running of the Båstad manufactory when Barbro Nilsson retired. Among her most famous hangings are *Bålbär Skansen* (1946) (for Svenska Cellulosa AB, Sundsvall), *Tånga* (1955) (for Direktör E. Wennerholm, Stockholm), *Mässhake* (1961) (for Markuskyrkan, Stockholm), *Nordstjernan* (1961) (for Skandinaviska Banken, Malmö) and *Guldhästen* (1965) (for Sydsvenska Kraftaktiebolaget, Malmö). Marianne Richter's designs have roots deep in folk art. In 1952 she created a drapery 200 square metres in area for the premises of the Social and Economic Council in New York's United Nations building, and combines tapestry techniques with other art forms: one of her early tapestries, *Tuppamattan orange*, woven in 1949, is in Berns' Salonger, Stockholm. Ann-Mari Forsberg has made a series of large tapestries which all have themes based on Swedish history, summer or culture. Her *Röd crocus* (1945) is in Stockholm's Nationalmuseum, as is her *Valdemarsskatten* (1955). Kaisa Melanton was artistic director of the Märta Måås-Fjetterström workshops from 1971 to 1975; one of her tapestries *Journey in Space* is in Huddinge Hospital.

Under Edna Martin's direction, the workshops of Handarbetets Vänner changed from high-warp to low-warp looms with tapestries designed almost entirely for public buildings. Through her position as a lecturer at the Stockholm School of Arts, Edna Martin exercised a profound influence on the mid-twentieth century generation of textile technologists, numbering among her students Helena Hernmarck (*see* Plate 34). Other outstanding tapissiers of recent times include Barbro Sprinchorn, Marin Hemmingson, Anita Dahlin, Margareta Hallek, Maria Triller, Agneta Flock, Elna Hansson, Eva Schaeffer-Ek, Elisabet Hasselberg-Olsson, Sandra Ikse-Bergman, Beate Sydhoff, Ulla Schumacher-Percy and Gunwor Nordström. Hans Krondahl, formerly the Director of the Textile Department of the Konstfackskolan (State College of Crafts and Design), is now locum tenens Director of the Textile Department of the Crafts College in Oslo, Norway. One of his most recent tapestries is shown in Plate 51. It measures 213·5 × 427cm (7 × 14ft) and is woven with a weft of wool, silk and linen on a linen warp.

Finland

Dating from Viking times some 1200 years ago, the ryijys, rya or tufted rug was a typical Scandinavian rural handicrafts product, and was initially woven in Finnish coastal regions from about the sixteenth century. Until the beginning of the twentieth century it was used as a sleigh, bed or wall-covering and the more ornamental and finely woven varieties were venerated as status symbols in many of the country's castles and stately homes. Rya rugs were also used for church decoration. From about 1910 rug-weaving gradually incorporated tapestry-weaves and by the 1930s designs increasingly were drawn before bobbin was put to loom. During the second half of the twentieth century the dividing line between hand-woven textiles, rya rugs and tapestries has grown increasingly difficult to define, with emphasis on intricate wall-hangings such as that illustrated in 80. Double-weave textiles are called täkänä although they may have rya characteristics. Notable tapestry designers and, or, weavers include Anna-Liisa Kuula-Vainio, M. Kolsi-Mäkelä, Laila Karttunen, Eva Anttila and Margareta Ahlstedt-Willandt. The main national organization responsible for promoting tapestry is the Finnish Society of Crafts and Design, whose headquarters are in Unioninkatu, Helsinki.

Norway and Denmark

In nineteenth century Norway, a renaissance in tapestry design and technique was led by the painter Gerhard Munthe (1849–1931) and by the weaver and student of archaic textile handicrafts, Frida Hansen (1855–1931), concurrently with the latter phases of William Morris's Merton Abbey activities in England. Gerhard Munthe and Frida Hansen tried to stimulate a lighter and more lively style based on Norwegian medieval tapestry. Subsequently weaving has turned

80 Helmi Vuorelma Oy, which wove this hanging in täkänä double-weave to the design of Maija-Liisa Forss-Heinonen, is one of Finland's main tapestry workshops. The name of the piece is *Joonas*, material is linen and measurements are 200 × 77cm (6ft 6⅜in × 2ft 6in) (*Helmi Vuorelma Oy, Lahti, Finland*)

into a widespread professional and hobby activity, with the largest manufactory at Norsk Biledvev, Oslo. Prominent tapissiers include Else M. Jacobsen, Ludvig Eikas, Karin Sundbye, Brit H. Warsinski and Hannah Ryggen (*see* 81).

Like Norway, Denmark has religious foundations which have acted as patrons of tapestry workshops, but the number of emigrant tapissiers suggests that the country is too small to support more than a few small workshops or that the cost of workmanship is uncompetitive with other countries.

Belgium and Holland

Several attempts were made in nineteenth century Belgium to re-establish tapestry weaving. The Count des Cantons de Montblanc (died 1861) opened a low-loom workshop at Ingelmunster and in 1856 was joined by the brothers Braquenié; tapestries included the *Siege of the Château at Ingelmunster*. The Braqueniés and M. Dautzenberg established a Royal Tapestry Manufactory at Malines, which wove a series of panels depicting *Trades of the Low Countries* after M. Geets, for the Hôtel de Ville, Brussels; another manufactory was at Héverlé. Brussels had a Royal Manufactory. In 1945, mindful of Lurçat's success in France, Louis Deltour, Edmond Dubrunfaut and Roger Somville—all painter-designers—founded the Forces Murales group of Tournai, which two years later was extended by the Centre de Rénovation de la Tapisserie Workshop. It had a short but influential life, closing in 1951. Present Belgian tapissiers include Raoul Ubac and Brigitte Leclerc.

Holland's major workshop is the E. de Cneudt manufactory at Baara. Prominent tapissiers include Herman Scholten and Margot Rolf (both of the Textile Department, Gerrit Rietveld Academy, Amsterdam), Marie van Derle van Gorp, Gerda Edens and Jan Bons.

Austria, Italy and Yugoslavia

During the last quarter of the nineteenth century attempts were made, with a modicum of success, to establish tapestry looms in connexion with the State Collection of Tapestries in Vienna. But in recent years, tapestry-weaving in Austria has largely centred on the workshops of J. Schulz and F. Riedl in Vienna, who use high-warp looms and are represented in several museums and private collections.

In Italy, tapestry studies and weaving have been encouraged by Professor Umbro Apollonio, of the Department of the History of Art of Padua University, the Armando Diaz Istituto in Rome and the Tapestry School founded in 1935 at Esino Lario, Como. A number of small workshops are engaged in producing traditional hangings and also possibly a larger number of rather shorter lived establishments engaged on weaving fabrics that are hard to classify despite the wish of their weavers to call them 'tapestry'; one of these workshops has gone to considerable expense to produce hangings based on mathematical calculations related to the area of the fabric and what the human eye is likely to observe at the optimum viewing distance. This is a technique based on the optimum distance at which one should view a television picture raster in terms of the picture frame so as to obtain maximum resolution without visual disturbance caused by the scanning lines; i.e., the weaver determines the warps per cm in terms of the size of the hanging and the resolution required at an optimum viewing distance. Workshops producing far less experimental tapestries are located in Milan, Florence, Turin and Rome.

Yugoslavia's tapestry-weaving activities have increased greatly during the

81 *By the Ocean of Debt* is a representative Norwegian tapestry exhibited at London's Royal College of Art in 1973. This humorous work is made with olive, brown and orange-hued yarns spun and dyed by the designer-weaver, Hannah Ryggen. Measurements are 145 × 180cm (4ft 9in × 5ft 10¾in) (*Royal Norwegian Embassy, London*)

second half of the twentieth century, and have been based on the designs and ideas of a previous colourful rural textiles industry that was mostly based on ordinary fabric and rug-weaving. Most tapestries of the last 30 years are only a few square metres in extent but are excellently woven, brilliant but not garish in colour and, although tending towards a typical national style, have obviously been influenced by the ideas of Lurçat in France, the Dovecot Studios in Edinburgh and the Art Nouveau movement of America. Milica Zoric's *Terrible Meal* hanging of 1960 is displayed in the Parliament House in Belgrade. Other notable tapissiers include Jagoda Buic (high-warp loom), Mateja Rodici, Bosko Petrovic and Nadja Voltko.

Australia

It is only natural that one of the world's main wool-producing countries should have a number of artistically inclined people interested in tapestry production. Since the mid-twentieth century small workshops have grown up in the main towns and also in rural areas. But the most ambitious of all projects was started in the mid-1970s and is making good progress.

The Victorian Tapestry Workshop in South Melbourne was established by the State of Victoria Government through the Ministry of Arts. The idea for this enterprise originated with Lady Delacombe, the wife of the former Governor of Victoria, and the then Director of the National Gallery of Victoria, Eric Westbrook. They felt that Australia's wool industries and rich artistic tradition should support a centre where works of fine art in the tapestry medium could be produced. The proposal for a workshop was supported enthusiastically by the State Prime Minister, Mr Hamer, and a suitable building was found. A former student of the Edinburgh Tapestry Company's Dovecot Studios in Corstorphine—Belinda Ramson—trained the 14 weavers who were to initiate production. Modern high-warp looms were installed. One of the

197

first large contracts was won competitively and consisted of an order for 30 square metres of hangings to cover the walls of Canada's Saskatchewan Centre for the Arts, to the designs of Canadian Alan Weinstein. The Workshop's director, Sue Walker, has defined their guiding philosophy in these terms:

> Our aim is to produce a living art extending from the creative language of both artist and weaver. Our people are artist-weavers, not artisans. All have a background in the visual arts. Most have diplomas or tertiary qualifications in art or sculpture. We make works of fine art, using the special qualities and possibilities of tapestry to interpret the visual imagery of the artist's work.

The Workshop's palette is standardized on 40 basic colours, each produced in four shades and two thicknesses of yarn. Weavers mix their yarns and shadings just as a painter mixes his colours, to obtain a desired result. The Workshop's dyeworks are at Geelong. The illustrations used in Chapter 1 to demonstrate weaving techniques were supplied by the Victoria Tapestry Workshop (*see* Plates 1, 2, 3 and 4.

Epilogue

In recent years tapestry has attracted countless people in every country; in fact, in far more parts of the world than it has been possible to detail here. The book was planned to serve the dual function of introducing tapestry to the person who has given this art little or no attention before, and of providing the specialist with a concise history extending from the earliest times to nearly AD 2000. Economic constraints have limited size and have, therefore, imposed on the author an obligation to define tapestry within certain limits. The majority of illustrations demonstrate the excellence attainable by masters of design and weaving who combine their skills to make a textile so arresting and so pleasing, that it automatically signals the inadequacies of anything called 'tapestry' but of lesser status.

Tapestry usually is a truer mirror of history than painted pictures. Those woven up to about the end of the first third of the twentieth century were often the work of a team of experts devoted to creating the best visual and textile product. The materials and dyes used were those commonly employed for making clothes, furnishings and other textiles of the times. Even the expressive faces seen in older tapestries are likely to be truer to life, for weavers used each other's features as models. The very size and the detail incorporated in hangings from, say, the early sixteenth century, provide a wealth of historical information unequalled by painted pictures from medieval times.

Despite the immensely valuable archives of history represented by tapestries, they receive in general far less care and attention than pictures by the old masters and lesser painters. Is it too much to ask that each nation should make far greater efforts to conserve tapestries more than a century old, and lavish on them the same care as that bestowed on valuable paintings?

Bibliography

Catalogue 15. *Ausstellung der Albrecht Dürer Gesellschaft*. Germanischen National-museum, Nuremberg (1971)

Catalogue. *Manufactura de Tapeçarias de Portalegre*. Galeria de Arte do Casino Estoril (1978)

Ceskoslovenská Tapiserie 1966–71. Czechoslovakia Ministry of Culture, Prague (1972)

Exhibition catalogue. *Modern French Tapestries*. Royal College of Art, London (1972)

Fougère, Valentine. *Tapissiers de Notre Temps*. Les Editions du Temps, Paris (1969)

Handarbetets Vänner 100 år. Liljevalchs Catalogue 315. Stockholm, Sweden (1974)

'Helena Hernmarck', *Fiberarts* (USA), pp. 32–39, no. 2, 1978

Lindkvist, L. *Design in Sweden.* Swedish Institute, Stockholm (1977)

Miralles, F. *Maria Asuncion Raventos.* La Gran Enciclopedia Vasca. Bilbao, Spain (1977)

Nelson, Karen. 'The Evolution of an Ethnic Craft', *Tradecraft,* January–March 1978

Poupet, Armelle. 'Tissages, Tapis et Tapisseries au Portugal', Études *Luso-Brésiliennes, XI.* Presses Universitaires de France, Paris (1966)

Raban, Josef. *Czechoslovak Form.* Orbis, Prague (1971)

Schwartz, Marvin. 'Arts and Crafts Movement 1876–1916', *Crafts Magazine* (USA), pp. 46–49, 74–76, December 1972

White, Bjorg K. 'Handicrafts and Technical Assistance: A Case Study'. *Tradecraft,* July–September 1978

Acknowledgements

Acknowledgement with thanks is made to the following for sending information: Alice Z'rebiec, Textile Study Room, Metropolitan Museum of Art, NYC; Elizabeth P. Holcombe, California; Mrs Beatrice Cruickshank, Louisiana; Terry Perram, Louisiana; H. Roué, Reims, France; Veronika Gervers, Royal Ontario Museum, Canada; The Royal Canadian Academy of Arts; Helen Frances Gregor, Toronto, Canada; Mona Prytz, ILO's Women's Handicraft Centre's Chief Technical Advisor, Abu Dhabi, United Arabic Emirate; S. J. Brushett, Winchester, Hants; Gloria F. Ross, NYC.

Appendix 1
Tapestry Identification

Like other popular or valuable art-forms, tapestries made for the powerful or famous were often copied by other than the originating workshop and it is difficult to confirm their pedigree. Just occasionally mysterious pieces are discovered when an ancient building is demolished, sometimes behind wall plaster, or used to block gaps between floorboards, skirting or panelling. Some years ago the author found an unlisted square of tapestry in Westminster Abbey which, before the Dissolution of the Monasteries, and in the interval before the Commonwealth, had many more tapestries than now. Friends of the monasteries and churches may, on these occasions, have secreted priceless tapestries and then forgotten to recover them or died with the secret of their hiding-place. It is always beneficial to be on the look-out for forgotten tapestries, especially when disturbing vaults, tombs, ancient cellars and roof spaces.

To safeguard the originality of tapestries woven for clients of high estate, workshops of the fifteenth century started to weave a distinctive mark or monogram into the border or selvedge; it had the status of a hallmark. The sixteenth century reputation of Brussels tapestry induced many lesser workshops to copy it and to try by dubious means to undercut its price. 'Counterfeit' arras or tapestry was often plain weave with painted designs or made with coloured silk instead of gold and silver weft, or made of dyed wool which faded quickly. Some tapestries felt rough, looked coarse after a short time or shed weft like a moulting animal. To protect their reputation the tapestry makers of Brussels appealed to the City's magistrates. On 24 April 1525, a decree required all Brussels workshops to conform to certain minimum standards of design and materials. Plagiarization continued, however, and a new decree of 16 May 1528 required pieces exceeding six ells in size to have on the lower part of one side the workshop, weaver's or client's mark, and, on the opposite side, a red shield or armorial similar to that of Brussels, flanked by the letter 'B' standing for 'Brussels' and 'Brabant'. The reversed '4' found on some pieces means, probably, they were made for a merchant or dealer. Despite infliction of heavy penalties on miscreants caught, plagiarization continued. In 1544, Charles V (*see* Index) extended the 1528 decree to cover all tapestries sold for more than a certain amount in all parts of the Low Countries, with the addition that the name of the place of origin should replace the Brussels mark. Plagiarization continued on a lesser scale. In 1560 the Council of Brabant heard a complaint from the tapissiers of Brussels that the tapissiers of neighbouring Antwerp were fraudulently using the Brussels mark. As several Brussels workshops had a branch in Antwerp, or weavers from one town were native to the other, this 'misuse' was hard to stop. In 1617 and 1619 the provisions of decrees were stiffened to make transgression more painful for offenders.

From the seventeenth century a tapissier's initials started to take the place of his mark or monogram (before this time few tapissiers could read or write or sign themselves other than by a mark). Later, tapissiers wove their signature or name into the fabric, or painted it on the selvedge or border. The importance of any form of identifying mark cannot be over-estimated. Twentieth century tapissiers often ignore this ancient custom. Of course, many modern so-called 'tapestries' might be marred by a mark—but perhaps some originators do not expect their creation to survive them? Or their style is so universally associated with their design philosophy that nobody is in any doubt as to the workshop and weaver; the style of William Morris and the Merton Abbey Workshops is a relevant instance. In the reverse direction, some modern weaver's names are so prominently displayed that the impression is that the piece is purely a vehicle for self-advertisement. Outstanding workshops, designers and weavers of the Middle Ages used small, distinctive or subtle marks, often placed so that one has to search in selvedge or border, and in the process, come to examine and admire their craft the more!

Workshops that produced a popular tapestry or set often made a copy of lower value than the original. Gold and silver threads might be replaced by coloured silk to ensure the unique character of the original. 'Unauthorized' copies sometimes may be identified by the differences in the weave—by a rougher or a coarser feel or appearance, or because colours have faded differently meaning that different dyes or methods of dyeing have been used. Close comparison of the marks of the original and copy may also disclose differences in calligraphy. The only fairly sure way to check identification and origins of a tapestry—apart from chemical and mechanical tests (by means of gas chromatography, spectroscopic measurements and nuclear magnetic resonance methods it is possible to find out much about the authenticity of materials)—is to record as many genuine versions as possible of a known mark and use it as a basis for comparison.

During the twentieth century a new terminology has emerged. Tapestries are now 'edited' and 'published'. For some persons the art has been aligned with the terminology of big business. An 'editor' commissions a designer who may be an artist without any grasp of the tapissier's repertoire of techniques and skills. It is the editor's task to act as middle-man, a translator between the inspiration and skills of a prestigious artist, and the workshop, which may be an ocean or continent away. When the tapestry is finished it is 'published'. If it appeals there may be orders for copies, which help to defray the cost of the original design. In general, this method of semi mass-production has been responsible for many mediocre hangings, which satisfy clients who believe it is better to have some sort of tapestry rather than none at all. The golden rule learned through the ages is ignored: that the best tapestry results from the closest co-operation between designer, dyer and weaver.

Some years ago authorities in France promulgated rules to regulate the copying of tapestry originals without impairing their status. Of the several obligatory rules the two most important are: (1) the order number must be woven into the piece; and (2) the reverse side of the tapestry must bear a certificate incorporating the workshop's distinctive mark, the date the tapestry left the loom and the signature of the cartoon designer. These rules should be adopted internationally.

In a volume of this size it is impossible to do more than list identification marks briefly. Analysis by countries is not feasible; boundaries have changed much in 500 years. The field of research may be narrowed by reconciling two or more unknown marks and then comparing the design and style of the tapestries to which each refers, and by comparing the history of each piece in the records of each owner.

Bibliography

American Association for Testing Materials. *Tentative Methods for Identification of Fibers in Textiles*. Philadelphia (1943)

Böttinger, J. *Svenska Statens Samling av Vävda Tapeter*. Stockholm (1895–6)

Ford, J. E. and Roff, W. J. 'Identification of Textile and Related Fibres'. Shirley Institute Memoirs, England. v. XXVII, 1954, pt. VI

Göbel, H. Wandteppiche: I. *Die Niederlande*. II. *Die Romanischen Länder*. III. *Die Germanischen und Slavischen Länder*. Leipzig–Berlin (1923–33). *Wandteppiche : und ihre Manufakturen in Frankreich, Italien, Spanien und Portugal*. Leipzig (1923)

Thomson, W. G. *Tapestry Weaving in England from the earliest times to the end of the eighteenth century*. London (1915)

82 Just sufficient of the selvedge of this tapestry – in a Swedish private collection – has survived wear to enable one to recognize the mark of the Brussels weaver, Jean Raes. Until a tapestry has to be identified the selvedge may look so unimportant that it is not as carefully preserved as the rest of the tapestry

	1	2	3	4	5	6	7	8	9
A						M+D+BOS			
B	I D								

83 BELGIAN (FLEMISH) TAPESTRY MARKS. Town or workshop mark of ANTWERP: A1, A2. Weaver's or merchant's mark (all sixteenth century): A3 Antoine van Berghe (?); A4 Cornelius van Bomberghen; A5 Gaspar van den Bruggen (?); A6 Michael de Bos; A9 Martin de Cordier (?). Weaver's or merchant's mark with tapestry subject: B1 *The Story of Cyrus* (Madrid); B3 *The reception of a woman and child by a king.*

84 BELGIAN (FLEMISH) TAPESTRY MARKS. Town or workshop mark of ATH: C1.
BRUGES weaver's or merchant's mark and tapestry subject: C3 *The History of Rome* by Jean
Crayloot in 3rd ¼ of 16 c; C5 *Armorial Tapestry*; C6 *Diana Hunting* – Bruges with Brussels
mark (Madrid). Town or workshop mark of BRUSSELS: C7 to J8; J9 Author's copyright
reserved mark. Weaver's or merchant's mark with tapestry subject: K1 to K5 *The History
of Ulysses* (Hardwick Hall, England); K6, K7 *Scenes from Ancient History*; K8 to L2 *The Story
of Polyphemus*; L3 *The History of Diana* (see also **90** LA7 to LA9); L4 *Paris wounding Menelaus*;
L5 *Vulcan*; L6 to L8 *Gombard and Macee*; L9 *Hercules*; M1 *The History of Theseus*; M3, M4 *Vert-
umus and Pomona* (Vienna); M5 *The History of Pomona*; M6 *Alexander the Great*; M7 *The History
of Alexander* (Madrid); M8 *The History of Alexander*; M9 *The History of Alexander* (Madrid); N1,
N2 *The Triumphs of the Gods* by François Geubels (Garde Mobilier, Paris); N3 *The Triumphs
of the Gods—Neptune*; N4 to N6 *The Triumphs of the Gods*; N7 to N9 *The History of Cyrus*
(Madrid)

	1	2	3	4	5	6	7	8	9
O									
P									
Q									
R									
S									
T									
U									
V									
W									
X									
Y									

85 BELGIAN (FLEMISH) TAPESTRY MARKS. Weaver's or merchant's mark with tapestry subject: O1 to O3 *The History of Cyrus* (Madrid); O4 *The History of Cyrus* (Sweden); O5 *The History of Decius;* O6 *The History of Tobias* (Madrid); O7 to O9 *The History of Tobit;* P1 to P3 *The History of Scipio* (Madrid); P4, P5 *The History of Scipio* by Jean Leyniers; P6, P7 the same subject and tapissier (Madrid); P8 *The Creation* (Burgos); P9 to Q1 *The Six Ages of the World* (Vienna); Q2 *The History of Rome* (Stockholm); Q3 *The History of Rome;* Q4, Q5 *Romulus and Remus* (Vienna); Q6 to R5 *Romulus and Remus,* by François Geubels (?) (Vienna); R6 same subject and tapissier; R7, R8 *Romulus and Remus* by Marc Cretif; R9 *The History of Caesar* (France); S1 *The History of Cleopatra* (Burgos); S2 *Anthony and Cleopatra;* S3 *Romans and Sabines;* S4 *Zenobia* (Vienna); S5, S6 *The History of Noah* (Madrid); S7 *The History of the Ark* (Hardwick Hall, England); S8, S9 *The Life of Abraham* by Wilhelm Pannemaker (Vienna); T1, T2 *The History of Abraham* (Vienna); T3, T4 *The History of Abraham* (Munich); T5 *The History of Moses and Joshua;* T6 *Moses Striking the Rock;* T7, T8 *The History of Joshua* (Vienna); T9 *The History of Jacob* (Madrid Museum); U1 Author's copyright reserved mark; U2 *The History of Jacob* (Vienna); U3 *The Triumph of David;* U4 *The History of David* (Burgos); U5 *The Old Testament* (Vienna); U6, U7 *The Story of Samson* (France); U8 *The Story of Samson* (Madrid); U9 *The Story of Samson;* V1 *The History of Gideon;* V2 *The Creation of Woman* (Florence); V3 *The Adoration of the Magi* (Madrid); V4 *The Ascension of Christ* (Munich); V5 to V7 *The Apocalyspe* by Wilhelm Pannemaker (Madrid); V8, V9 *The Apostles Preaching* (Madrid); W1 *The History of the Apostles* (Vienna); W2 to W8 *The Apostles* by Jean Raes (Munich); W9 *The Acts of the Apostles* (pre-1563) (Vienna); X1 to X4 *The Acts of the Apostles* by Nicholas Leyniers (?) (Madrid); X5 *The Acts of the Apostles* (pre-1563) (Vienna); X6 *The Life of the Apostles* (Vienna); X7, X8 *The Acts of the Apostles* (Vienna); X9 *The Life of Magdalen* (Madrid); Y1, Y2 *The Passion* by Wilhelm Segers (Vienna); Y3 *The Passion* (Vienna); Y4, Y5 *The Temptation of St Anthony* (Madrid); Y6 *The Incarnation* (Madrid); Y7 *The Story of St Paul* (Madrid); Y8 *Paul and Barnabas at Lystra*; Y9 *The Life of St Paul* (Munich)

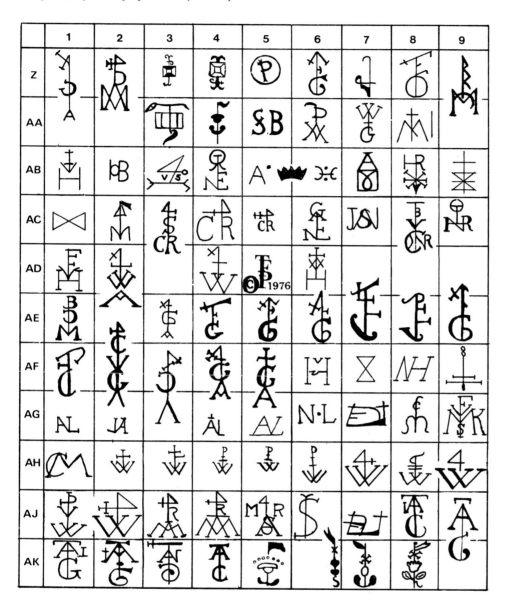

86 BELGIAN (FLEMISH) TAPESTRY MARKS. Weaver's or merchant's mark with tapestry subject: Z1 *The Conversion of St Paul*; Z2 *The Last Judgement* (Madrid); Z3, Z4 *The Seven Deadly Sins*, one set by Wilhelm Pannemaker; Z5 *The Seven Deadly Sins*; Z6, Z7 *The Seven Virtues* (Vienna); Z8 *The Cardinal Virtues* (Burgos); Z9 *The Triumph of Life*; AA3 *The Lucas Months* (Munich); AA4, AA5 *The Sphere* (Madrid); AA6 *The History of the Kings* (Stockholm); AA7 *The Hunts of Maximilian* by Georges Wezeler; AA8 *The Hunts of Maximilian*; AB1 *Hunting Scenes*; AB2 *The Ostrich Hunt*; AB3 *Hunting Scenes*; AB4, AB5 *Battle in a Forest*; AB7 *Garland of Flowers and Fruit*; AB8 *Garlands* (17 c) AB9, AC1 *Pastoral* (Vienna); AC2 *The Month of December* by Wilhelm Pannemaker; AC3 to AC6 *The Twelve Months* (Vienna); AC7 *Landscape*; AC8 *Landscape* (17 c) (Vienna); AC9 *Landscape* (Vienna); AD1 *Armorial Landscape*; AD2 *Verdure* (16 c) (Madrid); AD4 *The History of Abraham* (16 c) (Hampton Court Palace, England). Weaver's or merchant's mark: AD5 Author's copyright reserved mark; AD6 Henri van Assche (17 c) (see also **90** LG1 BRUSSELS weaver van Aelst); AE1 Jacob de Carnes (mid-16 c); AE3 Jacques Geubels (late 16 c); AE4 to AE9 François (Franz) Geubels (mid-16 c); AF2 Katharina Geubels (née van den Eynde) (late 16 c); AF3 to AF5 Jacques (Jacob) Geubels; AF6, AF7 Leo (Leon) van den Heck (Hecque) (pre-1576); AF8 Nicholas (Nikolaus) Hellinc(k) (2nd ½ of 16 c); AF9 Nicholas van den Hove (2nd ½ of 16 c); AG1 Jacques Leyniers (2nd ½ of 16 c) (see below and **85** P4 to P7); AG2 and AG4 Antoine (Anton) or Jacques (Jacob) Leyniers (2nd ½ of 16 c); AG5 Jacques (Jacob) Leyniers, from a document; AG6 Nicholas (Nikolaus) Leyniers (mid-17 c); AG7 Antoine or Jacques Leyniers; AG8 Hubert (Hubrecht) de Maecht (2nd ½ of 16 c); AG9 François (Frans) van Maelsaeck 1st ½ of 17 c); AH1 Cornelius Mattens (2nd ¼ of 16 c to 1st ¼ of 17 c); AH2 to AH9 Wilhelm (Guillaume) de Pannemaker (1535-78); AJ1, AJ2 Wilhelm de Pannemaker (?); AJ3, AJ4 Martin Reynbouts (17 c); AJ5 Matthias Roelants (mid-17 c); AJ6 Jan Segers (mid-17 c) (see **85** Y1); AJ7 Daniel Thienpont (2nd ½ of 16 c); AJ8 to AK4 Johan van Tiegen; AK5 to AK8 Georges Wezeler (Wescher) (last two queried, but see also **86** AA7)

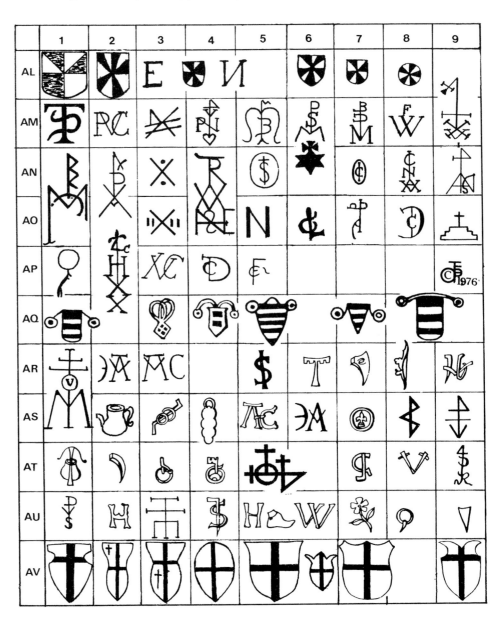

87 BELGIAN (FLEMISH) TAPESTRY MARKS. Town or workshop mark: AL1 to AL8 ENGHIEN. Weaver's or merchant's mark with tapestry subject: AM1 *Historical* or mythical subject; AM2 *Diana Hunting* by Philippe van den Cammen (Vienna); AM3 *Diana Hunting* (Munich) (see also **84** C6, L3, **90** LA7 to LA9); AM4 *Hercules and the Centaur* (Vienna); AM5

206

Vulcan (see **84** L5); AM6 *Minerva;* AM7 *The History of the Exodus* (Vienna); AM8, AM9 *Esther before Ahasuerus* (Vienna); AN1 *The Triumph of Love;* AN2 *Landscape* (see **86** AC7 to AC9); AN4 *Original Sin* (Madrid); AN5 *St Paul* (Vienna); AN7 *The Life of St Paul;* AN8 *A woman kneeling before a General* (Vienna); AO3 and AO5, AO6 *Armorial Verdure;* AO7 *Verdure* (Vienna); AO8, AP1 *Arabesque* (Vienna); Weaver's or merchant's mark: AP2 Henri van der Cammen; AP3 J(e)an van der Cammen (2nd ½ of 16 c); AP4 Nicholas de Dobbeleer (2nd ½ of 16 c); AP5 Quentin (Quentyn) Flascoen (Flaschoen) (2nd ½ of 16 c); AP9 Author's copyright reserved mark. Town workshop mark of OUDENARDE (AUDENARDE): AQ1 to AQ9. Weaver's or merchant's mark with tapestry subject; AR1 *The History of Hercules* by Michael van Orley (?) (Vienna); AR2, AR3 *The History of David* (Vienna) (see also **90** LB1, LB2). Weaver's or merchant's mark: AR5 Jacques Benne; AR6 Jean de Bleekere; AR7 Mathieu van Boereghem; AR8 Jean Boogaert; AR9 Jacques (Jacob) van den Brouke (Broucle); AS3 Guillaume (Willem) van den Capellen; AS4 Jean de Clynckere; AS5, AS6 Arnould Cobbaut; AS7 Remi Gruppen(n); AS8 Jean Dervael; AS9 Pierre (Peter) van Kercken; AT1 Arnould van den Kethele; AT2 Martin van den Muelenc (Muelene); AT3, AT4 Gilles Mathieus; AT5 Thomas Nokerman; AT7 Jean Pontseel; AT8 Pierre (Peter) van Rakebosch; AT9 Peter (Pierre) Robbyns (Robbins) (2nd ½ of 16 c); AU1 Pierre (Peeter) van Sin(a)y (1st ½ of 17 c); AU2 Hubert Stalius (Stalins); AU3 François (Frans) van den Steens (2nd ¼ of 16 c); AU4 Jean Talpaert; AU5 and AU7 Antoine (Anton) van den Neste or Jean de Waghenere; AU8 Josse Wal(r)ave; AU9 Pierre (Peter) Willemets. ENGLISH TAPESTRY MARKS. Town or workshop mark of MORTLAKE and LONDON (St George's Cross): AV1 to AV9

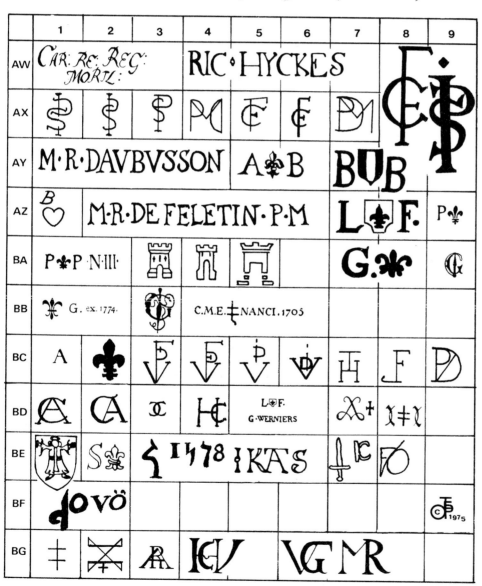

207

88 ENGLISH TAPESTRY MARKS. Town or workshop mark of MORTLAKE with royal inscription of 'Carole rege regnante. Mortlake': AW1; BARCHESTON: Richard Hicks (Hickes Hyckes) (2nd ½ of 16 c and 1st ½ of 17 c): AW4 Weaver's or merchant's mark with tapestry subject: AX1 to AX3 *The Acts of the Apostles* (Garde Mobilier, Paris): AX4 *The Five Senses* (Hardwick Hall, England). Weaver's or merchant's mark: AX5, AX6 Sir Francis Crane; AX7 Philip de Maecht; AX8 Sir Francis Crane's monogram; AX9 Peter Schrijuer's monogram (?). FRENCH TAPESTRY MARKS. Town or workshop mark of AUBUSSON: AY1 to AY5 (16 c to 18 c); BEAUVAIS: AZ1 (17 c to 18 c); FELLETIN: AZ2 (17 c); LILLE: AZ7 (18 c); PARIS: AZ9, BA1; TOURNAI: BA3 to BA5; Gobelins: BA7 (17 c to 18 c); Gobelins: BA9 (1st ½ of 20 c); Gobelins: BB1 (18 c); Gobelins: BB3 (19 c to 20 c); NANCY: BB4 (17 c to 18 c) (see BD7); AMIENS: BC1 (?). Weaver's or merchant's mark with tapestry subject: BC1, BC2 *The Translation of Elijah*; BC3, BC4 *The Story of Artemesica* (Madrid); BC5, BC6 *Arethusa Transformed into a Fountain* (Paris); BC7 *The History of Constantine* by Hans Tayer (Paris); BC8 *The History of the King* by Lefèvre (Lefèbure) (Gobelins); BC9 *Abraham's Sacrifice* (Paris); BD7, BD8 *The Battles of Charles V* woven at Nancy (?) (Vienna). Weaver's or merchant's mark: BD1 to BD3 Alexandre de Comans; BD4 Hippolytè de Comans; BD5 Widow G. Werniers, Lille: GERMAN TAPESTRY MARKS. Town or workshop mark of MUNICH: BE1; STRASBURG: BE2 (late 16 c); BE3 and BE5 Master's mark (late 15 c and 16 c, respectively); BE7, BE8 Master's mark; DANZIG: BF1 Master's mark. BF9 Author's copyright reserved mark. Weaver's or merchant's mark with tapestry subject: BG1, BG2 *The History of Moses* (16 c) (Vienna); BG3 *Scenes from the Life of Christ* woven in Alsace (1592); BG4 to BG6 *The Life of Christ* woven in Alsace (3rd ¼ of 16 c and 1st ¼ of 17 c)

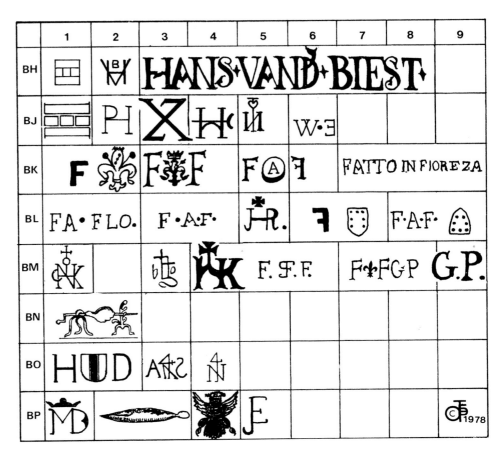

89 GERMAN TAPESTRY MARKS. Weaver's or merchant's mark: BH1 to BH3 Hans van der Biest, Munich (17 c); BJ1 Peter von der Gehüchtan; BJ2 Peter Hayman, Stettin (2nd ½ of 16 c); BJ3 Heinrich von der Hohenmuel (mid-16 c); BJ4 Jan van Kenss, Heidelberg (1st ¼ of 17 c); BJ5 Paul (Lukas) van Nieuenhove (Nieuvenhouen), Munich (1st ¼ of 17 c); BJ6 E. Wagner (Waghenere ?), Leipzig (mid-16 c). ITALIAN TAPESTRY MARKS. Town or workshop mark of FLORENCE: BK1 to BL3; FERRARA: BL5 (1553 with BRUSSELS mark also); FLORENCE: BL6 to BL8. Weaver's or merchant's mark with tapestry subject: BM1 *Grotesques*, Florence, by Nicholas Karcher (c. 1550). Weaver's or merchant's mark:

BM3 Rinaldo Boteram, Mantua and Ferrara (from a document); BM4 John (Jan, Hans) Karcher, Flanders and Ferrara (mid-16 c); BM5 Pierre Lefèvre (Lefèbure), Paris then Florence (16 c to 17 c); BM7 to BM9 Guasparri di Bartilommeo Papini, Florence (16 c to 17 c); Jean (Hans) Rost, Florence (mid-16 c). NETHERLANDS TAPESTRY MARKS. Town or workshop mark of DELFT: BO1. Weaver's or merchant's mark with tapestry subject: BO3 *The History of Tobias* by Armand Spierinck (Spierincx) BO4 *The History of Diana* by François Spierinck (Spierincx). SPANISH TAPESTRY MARKS. Town or workshop mark of MADRID Royal Manufactory: BP1; MADRID St Barbara Manufactory: BP2: Weaver's or merchant's mark with tapestry subject: BP2 *The Conquest of Tunis;* BP4, BP5 *Portière with figures;* BP9 Author's copyright reserved mark

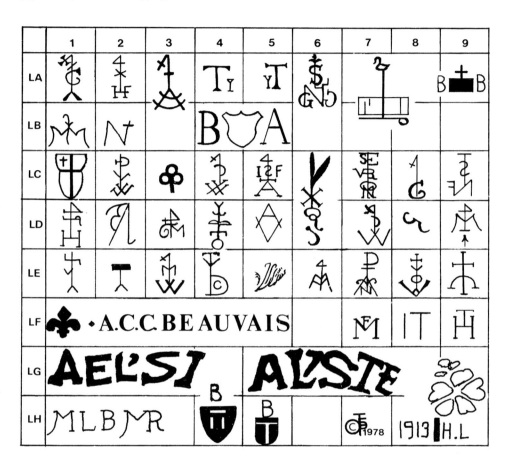

90 INDETERMINATE OR UNCLASSIFIED TAPESTRY MARKS. Town or workshop mark of BRUSSELS. Weaver's or merchant's mark with tapestry subject: LA1 Unknown but possibly Jakob Geubels; LA2 Unknown but possibly Jan van den Hecke (1st third of 17 c); LA3 to LA5 *The Acts of the Apostles* (Hardwick Hall, England, and Madrid); LA6 *The Life of Jacob* (Vienna); LA7 to LA9 *Diana Hunting* (Madrid). OUDENARDE (AUDENARDE). LE1 *The Return of Jacob* (Bowes Museum, England); LE2 *Hercules wrestling with Antaeus;* FLEMISH. LB4 *Ornamental tapestry.* MORTLAKE. LC1 *Unknown subject;* LC2 *The History of Julius Caesar;* LC3 *The Crown offered to Julius Ceasar;* LC4 *The History of St Paul;* LC5 *The History of Alexander;* INDETERMINATE MANUFACTORY. LC7 *The History of Hercules* (France); LC8 *The History of Alexander;* LC9 *The History of Cyrus;* LD1 *Tobias and Raguel;* LD2 *The Madness of Brutus* (Madrid); LD3 *The Death of Abraham;* LD4 *The Story of David* (Italy); LD5 *Esther and Ahasueras;* LD6 *Vertumnus and Pomona* by Georges Wezeler (?); LD7 *The History of St Matthew;* LD8 *The Hunt of the Leopard* (Bowes Museum, England); LD9 *Foliage with Animals* (Victoria and Albert Museum, England); LE1, LE2 *Foliage with Birds;* LE3 *Men attacking a Hydra;* LE4 *The Seasons* (Italy); LE5 *Landscape* (Bowes Museum, England); LE6 *Armorial tapestry;* LE7 *Woman supplicating for her child;* LE8 *Figure subject* (Bowes Muesum, England); DANZIG (GDANSK) town mark (?). LE9 Unknown subject. BEAUVAIS. LF1 Tapestry with initials of workshop's director, André Charlemagne Charron (c. 1750-1800). PARIS: St Marcel Manufactory. LF6 to LF8 *The Baptism of Constantine* (c. 1600-25); LF9 *The Battle*

209

of the *Milavian Ridge* (c. 1600–25). BRUSSELS. LG1 to LG5 The *Passion,* by Peter van Aelst (Ael'st, Al'ste, Alst) (Angers) (c. 1475–1515). SWITZERLAND. LH1 *The Adoration by the Three Kings at the Nativity* (1597). UNITED STATES OF AMERICA. LH4, LH5 William Baumgarten Manufactory, NEW YORK (1897 and 19 c to 20 c, respectively); LH8, LH9 Albert Herter's design and, or Manufactory, NEW YORK (20 c); LH7 Author's copyright reserved mark

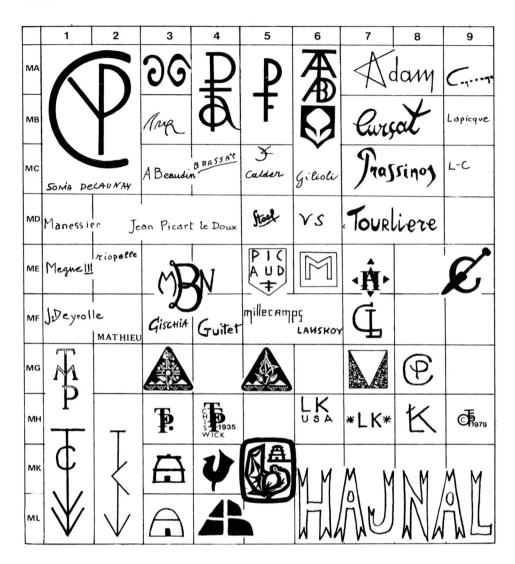

91 TWENTIETH CENTURY TAPESTRY MARKS. FRANCE. Manufactories: MA1 Atelier Yvette Cauquil Prince, PARIS and CORSICA (1959–); MA3 Atelier Goubely-Gatien, AUBUSSON; MA4 Atelier Picaud, AUBUSSON; MA5 Atelier Pinton Frères, AUBUSSON; MA6 Atelier Tabard Frères et Soeurs, AUBUSSON; ME3 Manufacture Nationale de Beauvais; ME5 Atelier Picaud, AUBUSSON; ME6 Atelier Marie Moulinier, PARIS; ME7 Atelier Hamot. AUBUSSON; ME9 Manufacture des Gobelins, PARIS; MF7 Atelier C. et P. Legouiex, AUBUSSON; MG8 Atelier du Marais, PARIS (see also MA1). Designer's or weaver's mark: MA7 Georges-Henri Adam (1904–67); MA9 Jacques Lagrange (1917–); MB3 Jean Arp (1887–1966); MB7 Jean Lurçat (1892–1966); MB9 Charles Lapicque (1898–); MC1 Sonia Delaunay (1895–); MC3 Andre Beaudin (1895–); MC4 Brassai (1899–); MC5 Alexandre Calder (1895–); MC6 Emile Giloli (1910–); MC7 Mario Prassinos (1916–); MC9 Charles-Edouard J. le Corbusier (1887–1965); MD1 Alfred Manessier (1911–); MD3 Jean Picart de Doux (1902–); MD5 Nicolas Stael (1913–55); MD6 Vera Szekely (1919–); MD7 Michel Tourliere (1925–); MF1 J. Deyrolle (1911–67); MF2 Georges Mathieu (1921–); MF3 Léon Gischia (1903–); MF4 James Guitet (1925–); MF5 Yves Millecamps (1930–) MF6 André Lanskoy (1902–). PORT-UGAL. PORTALEGRE; MG1 Manufactura de Tapeçarias de Portalegre Limitada (Fábrica de

Lanificios de Portalegre). UNITED ARAB REPUBLIC OF EGYPT. ʜᴀʀʀᴀɴɪᴀ. Studio
Ramses Wissa Wassef, near Cairo: MG3, MG5 European and Arabic marks, respectively.
AUSTRALIA. ᴍᴇʟʙᴏᴜʀɴᴇ: Victorian Tapestry Workshops: MG7. SCOTLAND. ᴄᴏʀsᴛᴏʀ-
ᴘʜɪɴᴇ: The Dovecot Tapestry Studios (pre-1954): MK3, MK5, ML3; The Edinburgh
Tapestry Company (c. 1954-): MK4. Designer's and Weaver's marks: MH-MK-ML1
William George Thomson (1865-1942) Corstorphine and Chiswick, ʟᴏɴᴅᴏɴ; MH-MK-ML2
Ronald Cruickshank (1898-1969) Edinburgh and USA; MH3, MH4 Francis Paul Thomson
(1914-); Chiswick Loom, ʟᴏɴᴅᴏɴ; MH6 to MH8 Edgewater Looms, USA (1913-15,
1815-20, and 1920-, respectively); ML6 Archie Brennan, Edinburgh Tapestry Co (1931-).
HUNGARY. ʙᴜᴅᴀᴘᴇsᴛ. MK-ML6 Gabriella Hajdal. MH9 Author's copyright reserved

Appendix 2 Glossary

The following are expressions commonly used in describing tapestry; many are archaic and do not appear in modern dictionaries.

alb a tunic of white cloth like that worn by some priests

aniline a dye produced from coal or coal-tar

appliqué *see* Chapter 1

armorial to do with heraldic arms. A tapestry with a coat-of-arms is said to be an armorial tapestry

Arras, arras, arrazzi *see* Index

asa, ASA, A.S.A. American Standards Association = American Standards Institute

Ångström unit 1 A.U. = 10^{-10} metre. The unit of measurement of light wavelength; red has a long wavelength and blue a short one

Aubusson *see* Index

banderole a ribbon-shaped scroll or flag; long and flat band with writing on it

bar a metal bar to hold warp-ends in the loom roller-groove

bar-loom an archaic loom with warp tension regulated by turning the top roller (high-warp loom) or back roller (low-warp loom) by means of a lever or bar

bast fibre a fibre from the inner bark of a tree or inside a plant's stalk, like linen fibre from flax plants

batten the frame holding the reed on low-warp and some high-warp looms

beater a comb-like tool of wood or metal used to push the weft against the woven material

binder a thread which is interposed between weft threads of different colour to bind them

bobbin a concentrically slotted wood or plastic holder used to introduce the weft thread wound round it in the slot, into the shed between warp strings. The bobbin blunt end may be used to push the weft against the woven material

border decorative motif in the shape of a band that is integral with the rest of the tapestry, and has the effect of framing it. Ancient tapestries usually have a plain weave border

brocade a textile fabric with woven parts raised above the general surface. Often looks like tapestry, or may be used to make counterfeit tapestry

BS or **B.S.** British Standard as approved by the British Standards Institution

busk stiffening materials such as splinters of wood, bone or canvas

byssus an exceedingly fine and much valued cloth woven in ancient times from flax or, occasionally, cotton or silk

calibre a unit of measurement indicating thread thickness and computed from the length in metres of a thread spun from one kilogram of wool, etc. When the thread is multi-stranded silk or wool, the calibre number is preceded by a number indicating the quantity of threads; when the material is cotton the reverse sequence applies—e.g., the calibre may be 16 or 24, to indicate the spun length was 16 000 or 24 000 metres; wool or silk shown as 3/24 means a thread of 3 strands of 24 calibre, while 24/3 cotton means 3 strands of 24 calibre cotton

canvas a roller-width of cotton, linen, or hemp canvas wound with the tapestry (to protect it) on a low-warp loom front roller

cartoon a full-scale drawing of the tapestry, in black-and-white or colour and sometimes with parts numbered to indicate the rosary colour issued to the weaver. The cartoon may be drawn or photographed (as an enlargement of the original) on stout paper or line sheet. The cartoon is the weaver's guide to design and is placed behind a high-warp loom, or beneath the warps of a low-warp loom, from which its outlines are copied on to the warp strings in dark ink. The cartoon is left beneath the warps of a low-warp loom and behind the weaver of a high-loom

catch a piece of metal shaped to limit the turning of a loom roller against the roller ratchet. Until a catch is swivelled clear the roller may be turned in one direction only

chamber a suite of tapestries designed for a particular room and possibly comprising (for a bedroom) a bed canopy, headboard and covering, wall and door hangings

chevillon a wood stick used with a spar to remove wool immersed in a vat of dye

cithara an ancient musical instrument shown in some old tapestries; the instrument is triangular, with from 7 to 11 strings and resembles a lyre

clamps metal fasteners placed in loom roller grooves to hold warp bars

cloth beam an American term for the loom roller on which finished tapestry is wound

colour code a system for the identification of colours by encoding each with an alphanumeric code or other means of easy recognition

colour guide *see* rosary

colourimeter a scientific instrument which measures or matches colours

colourist a specialist in colour matching or dyeing

comb a tool used by the weaver to push the weft down and ram it over the warp threads or strings. In some Asian countries women weavers' finger-nails are cut in a sawtooth shape for use instead of a comb

corde a unit of measurement. A corde of wool is 4 or 5 skeins of wool with a total weight of about 0·55kg

cross the cross of the threads at either or both ends of the warp, which prevents tangling and holds them in place during warping

cross rod the rod separating the even set of warps (high-warp loom)

crossing either the method of joining the edges of two adjacent colour areas parallel to the warp during weaving so that 'relay' joins are unnecessary, or the gap between alternate warp threads through which the bobbin or shuttle passes

cubit an old measure of length, from the elbow to the tip of the middle finger

cushion either a cushion placed for the comfort of the weaver on his bench or to raise his sitting position, or a pad some 60cm (3ft) long by 25–30cm (10–12in) diameter placed between the front roller of a low-warp loom and the weaver's throat or chest, to help him remain in a particular position

damask a rich silk fabric woven with elaborate designs and figures. A twilled linen fabric with designs which are emphasized by opposite light reflections from the surface

dents the gaps between the vertical members of a reed through which the warp passes, like threads between the teeth of a comb

dose the quantity of dye measured out for dilution

double-bracket a wooden support for wool skeins suspended over a dye-vat to facilitate their removal

dressing the process of preparing a loom for weaving

driadi a knotted stitch involving two warps, which helps to strengthen and fix non-linear design features

dropping warp threads are 'dropped' by the weaver when working on a progression in an unpatterned area so as to make the superimposed double passages increasingly short; the woven area takes on the appearance of an isosceles triangle

drum a slatted reel used when unwinding a skein

dupion fine quality raw silk taken from a single cocoon woven by two silkworms

dyer's weed weld (a yellow dye)

ecru raw, unbleached

edging an edging composed of several passages of a bobbin loaded with the same thread as the warp, laid down before a tapestry is started. The edging provides a foundation to hold the warp threads parallel and equidistant from each other

ell an ancient measure of length not standardized internationally, but related to the cubit. 1 ell (English) = 114·3cm (45in); 1 ell (Scottish) = 94·4cm (37·2in); 1 ell (Flemish) = 68·6cm (27in); 1 ell (Netherlands) = 100cm (39·4in)

embroidery *see* Chapter 1

enlevage a French term meaning part of a weave that is overlaid with another type of weave

entre-fenêtre(s) a narrow length of tapestry intended to be hung between windows

filling *see* weft

flat patch a uniform wave with no relief modelling

flat sticks long laths of wood, etc., with which the warp is beamed before weaving starts

floss silk from the outer layers of a silkworm cocoon, of comparatively low quality

freeing the action of cutting a tapestry from a loom, by cutting the spare warp threads

fugitive colour a colour that is not fast

grain the texture of a tapestry is determined by the number of warp threads per unit length, which gives it the appearance of being either smooth or grossly ribbed

groove the recess into which the roller bar, holding the warp threads, fits

guilloche an ornament in the form of intertwined ribbons, bands or threads, or one in which the form of bands twisted over each other repeat the figure in a continued series, by the spiral returning of bands

gules red as one of the heraldic colours, or ermine dyed red

hachures a special weave in which the colours are interposed to give marked contrast and tone shading; woven in the direction of the weft, there are spike-like interchanges of the two colours

heddle a string or wire with a loop at one end, through which a warp string passes; at the other end the heddle string or wire is attached to a bar. Each warp of a low-warp loom passes through the **eye** (loop) of a heddle and all the even-numbered warp heddles are attached to the same **heddle bar,** and likewise with respect to the uneven-numbered warps. Each heddle bar is coupled by means of a dowel, harness and section-rod to a treadle (or pedal) operated by the weaver's feet, which lower one set of warps relatively to the other, to create a shed through which to pass the bobbin and lay down a pick of weft. Only the back series of warp strings of a high-warp loom are encircled by heddles. A heddle may be called a **liss** or a **lisse** (*see* 1 and 2)

high-warp or **high-loom** the principal characteristic of the loom is that warp threads or strings are stretched parallel and vertically between the top and bottom rollers. The heddles are attached to a heddle bar above the weaver's head and manipulated by his/her left hand. The cartoon is placed behind the weaver for reference. Until recently it was customary for the tapestry to be woven from the back, and for the weaver to watch the progress of his work—as seen from the front—by seeing a mirror-image of it

infra-red light rays of light similar to visible light but of longer wavelength and felt as heat. Photographic film specially sensitive to infra-red may disclose features not visible to the naked eye, such as patches of tapestry touched up with paint, or weft not made of the same material as the main part of the fabric

infra-sonic very low frequency sound. A type of energy sometimes used for cleaning

inkle loom a loom with a narrow frame, used to weave braid

jack part of the treadle (or pedal) control linked with the section-rod

jewelled spots of intense colour in a tapestry design

lam part of the treadle or pedal mechanism of a low-warp loom; in particular any of the levers coupled by cords to the treadle/pedal, or lever connected to the harness

lea linen measured by the yard (36in)

leash a single loop of thread or twine used instead of a heddle

liss, lisse *see* heddle

lissoir a bar from which skeins of wool are suspended, or moved, in a dye-vat

loom the framework, instrument or machine operated manually or by automotive means, which is used to construct fabrics by a process of weaving in one or more of several ways. In the case of tapestry, the process of weaving entails intertwining one set of threads at right-angles to another set of threads, or as nearly at right angles as circumstances permit, so as to build up a fabric

low-warp or **low-loom** the principal characteristics of a low-warp loom are parallel but horizontal warp threads or strings, heddles located beneath the upper plane of the warps, each of which is accessed by a heddle; and control of all warps by means of foot-operated pedals

merino a fine wool from sheep originally native to Spain

mordant metallic salts, such as potassium alum, and salts of copper, zinc and iron used to enhance the dyeing qualities of various pigments

mottle a method of weaving a gradual change from one colour to another. A bobbin is filled with weft threads which change colour gradually; i.e., a thread composed of, say, 3 strands of black is changed to 1 of white and 2 of black, then 2 of white and 1 of black, and finally 3 of white. The transfer from black to white is made by means of 2 very small speckle-like black-white gradations that look like greys

ogee a wave-like form having an inner and an outer curve like the letter B, a pointed arch each side of which is formed by a concave and a convex curve

passage the journey made by the bobbin when carrying the weft thread between and across the warp threads. A so-called double passage is made when the warp threads have been crossed once in each direction

pastel a plant that produces blue dye

petit-point an embroidery stitch used in making pictorial pieces; at first sight these may look like tapestry

pick a single pass of weft thread across the warps

pinhead design weaving that produces a very small two-colour check pattern

pique the weave resulting from mixing two contrasting colours on one bobbin

plain weave warp and weft interlaced closely to produce a plain tapestry material

ply the number of fibres or strands spun or wound together to make the yarn or thread

portee a quantitative measure of warp threads; 1 portee = 12 warp threads. Tapestry texture depends to some extent on the number of portees per 'section' (*qv*)

portière a tapestry woven specially to fit over a door

positioning line a pencil line drawn on the cartoon at right-angles to the horizontal edge on which the weaving is to start. The line is synchronized precisely parallel with one warp thread, thus providing the weaver with a geometrically accurate reference

pricker a metal tool used to equalize the distance between warp threads on the roller

progression an area of tapestry worked in advance of the rest to facilitate design development or working of other parts, e.g., verges

pull in high-loom weaving, the manipulation of the heddles which produces the cross of the warp threads

rack a board on which spools thread for weft are mounted on equidistantly spaced pegs or spikes, until required. Shades of colour are arranged according to a particular plan or code, thereby simplifying colour-matching or mixing

rake a rule with a spiked edge used to arrange warp on a loom

reed a comb-like metal tool used to space out warp and, on some looms, to beat the weft over the warp. By holding the warp threads an equal distance apart, the reed also helps determine the stiffness or firmness of the material

reed hook a hooked tool used to direct warp thread through the reed dent

relays when a weaver has not used the crossing or interlocking technique to bind together adjacent areas of different colour, a slit appears between adjacent warps. The slit or relay may be left open if small and its presence contributes to the contrast of colour required. Alternatively the relay (French: 'relais') is stitched together by hand to give continuity of texture

reticular resembling a mesh or net

rippling differential tension in warp threads as a result of faulty or careless weaving may cause puckering or bunching of the tapestry surface, called rippling

rod the wooden rod of high-looms, which separates the warp threads into two series comprising the even- and odd-numbered warps. The rod of low-warp looms may be 50·8cm (20in) long and coupled to the heddle-bar, which, on pressing the foot-pedal, lowers a warp section commonly some 40cm (15·7in) wide. The coupling components may be referred to as the harness

rod shed the shed or space between alternate warp threads

roller the roller on which the warp or tapestry is wound and which, as weaving progresses, is respectively unwound or wound on incrementally

roll or **core** the cardboard or plastic core on which thread is wound for storage

rosary this may be: (1) a sketch of the tapestry design together with colour samples of the various threads attached over the field where each colour is to appear, thus providing the weaver with a convenient reference; or (2) a range of thread colour samples that correspond with colours chosen for use according to the cartoon. Samples may be made up in small skeins and strung together in use-sequence, like the beads of a rosary. When a cartoon is colour encoded each small skein is numbered according to its identifying code. It is usual to make three rosaries: one for the artist-designer, one for the weaver, and one as a reference-standard

saie a kind of cloth

sampler a tapestry or embroidery usually worked by a student or apprentice to demonstrate ability in all techniques of the craft

sampling part of the preparation for weaving. Coloured threads are called up to check whether they correspond with those the cartoon calls for. Eventually the rosary is compiled

Savonnerie manufactory when du Bourg and Girard Laurent moved their Faubourg St Antoine tapestry manufactory to the Louvre, Paris, in the early seventeenth century, a neighbouring atelier conducted by Pierre du Pont produced carpets and rugs 'tapis à la façon du Levant'. This workshop made some tapestries but eventually concentrated on very high quality carpets

scraper a metal or wooden flat comb with hooked teeth used in low-warp weaving to insert the weft thread into the warp, and push it down to lie against the material already woven

section a measure of weaving-width for low-warp looms; 1 section = 40·64cm (16in). The width of a low-loom is expressed in terms of the number of workable sections; e.g., a 3-section loom could be used to weave tapestries 121·9cm (4ft) wide

selvedge or **selvage** a tapestry edge or border constructed so that it does not fall apart, unravel or fray; i.e., the edge does not need binding to remain compact as woven. The selvedge is often woven in a distinctive colour associated with a particular workshop; for example, Morris's Merton Abbey Workshops used a deep but bright blue

separate the criss-crossing of warp threads between finger and thumb during the preparatory warping procedure, to separate the even-numbered threads from the uneven-numbered ones. Thereafter the threads are slipped off the fingers on to the pegs or pins of the warping machine

series the total of even-numbered warps, or the total of both even- and uneven-numbered threads

sewing the process of stitching up relays in a tapestry. The tapestry may be tensioned on a small loom to facilitate this operation and to prevent rippling

shaft two lathes of wood, etc., on which heddles are looped

shed the space between the two series of warp strings through which the bobbin or shuttle is passed to lay down the weft thread

shrinkage foreshortening of the tapestry when cut from the loom. Caused by contraction of the previously stretched warps. Foreshortening across the width may result from contraction of weft threads if interlocking has been badly done. Shrinkage may also be caused by a radical change in environmental conditions compared with those prevalent during weaving

shuttle a tool loaded with weft thread, like a bobbin or a spindle. There is some benefit in using the name 'bobbin' for tapestry-weaving as a shuttle is often used to weave ordinary cloth by manual or mechanical means, and a 'spindle' is more often associated with spinning

side-beams the loom frame which supports the rollers

skein yarn wound in a coil folded and knotted to minimize thread displacement in storage

slay another name for the reed-like component that separates and guides warp (*see* reed)

sleeve a metal component comprising two rings fixed to the roller of archaic bar-looms, through which the lever was inserted

slide-block the worm-screw mechanism which positions one roller in relation to the other. The mechanism is locked in a side-beam

sourmak a particular type of knot used in making carpets, but used occasionally in tapestry-weaving to introduce contrast, or as an over-weave for emphasis

spar a conically-shaped piece of wood which is used to wring out wool skeins removed from a dye-vat, or to twist skeins before storage. Used with a chevillon

stay a metal bar or strut used to reinforce the loom framework so as to ensure uniform separation between the two rollers over their entire length. The stay is placed down the middle of the loom between the rollers and at right-angles to them. On large looms the rollers may tend to bend under strain of the warp threads stretched between them

strings, warp an alternate name for warp threads or warp cords

tabby weave plain weave

tache a hook, clasp, fastening

tease to comb or card wool, flax, etc. To brush apart the fibres or to separate the fibres so they may be made to lie parallel in the same direction

teasel or **teazel** a thistle-like plant with heads of stiff and hooked spikes or burrs, which from ancient times were used to tease wool, etc.

temple or **tenterhook** a tool used to help maintain an even width of material during weaving

tensioner a device that varies the warp tension

texture the arrangement of threads in a woven material; often used to indicate tapestry warps per unit length

thrown referring to several fine threads twisted together in one direction, and then united with other like threads by twisting in the reverse direction, which is a process in preparing cotton thread to be used for warp; also called a **twist**

transit shade a compromise between two colours. Obtained either by using a third colour or by hachures (*qv*)

transom the part supporting the jack of low-looms. Transom ends rest in metal stirrups fixed to the side-beams, to fix it parallel to the rollers below, some 51cm

(20in) from warp threads, and about midway across the loom

treadles the foot-pedals or treadles of a low-loom are coupled by cords, levers and section-rods to the heddle-bars through a jack

trough the recessed part of the transom which accommodates the jack

turn when a completed portion of a tapestry is wound on the (low-loom) front roller or beam, or the (high-loom) bottom roller or beam, it is a turn. A corresponding length of new warp must be discharged concurrently from the roller on which it is wound. Alternatively, a 'turn' is the process of weaving round a design motif contour

verdure a tapestry displaying substantially landscapes or with a dominance of green plants and trees

verge the intervening area between warp edges of two sections woven on a low-loom which, to make a verge, must have its pedal mechanism adjusted to control simultaneously the warp of adjoining sections

w (abbreviation) warp; **w/cm** = warps per centimetre

warp-face or **warp-ribbed tapestry** a tapestry with warp closely spaced so that the weft is covered entirely. A technique used by some modern weavers, especially those using low-looms

warping or **warping-up** the process of assembling the bundles or sheaves of separated warp on the warping machine and, or, dressing the loom with warp; i.e., warp mounting

weft, woof or **wouf** the thread laid down with a bobbin or shuttle between warp strings to make the tapestry by filling in and covering the warp. The preferred term is weft

weld a plant that produces yellow dye

wheel a colloquialism for a machine used to wind skeins on to spools or to load a bobbin from a spool of weft thread. Sometimes similar to, or actually a spinning wheel

winch ancient low-looms had a winch fixed to the side-beam to facilitate rotation of the back roller or vary warp tension

wind-up a means of increasing warp tension of old bar-looms, by using a lever to turn the rollers

woad a blue dye (*see* pastel)

wy (abbreviation) weft yarns; **wy/cm** = weft yarns per centimetre

Appendix 3
The Art of Dyeing

Well preserved ancient tapestries from Peru and the burial grounds of Egypt and Europe all bear witness to the astonishing mastery of materials and techniques possessed by the dyers of old.

The earliest textiles were coloured by the inherent shades of materials, although a different hue might be seen depending on whether the thread was dry, damp or oiled. In Europe and Asia the vegetable fibres used first were: ramie (or rhea), a plant of the nettle family found in sub-tropical regions which provided strong thin threads with a silk-like gloss; wild and then cultivated cotton; flax, which provided linen thread; hemp, which is a member of the cannabis family; and, more recently, jute, derived from the bark of the Indian *Corchorus capsularis* or *Corchorus olitories* plants. Animal-derived fibres included various types of wool, fur and silk. In the Americas, vegetable fibres were obtained from the flax, hemp, cotton, sisal, yucca, maguey, bullrush and palmetto plants; threads were made from the bark of mulberry and cedar trees and the sage-bush. Animal-derived fibres included wool from vicuna, alpaca and the mountain goat, fur from rabbits, and hair from bison. The natural shades of all these materials varied from different purities of white, through creams, greys, browns and reddish tints to black.

It was indeed extraordinary that three widely dispersed and fairly easily grown plants should have been found capable of producing ingredients to make dyes of the three primary colours: red, yellow and blue. It is equally remarkable that people living so long ago discovered dye-making processes and that the addition of copper, zinc and aluminium improved the qualities of dyes. About a thousand different plants, shrubs and trees were found to be capable of producing a dye.

Blue was possibly the most widely used colour initially. In Asia, the *Indigofera* plant was processed from the earliest times to give indigo, a colour midway between blue and violet. The processes involved in producing the dye were complex and required a combination of skill and instinct if the end-product was to be of the best. Indigo was brought to Europe from India during the sixteenth century, but was known in pre-dynastic Egypt. Until indigo was introduced, dyers in Europe used the plant *Isatis tinctoria,* which appears to have been grown in Asia concurrently with the indigo plant. *Isatis tinctoria* leaves give a different hue according to their age, the older the leaf the darker the blue, known as woad. The plant is related to mustard. American Indians discovered a similar plant which they used as a blue-violet skin pigment. Blue crepe cloth from the pre-Inca era, and cloth in various intensities of blue (and other colours) from the Tiahuanaco period (AD 700–1200) show that the art of dyeing was as advanced in the Americas as in Europe and Asia, although indigo does not appear until it was introduced by the Spaniards after which, as elsewhere, it was mixed with woad.

Yellow was obtained from weld or *Reseda luteola*, the so-called 'dyer's weed', a plant resembling the flower gardener's mignonette. Another source of yellow was the flower pistils of *Crocus sativus,* which appears to have originated in Persia, from where it spread along the trade routes to China, Greece and Rome. Modern bakers use this dye's raw material—saffron—to colour and flavour special types of bread and buns.

Red came from the *Rubia tinctorum* plant, and was made from prehistoric times. Egyptians used this dye—madder—for pre-dynastic mummy wrappings, and it was known to the Persians, Greeks and Romans. Later, brazilwood or *Caesalpinia echinata* was also used; it produces a bright red dye.

Mordants gave greater colour permanence and richness, and helped to produce a special shade. Dark green was made by mixing woad and weld and aluminium or oxide of iron mordant, although good dyers avoided using iron if possible since it could cause rot. Wool and silk dyed differently. Dyes like that obtained from the Central American logwood tree (*Haematoxylon campechianum*) coloured wool mauve or purple, cotton blue or bluish-black, and silk black.

In more recent times vegetable dyes in common use have included yellow tints obtained from birch trees, scabious, apple-tree bark, and the American fustic tree (*Chlorophora tinctoria*); brown tints from birch and black oak tree bark, marjoram, coffee, cutch (*Acacia catecha*), *Rhamus catharticus* berries, and sphagnum moss; green shades from *Bromus vulgaris,* and young fustic or *Rhus cotinus* wood; purple or mauve from the lichens: *Rocella tinctoria* and *Lecanora tartarea*. Some dyes are more colour fast than others.

Dyes from organic sources have been used almost as long as woad and madder. The legendary son of Aloemene by Zeus, Heracles of Tyre, is said to have discovered a purple dye when his dog bit into a shell-fish like a mussel, when they were walking on the shore of the Mediterranean Sea. Heracles (Hercules) had a tunic immersed in the brilliant red stain from the purpura shell-fish, which dyed the tunic to what since has been called 'Tyrian purple' or 'murex'. This magnificent pigment was exploited throughout the Mediterranean area some 3600 years ago, and formed a major trading activity of the Phoenicians, who carried the highly-prized 'royal purple' textiles as far as the west coast of Europe, possibly as far as the British Isles. The Aztec and Maya peoples of America used the cochineal insect to make a brilliant crimson dye. In the Orient, the kermes louse yielded a similarly brilliant red. As the colouring properties of minerals and earths were discovered, a wider variety of tints came into use, although many dyers mistrusted colorants not of animal or vegetable origin believing that mineral dyes rotted fabrics. The discovery of chemical bleaches helped to create greater colour contrasts.

The ancient Greeks initiated studies into the science of colour and its standardization. Fairly early on the discovery was made that the primary colours of red, yellow and blue were the constituents of white and, of course, mixing these three could create orange, green, mauve, grey, brown and so on. It was observed that the association of one colour with another beside it produced a complementary tint; for example, if blue and yellow are placed side-by-side, the blue will take on the yellow's complementary colour of violet, and the yellow will take on the blue's complementary colour of orange. Under certain circumstances the eye would try to compensate for the colour missing from the full spectrum represented by white. A full understanding of how colours influence each other, or the eye can be made to see a colour not actually there, proved invaluable to designers. By mixing threads of different colours, and by spinning threads unevenly so that one colour was more prominent than the other(s), or by dyeing a thread unevenly, many combinations that appear minutely as single-colour specks in a tapestry could be made to produce what looked like a third or fourth colour. The Persians and Chinese, in particular, made a speciality of harmonious pastel shades of great delicacy, which produced as much dramatic contrast as the vigorous use of brilliant colours.

Modern dyeing material and techniques stem from research into the physics and chemistry of dyestuffs initiated during the seventeenth century. Attempts were made to synthesize colorants with a view to exercising better control. Towards the end of the eighteenth century a group of French chemists attempted to improve the range of colours especially suitable for tapestry wools and silks. In 1824 one of their number, Michel Eugène Chevreul, was appointed to direct the dyestuffs laboratory of the Gobelins Tapestry Manufactory in Paris, a position he held until 1889. He created a palette of ten clear colours. Each colour was divided into 72 'scales'. Each scale, in turn, was divided into 20 tones. By this means Chevreul standardized 14400 colour variations. Although the difference between adjacent tones was scarcely perceptible, the variations were thought to be necessary for the work of Gobelins' designers and weavers. By spinning two threads of different colour together, Chevreul then created a choice of nearly 200000000 colour variants. The letter written in 1923 to the Marquis of Bute's secretary, by David Anderson of the Dovecot Workshop, shows that the Gobelins' dyer was still working with a huge range of tones (*see* Index).

By way of contrast, the fourteenth century manufactory that wove the magnificent. *Apocalypse* tapestries managed to make do with no more than some 15 to 20 dyes for these all-wool hangings. The gold, silver and Granada silk weft of the *Conquest of Tunis* tapestries woven by William Pannemaker, and finished in 1554, are coloured by 19 dyes each diluted to give between three and five shades, making a total of between 57 and 95 colour variants.

The gradual development of alternatives to vegetable and animal dyes, which started in 1834 with the German chemist Runge's discovery that the aniline by-product of coal-tar produced a brilliant blue when bleached, followed in 1856 with the founding of the aniline dyestuffs industry by Sir William Henry Perkins (1838–1907), who discovered the first aniline dye—a vivid purple—were the first steps on the way to producing a vast new range of pigments.

Despite this range of easily used and relatively fast colours, many tapissiers still prefer the old dyestuffs for, they argue, insufficient time has elapsed to find out the extent of reaction between aniline dyes and wool, silk, etc., warp and weft. It is known that some aniline dyes do rot fabrics, or change colour. In particular, the colour-fastness of synthetic dyes produced up to the end of the nineteenth century was not as good as madder, woad, weld, kermes and brazilwood.

Mid-twentieth century research into the molecular structure of fibres and dyes has produced materials wherein the pigment is fixed fast in the fibre so as to withstand the effect of light and washing without change. These are the fibre reactive dyestuffs.

When considering the authenticity of a tapestry it is desirable to check whether vegetable or aniline dyes were used. Characteristics of vegetable-dyed material are:

1. where there is a large field of colour that should be uniformly the same, variations may occur because hand-dyeing did not give even-dyeing and so there is variation in dye intensity. Note should be taken of the fact that some aniline-dyed materials are treated to fake this effect;

2. bright colours should be bright and clear;

3. hand-spun threads should all be of about the same colour unless it is obvious that several discrete colours have been spun together for effect;

4. materials should have a depth of colour and not display a patina or a metallic-like shine;

5. the mauves and blues should be the first to show signs of fading;

6. fibres examined under a magnifying glass should show signs of uneven dyeing. They should feel 'natural' and not cloying. Watch for split ends caused by harsh acids, etc., sometimes used with artificial dyes.

Artificial dyes tend to fade with time; colours may look lifeless after a few years or make the fabric brittle.

Bibliography
Bronson, J. & R. *Weaving and Dyeing*. Bailey Bros., London (1949)
Lemberg, M. 'Beispiele der Textilkonservierung am Bernischen Historischen Museum'. *Jahrbuch des Bernischen Historinischen Museums*. v. 37–38, pp. 138–42; 'Zur Restaurierung des vierten Caesarteppichs'. v. 53–54. Berne, Switzerland

Index